hamlyn

rock'n'roll people

consultant editor: david sandison

foreword: allan jones

the pioneers of pop in their own words

Executive Editor Mike Evans
Senior Editor Trevor Davies

Creative Director Keith Martin
Executive Art Editor Geoff Fennell

Picture Research Zoe Holtërman
Production Controller Louise Hall

First Published in Great Britain in 2000 by Hamlyn
an imprint of Octopus Publishing Group Limited
2-4 Heron Quays, Docklands, London E14 4JP

A catalogue record for this book is available
from the British Library

Produced by Toppan Printing Co Ltd
Printed in China

6   foreword

I'm a year out of art school, recently on the dole, but now working in the Dickensian gloom of the mail order department of a central London bookshop, when I see an ad in Time Out, the listings magazine. Melody Maker's looking for a new writer – no previous journalistic experience necessary, they say. Which is fine by me, because I don't have any. They're looking for someone who's under 21 and highly opinionated. At the time, I'm both. I duly write to the editor, the late Ray Coleman, to tell him as much.

To my vast and eternal surprise, I'm first interviewed and then offered a job as junior reporter/feature writer.

Not long after this, I'm swanning down the Brompton Road with Bryan Ferry, meeting Leonard Cohen for lunch in Sloane Square, getting drunk with Alice Cooper at the Savoy. The drugs, knife fights and hysteria in the backs of taxis are all in the future – for the moment I'm having the time of my life. Rather grandly – it seems to me – MM's offices at the time are in Fleet Street. I don't feel intimidated by this, however, as much as at home. Melody Maker has already been a big part of my life. I've been reading it for the best part of the last 10 years and know it and its staff of writers with a familiarity born of something approaching obsession.

Where I grew up in the Sixties, nothing much happened apart from the slow passing of time. Melody Maker put me in touch with a world that seemed exotic, different and dazzling with opportunity. It was 1965, and I loved The Who, The Kinks, Tamla, Stax and the Stones. I was already, in Neil Young's immortal phrase, a prisoner of rock'n'roll. I spent every penny I had on records. And when I didn't have any money, I spent hours in record shops mesmerised by the covers of LPs I couldn't afford. I memorised sleeve notes, engineering credits, catalogue numbers.

I wanted to know everything I could about these records and the people who made them. Of course, there's only so much you can learn about music from an album sleeve. For a real insight into the people and personalities behind the noise you were listening to, you had to read the Melody Maker. It arrived every Thursday and every week I'd devour everything in it, from Folk News to the loon pants ads. And when I'd finished reading it, I read it again.

I'd never previously entertained the idea of writing for MM, or anyone else. But here I was – a fan let loose in a fabulous world – and it's where I stayed for the next 20-odd years, 12 of them as editor. Things change, though. Melody Maker is no longer quite what it was, and neither am I. By May 1997, it was time to move on. I've got another gig now, and Melody Maker, still doing its best, is a different kind of music paper. This lends a certain poignancy to the majority of the pieces of its history collected here, even the most recent of which seem to belong to another time. Without wanting to sound wet-eyed for a past that was never really there – some spurious golden age – you really won't find stories like some of the ones in this anthology in what's left of the weekly music press.

It's a question of access, as much as anything. These days, you can't get near anyone who matters without first enduring protracted negotiations with small armies of overprotective flunkeys, shamelessly manipulative PRs acting as campaign managers of complex media strategies, usually only there to keep a safe distance between the press and the people whose payroll they're on.

Gone, mostly, are the days when you were genuinely in the front line – in the studio with John Lennon and Phil Spector, on a movie set in Mexico with Sam Peckinpah and Bob Dylan, on the road in Texas with Bruce Springsteen, being nicked by the law in London with The Sex Pistols, drinking New York dry with Lou Reed, or carousing all night and paying for it the next day with Elvis Costello.

It just doesn't happen any more like it did back then. But it did happen once, unforgettably for a lot of us who were there, with Melody Maker in the thick of it, both guns drawn, noise everywhere, everything happening at once, bringing the music of the hour to the people of the nation.

7

ALLAN JONES, LONDON, FEBRUARY 2000.

Bob Dylan's refusal to give interviews, his switches of musical style and the inconsistency of his work combine to make Robert Allan Zimmerman in 1941 an enigma. Add an unwillingness to follow accepted rules of pitch and phrasing and you'd be hard pressed to understand how he became one of the most influential musicians of his generation.

Raised in the Minnesota mining town of Hibbing, Dylan (from the Welsh poet, Dylan Thomas) played in local rock bands during his teens but converted to being a radical folk singer at university in Minneapolis, when he discovered the work of Woody Guthrie. Moving to New York in 1959, Dylan became a stalwart of the Greenwich Village politico-folk movement. Texan singer Carolyn Hester recommended Dylan to veteran Columbia Records producer John Hammond, and in 1962 Dylan's debut album was released.

That, and its immediate successors, Freewheelin' and The Times They Are A'Changing blended semi-traditional songs with Guthrie-like 'talking blues' which marked Dylan as a witty wordsmith. Openly political, he stamped his mark with powerful 'message' songs like 'Blowin' In The Wind', 'Masters of War' and the acid-bitter 'A Pawn In Their Game'.

Although acclaimed star of the 1963 Newport Folk Festival, Dylan lost the affections of purist folk fans with his 1964 album Another Side of Bob Dylan and the 1965 set Bringing It All Back Home, which saw him begin working with amplified instruments.

Dylan was one of many US artists affected by the dominance of British rock groups, especially when The Animals, Them and Manfred Mann had hits with covers of his songs. American bands, too, were drawing on his catalogue, and The Byrds' hit versions of 'Mr Tambourine Man' and 'All I Really Want To Do' introduced him to a vast new audience.

Many people at the 1965 Newport festival were outraged when Dylan went on stage with The Paul Butterfield Blues Band. Similar heckling and confusion came later in the year when, supported by The Hawks (soon re-named The Band) Dylan toured Britain for the first time. A film of that tour, Don't Look Back, offered a rare glimpse into his private world.

In Nashville, Dylan produced two seminal albums, Highway 61 Revisited and Blonde on Blonde. These remain the yardstick by which his early work should be measured.

In 1966 Dylan vanished from view for nearly two years, during which he recorded with The Band in the basement of their house in Bearsville, New York. Extensively bootlegged, these recordings were only officially released in 1975 as The Basement Tapes. Dylan reappeared in 1968, at a memorial concert for Guthrie that coincided with Dylan's John Wesley Harding album, a return to the sparsely backed days of his early electrical forays.

A year later, Nashville Skyline left critics and fans puzzled. Equally confusing were the 1971 set, New Morning and his experimental novel, Tarantula, which fuelled speculation that he'd lost the plot. Typically, he confounded everyone with a fine guest appearance at George Harrison's Concert for Bangla Desh at Madison Square Garden and made a cameo appearance as the outlaw 'Alias' in Sam Peckinpah's Pat Garrett and Billy The Kid, a movie for which he also contributed a score featuring the haunting 'Knockin' On Heaven's Door'.

Leaving Columbia, Dylan released Planet Waves on Asylum Records, toured America with The Band and released the double in-concert album Before The Flood. His return to Columbia in 1975 was marked by the multi-million selling Blood On The Tracks, still deemed a classic.

The Rolling Thunder Tour, a deliberately shambolic trans-America jaunt, resulted in the TV special Hard Rain and the self-indulgent, self-financed movie, Renaldo and Clara.

Dylan's continued ability to write commercial material was proven by Street Legal, which included 'Baby Stop Crying', a UK Top 20 hit. Dylan then announced that he'd converted to Christianity. Two preachy albums – Slow Train Coming and Saved – were followed in 1981 by the less challenging Shot Of Love in 1983 and Infidels a year later.

The release, in 1986, of the 53-song boxed set Biograph did much to place Dylan's back-catalogue and his importance in their proper contexts. It was a revaluation amply supported by the coincidental release of the excellent Desire.

As the 1980s drew to a close, Dylan became part of the Traveling Wilburys with George Harrison, Tom Petty, Roy Orbison and Jeff Lynne. While his solo output of the last 10 years or so has seen him work, with varying degrees of artistic success, in the company of The Grateful Dead, Tom Petty's Heartbreakers and producer Daniel Lanois, the only real guarantee his fans now have is that Bob Dylan remains a fascinating live performer, constantly turning his 'greatest hits' on their heads with often bizarre arrangements.

Infuriating, exasperating and often obtuse, Bob Dylan has never been boring. He's not about to start now.

Previous page: **Dylan takes the stage during his 1966 British tour. His first with The Band, it was marred by heckling from folk purists who believed Fender Stratocasters to be the devil's tool.**

February 3 1973 Michael Watts

THE MAN CALLED ALIAS

Under any other circumstances the remark wouldn't have been unusual. But today, riding this plane 20,000 feet above the Mexican desert, with these people, wow, the normality of it struck a freaky note.

The little guy with the pale, wispy beard and the worn black stovepipe hat, who had not spoken much to anybody else these past few weeks, had sidled cautiously down the aisle of the aircraft and nudged me abruptly in the shoulder.

The distant view of the mesas, like red, swollen welts, lying thousands of feet below, switched suddenly to a close-up of blue, almost translucent eyes.

"You with Melody Maker?" he demanded. Surprised nod. "Is Max Jones still working there?" Max Jones? Yes, sure he was, but...you remember!

A slight, unsmiling inclination of the fuzzy, black-topped head leaning over the seat. It stretched back all of ten years now to the time when this young folkie played the Royal Festival Hall.

He was only a kid then, but he'd stayed at the swanky Mayfair Hotel. He drank Beaujolais, wore jeans, boots and a leather jacket. He told everyone he wrote "finger-pointing" songs. He told Max Jones.

As a matter of fact, it had been the first time Bob Dylan was ever interviewed in Britain.

Rodolfo the Glasses knew all about Durango.

He had carried my bags to the room on the fourth floor of the Camino Real Hotel, the most space-age in Mexico City, where the swarthy porters wore black capes printed with gold lozenges. Rodolfo was fussing with the curtains whilst waiting for his tip.

"Durango? Si, si." He pushed his dark glasses further back on his nose, a short, stocky Mexican, eager to please as always the Americanos.

"Very, very hot, very dry." His hands moved like butterflies. "Make lots of films there." A pause. He brightens. "You go for film?" His face split into two rows of white teeth.

Sam Peckinpah, I muttered.

Above: **Dylan gets down and with it at the Isle of Wight Festival in 1969. Backed by The Band, he topped a folk bill that included Ritchie Havens, Tom Paxton and Julie Felix, offering the 100,000 crowd a taste of his recently released *Nashville Skyline* album. Legend has it that the white suit was loaned to him by John Lennon...**

Left: **A bearded George Harrison with Dylan during the latter's segment of 'The Concert for Bangla Desh' fundraiser, staged at Madison Square Garden in 1971.**

Left: **Doing what many of his fans would still prefer him to do all the time – Dylan in acoustic mode. He also proves, once more, that he's never made much of an effort to make 'The World's 10 Best Dressed Men' lists...**

"Sam Peckinpah!" he burst out. "Sam, he my friend!" It was if the name of his own father had been invoked. "He stay here. Great man – he drinks, drinks mucho." He put one hand to his lips and tilted back an imaginary glass, then shook his head in pure delight. I slipped the coins into his free hand.

"Thank you, senor, muchos gracias." He moved away. "Tell him, when you see him," he said, closing the door, "you saw Rodolfo." He pointed to his eyes. "He remembers the glasses." I could hear his faint chuckle as he disappeared down the corridor.

Sam Peckinpah! The terrible, if no longer the enfant, of Hollywood, the apostle of ultra-violence, even before Kubrick, the director of The Wild Bunch and Straw Dogs, the boozer, the wildman, the misogynist – that devil!

In these days of spoof Westerns, comedy Westerns, black Westerns, fag Westerns a la Warhol, neo-Realism Westerns, anything-to-be-different Westerns, Peckinpah remained a hardliner in his attitude towards how cowboy movies should be made.

He believed in physicality and hard-core action, adhering to the myth of the Western but intent at the same time to stir it up, just to show some of the scabby underbelly. His pictures were made for men, just as surely as he was a man's man, and his tough outlook on both life and movies had spun a cult around him that had not been achieved without mishaps along the way.

After his first two pictures, The Deadly Companions and Ride The High Country, he had made Major Dundee in 1964 with Charlton Heston but the producer, Jerry Wexler (of Atlantic Records fame) had it re-edited.

He then went through a period of disillusionment. The producer of The Cincinnati Kid, Martin Ransohoff, sacked him, he lost a lot of dough, went in for hard drinking and had wife trouble (he's twice married and divorced his Mexican wife, Begonia, and wedded in the middle of last year a 29-year old blonde, English secretary Josie, whom he met in Twickenham whilst in England for the shooting of Straw Dogs).

Then, after a period in television, he made The Wild Bunch with William Holden, which capitalised in a tremendously successful fashion on the atmosphere of acceptable violence that was permeating motion pictures.

It turned around his ailing reputation at the same time that his slow-motion depiction of carnage made him the controversial eye of a critical whirlpool surrounding his bloody permissiveness.

"I want to rub their noses in violence," he told Time magazine. "I regard all men as violent, including myself." He had gone on to direct Dogs with Dustin Hoffman and Junior Bonner and The Getaway with Steve McQueen, all of which delineated further his buckets-of-blood approach to movie-making.

But now! No film of his had whipped up such pre-release speculation as the present one, Pat Garret And Billy The Kid, not so much because of him this time, or his celluloid theories, but because of a certain "actor".

I mean, James Coburn had done scores of films, like The Magnificent Seven, and Jason Robards Jr was in Peckinpah's The Ballad of Cable Hogue, and Kris Kristofferson might be a famous folksinger, but he'd acted already in two movies, Cisko Pike and Bloom In Love (with George Segal, which is to be released in May).

But Bob Dylan! Bob Dylan and Sam Peckinpah! At first glance it was old America meeting the new, the traditionalist values of the West encountering the pop surrealism of the East. It was a symbolic meeting of two vastly different generations, of two attitudes to life. It was all this, but more. Beneath the skin depth lay other meanings.

For Peckinpah, the inclusion in his movie of Dylan and, to a lesser extent, Kristofferson (whose lifestyle may be rock but who has much of the traditional about him), represents a mellowed acceptance of the youth culture and its totems, a phenomenon to which he has been totally deaf in his past work.

Doubtless he has been somewhat persuaded by their box-office appeal to the rock generation, which MGM Studios, his financiers, will have pointed out.

But to Dylan the role is of much more momentous importance. He is the ageing and long-appointed prophet, who has grown old and increasingly distant in a role which for years has held for him no relevance yet which seems effectively to have constrained his talents.

It is more than two years since he made his last album, New Morning, and there are no apparent plans for another solo venture; his contract with Columbia Records has run out, although he can't deliver an album to another company unless he wishes to forego huge royalties CBS are holding.

He has consistently intimated to friends that he is tired of the music business, that he has no desire to play live anymore, and he takes little active part in it, except on a casual basis when he appears on the albums of friends like Doug Sahm and Steve Goodman.

Moreover, he has been away too long now to return to the heart of the action with the same pertinence as before, even if he wished to. And, as Grossman astutely realised, his past performances were so often uneven, anyway, as to necessitate them being infrequent.

He is Bob Dylan. But who is Bob Dylan? As the myth of the musician and the generation symbol rises like creeping fog, he casts about for some direction, for a new purpose to it all.

He sees other pre-eminent musicians, like Lennon and Jagger, involved in movies. An old mentor is Warhol. While down in Mexico a newer friend, Kris Kristofferson, is making a film. About Billy the Kid.

Billy the Kid! Whatever the nature of fact, Billy the Kid is part of American legend. As was John Wesley Hardin(g), and him he knows about, from the past, from an idea he once used. Down in Durango, Mexico, visiting Kristofferson on the set, he writes this song about Billy and plays it to the cast. It only follows that he should get a role in his first full feature film.

He got the part, in fact, through a combination of circumstances precipitated by Bert Block, Kristofferson's manager. Block, an old music pro who at one time managed Billie Holiday, was the guy who looked after arrangements when he played the Isle of Wight. He's the nearest thing Dylan has had to a business manager since he let his contract with the Grossman empire expire (Grossman and Block were business partners for a while, indeed, and handled Janis Joplin together).

Block mentioned to Dylan that Kristofferson was in a movie and suggested it to him as well. He also spoke to Gordon Carroll, the producer, who was delighted at the proposition.

Dylan had talks with Rudy Wurlitzer, the screenplay writer, and went to a private screening of The Wild Bunch. He was sceptical of the project at first. He only intended to see one reel. But then it stretched to three, to four...Dylan came out of MGM's theatre with a celluloid monkey riding on his back.

He was fascinated with the idea of a movie part as much as he was daunted by his feeling of inadequacy towards doing it. Before there had only been documentaries. And Peckinpah was a frightening genius!

But he went down with Bert to Mexico to exorcise his doubts. The first night they dined at Peckinpah's house on a meal of roast goat. Then he was shown around the set. He was particularly captivated by the wardrobe of Western clothes, trying on the hats and costumes like a kid dressing for a fancy dress party.

He looked around for a while, and then, on that second day, quietly picked up a guitar and sang to Kris and Coburn and Peckinpah this song he'd made up called 'Billy the Kid'. Peckinpah offered him a part there and then.

It's a small part as one of Billy's sidekicks, but it would have been expanded any time he wished. The fact that he hasn't asked illustrates his tentativeness. He plays, with the most fitting of poetic justices, the part of Alias.

In the public life of the musician he is the man of uncertain identity. In the movies he is the man with no name. He continues to play the game of "famiousity", as he once called it. But he may well have found that new direction which has been eluding him. People on the film say he would like to continue the part of Alias in succeeding movies, jokily preserving that anonymity.

In a sense Dylan is like Brando. The one is to the sixties what the other was to the fifties: a representation of their style and mood. In the late sixties, however, the charisma of both began to erode a little. They began to go out of fashion and the criticisms increased about their performances, the one in films, the other on records.

The difference is that Brando has recently sought, and successfully achieved, his rejuvenation with The Godfather and now Last Tango in Paris. Dylan is still in the process.

This movie is an enormous step in switching media to test the viability of his talent, not necessarily in transforming him into an actor but more in enabling him to ascertain for himself his filmic sense. It's a training ground for a possible directorial debut.

When I arrived in Durango he had been there for three months, since November 23. He had with him his wife, Sara, five kids and Rover the dog.

She had taken the children to Yucatan, a neighbouring state whose inhabitants, direct descendants of the Maya Indians, like to think of themselves as a separate entity from the rest of Mexico. They have a daughter, Maria, aged 11, and their eldest son is Jesse Byron, who's seven and reputedly something of a wild kid.

Maggie Netter, an MGM publicist, said she went riding with the boy on Sundays. "He's so intelligent! They all are. But they let them run wild, they don't look after them especially. They just let them do what they want. If they're going home they tell someone to bring the kids back with them, so they're always around people."

Wandering around Durango, in fact, and finding myself in one of the many banks, I came upon a Texan schoolmaster who was teaching at an American school there. Jesse was one of his pupils for a month.

This Texan was large-boned, wore a red, V-necked sweater and horn rims, and had an accent like the twang of a plucked bow-string.

"You must've taken the wrong turning somewhere," he smiled pleasantly after the introductions, and waved his hand generally at the town. The movie was mentioned. "I s'pose you're out here then for Bob Die-lan," he twanged, and then remarked about teaching Dylan's kid. The way he said it reminded me of ten years ago when no one in England seemed to know how to pronounce the name correctly.

I asked about the kid. He just gave a slow, Texan smile and muttered something inconsequential. Then I changed the subject and asked how people amused themselves in this place at night. Dull wasn't a strong enough word for my initial impression of Durango.

He looked at his companion, another schoolteacher, a Mexican woman in glasses, and said, "How do we amuse ourselves, Juanita?" and she shrugged her shoulders and smiled, and he smiled again. I couldn't guess what there was to smile about so much in this one-hoss city.

Durango is, indeed, a city, the capital of the state of Durango. It has the highest homicide rate in Mexico. A hundred and sixty thousand people live there digging out gold, silver or iron (particularly) from the mines, or else working in the numerous small stores that serve the community.

It seems incredible that there can be so many human beings cast out into this arid wilderness, 600 miles nor' nor'west of Mexico City, fringed by the Sierra Madre range that, from the only plane flying daily from the capital, the 6.45 am, is like a series of grey-red hummocks under a thin blanket of mist.

But beautiful, yes. You step out onto the tarmac from the plane, which is always full, and the pale red stripes of dawn have now dissolved into the horizon, and the spicy January air is like a cold douche, and you

Below: **The artist at work: a rare studio shot of Dylan during the recording of his Self Portrait album in 1970.**

Right: **Dylan goes Southern Plantation. A touch of the Tom Wolfes in this shot by Elliot Landy, probably taken outside the Nashville studios where most of Self Portrait was recorded. Nice ensemble...except for the footwear.**

suddenly become aware of all these people, these kids; with eyes that are eating up this huge metal thing which has dropped once again out of the skies, and you know it's a cliché but you find yourself wondering about their thoughts. *What's it like out there, beyond the mountains?*

An odd feeling for the traveller, because if you believe the books, something like this happened before, aeons ago, when the gods descended from spaceships among the Mayans and the other primitive Indian tribes, and told them to build pyramids and roads, to be the cradle of civilisation, and…hell, if God was an astronaut and felt as bleary as me this January morning, he'd get his blue ass back onto that thing and light out for Los Angeles, a thousand miles north, because in the year of our Lord 1973 there seemed precious little here to do.

The city of Durango is a wide, two-lane highway, shimmering metallically in haze of heat and dust as the sun winches upwards, with numerous smaller roads intersecting off it. It is pale stucco churches and banks, and a huge square flanked by finely-clipped yews. It is the Old World and it is the New.

The little shoe-shine boy at the pavement's edge puts spit on the toecap of his customer's shoe and lights a match, pausing an instant while the flame spurts up before applying his rag.

While next door, almost, here is a massive supermarket, the Soriana, larger than any I've seen in the States, which could supply the whole populace. The wire shopping trolleys outside the window are serried ranks, poised to trundle into action.

But most of all it is Hollywood – it is the myth of the Western movie made flesh there amidst the vista of cacti, scrub, old lava stones and brown, rolling plains. Today in these parts God is not an astronaut, he is a cowboy who rides into town on that plane for a couple of months and shoots his motion pitcher, for which you're paid so many pesos a day as an extra.

In the office of the best hotel in town, the Campo Mexico, one of the three there, which consists of a number of one-storey rooms slung together in a wide semi-circle, are hung signed portraits of the stars who've made movies in this area. "Hasta la vista – Glenn Ford"; "Many thanks – Kirk Douglas"; "Best wishes – John Wayne".

Wayne, he even has his own spread outside of town where he makes films. In fact, he's only just left. It would have made a great picture for that wall, him and Sam, and Jim Coburn, and Kris, and…Bobby Dylan.

Dylan and the other leading figures in the movie have their own houses close to each other in Durango. Maggie tells me this as we drive out this Saturday morning for the location site, El Suaz, which is about 20 to 30 minutes from the Campo Mexico.

She also informs me that Dylan is "very strange" and if I'm looking to speak to him…she smiles very prettily but adamantly. It seems there are strict instructions that his privacy not be so much as tampered with.

Expressly no cameras, except for the stills photographer and John Bryson, a former Life picture editor and an old friend of Sam's, who was given a chunky role in The Getaway.

Maggie says that Dylan talks to no-one, unless he wishes to. Like, he's a big friend of Kristofferson, they share a trailer together on the site, but some days he won't speak to him at all. He's the same with everyone.

"It's not just that he's picking on you, but he's…" she searches for the right adjective…"he's just *rude*." Ah! The mucho mysterioso quality.

They all tell me the same. "Dylan? Forget it! He won't talk." Casually mention his name in a conversation and a veil of protectiveness

descends. He's like an ever-present wisp of ectoplasm floating in the consciousness of all these assembled people, a thing intangible which needs to be preserved from the prying outside in case it blows away.

But it's not simply that no one wants to be the person to reveal anything. No one is sure if they have anything to reveal! They're uncertain about their own reactions to him and, even more, what their reactions *should* be.

One minute he's the breathless myth, set down exotically in the land of Quetzalcoatl, the next he's just a guy working on a movie like the rest of us, isn't he? *Isn't he?* About the only thing they are sure of is they're not gonna say too much, just in case.

It was eerie, those first few moments of arriving on the set.

The car pulls up into a large open space in front of the preserves of a big, crumbling stone building which was constructed as a cavalry fort some hundred years ago and is now renamed Fort Sumner.

Dotted around are a few smaller ruins – walls, mostly, that have long since ceased to support houses. The skull of a dead cow shines bone-white by a gate. And a Mexican is propping up a long pole with a red flag hanging stiffly at its mast and a white one trailing in the dirt. Red meant shooting was in progress.

It was extraordinary the effect this pole had on people. As soon as that red rag poked up into the cloudless sky everyone's conversation fell to a dead whisper, mouths were in suction with ears and footsteps were as timid as if the slightest noise would precipitate a wrathful earthquake – which it would, as we shall see.

There must have been 200 or more people – actors, Mexican extras, film people, women and kids – wrapped up in these mute, stony poses, or else gliding in concentrated slow-motion in and around the old lumps of stone that once rang out to the sounds of army life.

A silent frieze, while the birds twittered, horses snuffled in the pens inside the fort, and a couple of vultures wheeled obscenely in the sky. Here was a true conspiracy of silence. It was broken only by the man who held the right.

In one of the fort buildings, its blank windows shielded by black back-drops, Peckinpah was shooting and rehearsing his actors. He was out of sight, but the authority of his voice left no doubt as to its identity.

Coburn appeared, a lean handsome face with greying hair. He was wearing a Mexican coat in coloured patterns over a black vest and pants, and a black hat was perched on his head. He walked out of the door three times, on each occasion using the same movements and talking behind his shoulder as he did so.

Left: **Taking a break from the craziness of the road. Dylan on the 1965 US tour – his first with The Hawks, later to become The Band – after his controversial Newport Folk Festival appearance earlier that summer.**

"Right, like this, you say. Like this?"

And then Kristofferson. His face orange-brown with make-up and, minus his beard, looking about ten years younger. He was rangy in his dark, faded pin-stripes with the gun hanging off his hip. Sheriff Pat Garret and Billy the Kid. Meet the stars of the show.

And finally Sam Peckinpah came out. Not as tall or as big as you might have expected, but fierce, like an old bristling lion, with a thick white moustache and hair of the same colour wrapped around at the forehead with a green bandanna. He was the ferocious Anglo-Indian major of all those Kipling stories, leading his men over the Khyber Pass, sword in hand and a curse on his lips. It was easy to see why he scared the shit out of all and sundry.

He walked out the door and spat dramatically in the dirt. There was a loud phut! as the spittle hit and settled.

Later, when the scene was over and the white flag was up, I met Rudy Wurlitzer. He was the 36-year old author of three novels, one of which, Nog, has achieved cult status in England and America. He was also the writer of the screenplay for the James Taylor vehicle, Two-Lane Blacktop, never shown in Britain.

And now this movie. Wurlitzer was involved in this one as an actor, as well. He played another of Billy's gang. To this end his tall body was dressed in cruddy clothes and leather chaps, he had make-up like Clearasil smeared all over his face, and a battered top hat sat on his head. In his hand he twirled a Colt. He looked a real mean dude.

In reality he wasn't too happy, I learned, as weren't a good many on this film. It was two weeks overdue and a million dollars over budget, largely through technical problems; almost a fortnight's filming had been spoiled because the cameras were found to be out of focus.

Peckinpah was always in a huddle with the producer, Gordon Carroll, a tall, thin, snappy-looking man with light glasses. They were worried. And MGM was worried. The studios had sent down three executives already from Culver City to investigate the reasons for the late schedule. Peckinpah hated the studios with as much venom, but more realistic cause, than was contained in that gob of spit. He felt betrayed by them.

And then, if that wasn't enough, there was always Durango. Godddddd, Durango! The soullessness of the place, the boredom! The frustration of nothing to do, nothing to occupy the mind beyond memorising lines and that day's shooting, lay like an implacable, heavy hand over the set.

"Durango...it's a strange, dark place to make a film," Wurlitzer said. "Everyone gets so exposed." He whispered the last sentence.

We were sitting in one of the out-houses which had been roughly converted into a canteen for the crew. Outside they were shooting again. The voices came softly on the afternoon breeze. This and Two-Lane Blacktop, he muttered, were both horrible movies to work on, but in different ways. At the memory of the one he shook his head.

"James Taylor wasn't given a chance, no chance at all. He got no direction from Monte Hellman (the director) at all, which was what he desperately needed. Two-Lane Backtop was a better movie than people thought, but it forgot about two essentials: the road and speed. Monte didn't have too much strength to get it on. The original script was a little too original in a way.

"There's no doubt this is a better film, even if it turns out to be one of Sam's worst, because he has energy. What Sam does to language, for instance...he makes it more theatrical because he's innately theatrical.

17

It's like he's almost old-fashioned in what is the most effective. He imposed three scenes in the beginning of my script so that it works better from a film point of view. In my version, Pat and Billy never meet until the end. Here they do so at the beginning and the end."

To him, he explained, Pat and Billy were two gunmen who essentially felt a kinship but had chosen two diametrically opposed roles in life, the former as a sheriff, the latter as an outlaw. Thus they were the symbols of a changing America in the last century: the one a roving free spirit symbolising the pioneer nature of the Old West; the other selling out to the Establishment for a steady job and security, representing, therefore, the solidifying respectability of the new America.

And Dylan?

"Dylan is great," Wurlitzer whispered without any hesitation. "He's come down here to learn, he's turning in stuff and it's been really impressive. I think he's completely authentic. No, I don't know what he really wants to do but I would hope he would do his own film because he's an artist and he can't help it. He's just finding out about films."

Dylan and Peckinpah? He cocked an eye at me. "That's the really interesting thing," he replied thoughtfully, "what's going on between Peckinpah and Dylan. Sam is really Western, like an outlaw, looking to the wide-open spaces, and he didn't know about Dylan before.

"Dylan, you could say, was Eastern. He brings a different point of view, especially to a Western. The part is small but it's important in a funny sort of way. Do the two of them have any common ground to meet on – *that's* the big question."

Dylan, I'd been told, played the part with a stutter. "Yes, but it will have to be taken out. It becomes too much of a big thing if you only have a small part, and…"

Outside, here had been almost total silence except for faint, almost inaudible words, there now came a sudden angry bark and a command like a grating snarl. "Get outta that truck," it rapped with terrifying evenness. And then higher. "Get out! All of you!! Over there, behind the wall!!" There was a pause and then the rapid sound of many feet, and then quiet again.

A crew member tiptoed into the canteen with a ferocious grin on his face.

"He's the only person that can clear all the people outta one country just to make a f…ing pitcher," he breathed gleefully. There had been too much noise for Peckinpah.

They love Sam and they hate him. One bit player proclaimed proudly, as if he'd been granted his flying colours, "I bin 16 weeks with him on The Wild Bunch." But he can be as mean as snake juice when that devil bubbles to the surface.

Kristofferson spoke more fondly of him. "He's always gentle with his actors. He only bawls out one or two who know him well and have worked a lot with him before."

We were talking on the nightly plane from Durango back to Mexico City. He and all the other leading actors and members of his band were flying out for the rest of the weekend. It was Saturday evening. The final of the American World Series football championship was being televised on Sunday afternoon – there were no televisions in Durango. And Dylan was going to record with Kris's band that night at Columbia's studios in Mexico City.

I sat across the aisle from Kristofferson and we cradled a bottle of Jamieson's between us. On his other side was Rita Coolidge, who plays one of Billy's ladies in the film, as in real life. Her black hair was still pulled back into twin braids and she wore the rough, grey-patterned wool coat that costumes had given her, while Kristofferson was still in his movie duds; everyone had had to make a dash for the plane.

Leaning across the gangway, shouting above the noise of the engines, I was close enough to observe his pale blue eyes, which seemed oddly sightless, swimming a little with the effects of the whisky.

And there, in the seat behind him, was a little guy from Minnesota named Bob Dylan.

I had seen him fleetingly on the set that day. He had been wearing a scrape and an old grey top hat, but as he wasn't filming he flitted occasionally around the outskirts of the location, saying a few words to the odd people he knew well enough, but generally mute-faced and unsmiling. He looked skittery and ill-at-ease, and people seemed to avoid confronting him, as if the moment might be too charged with electricity.

But it was so obviously him! That face the colour of sour milk, and the full, sensuous nose, now pronouncedly Jewish, and the whole appearance of him that was nondescript at the same time that it was illuminated with the magnitude of him and our experience of him.

He was a whole era of youth coiled into one man and now slowly winding down into the years past 30, and the consciousness of this had escaped no-one, least of all him, with his eyes set straight and stonily to the front lest he be forced to pick up those curious side-long glances, as a magnet does iron filings.

Even on this plane his inviolacy was to be preserved to the full. He'd boarded with James Coburn and as they walked down the aisle together a seated passenger had asked for an autograph…from Coburn.

He hadn't been recognised in his rimless glasses, baggy beige parka and straw hat. But then, as the plane was taking off and I began to speak to Kristofferson, he got up jumpily from his seat and went to sit in the back.

We had begun to climb as he reluctantly dumped himself down again behind Kristofferson and next to Wurlitzer. He pulled his hat down right over the front of his face, which was odd because his body was rigidly upright in his seat, cocked and attentive.

We were touching down in Mexico City, with the Irish stuff two-thirds gone, and had had all the stories about his last English tour, his old landlady in Oxford and his ups and downs with Rita at the time, when Kristofferson's head came halfway across the gangway again and

Above: **In conversation with Pop Art superstar Andy Warhol. An aspiring movie maker himself, Dylan admired Warhol's attempts at making art through film. While none of his self-directed movies came to anything, Dylan would go on to make a number of big-screen appearances as an actor. None would trouble the Oscars judges.**

motioned behind him. He had just offered the bottle to Dylan, who had waved it away.

"Listen," he said, "this guy can do anything. In the script he has to throw a knife. It's real difficult. After ten minutes or so he could do it perfect."

He leaned over further. "Listen, he does things you never thought was in him. He plays Spanish-style, bossa nova, flamenco...one night he was playing flamenco and his old lady, Sara, had never known him do it at all before."

I looked back at the crown of the straw hat in uncompromising full-frontal. I said I was too scared to talk to the man right now.

"Sheeeeit! man," Kristofferson roared. "You're scared. I'm scared, and I'm making a pitcher with him!"

I began to feel more than ever like the lead in 'Ballad of a Thin Man'.

They recorded until seven the following morning on Dylan's 'Billy The Kid' and some other stuff he'd written down there in Durango.

Nobody knew if the material would be the basis of the movie soundtrack, or if Kristofferson's own song, 'Pat Garret', would be included, but a good deal of it was instrumental and it featured some trumpet men to give it a Mexican flavour.

Yet Jesus! It was so awkward with all those people in there, all those Mexican studio men come to see Bob Dylan play and sing. It began to be apparent that the stuff would have to be re-done, maybe in LA, after the movie.

Left: **Dylan and Joan Baez pour out their hearts during one of the many publicity and fund-raising benefits Dylan staged in 1975–76 to protest the innocence of former boxer Rubin 'Hurricane' Carter. His conviction for a triple murder not over-ruled until some years later, Carter would be portrayed by Denzel Washington in a 1999 movie in which Dylan's 'Hurricane' – originally released as a single in 1976 and featured on the Desire album – was given a much-deserved reprise.**

The following day, though, it was Sunday and in the afternoon practically everybody went over to the Fiesta Palace Hotel, where a suite had been booked, to see the Miami Dolphins beat up the Washington Redskins.

The Sheraton Hotel, where they were all staying, hadn't got television either. The hotel was always full of Americans and they never usually wanted to see Mexican television, which was filled out with the starch of Yankee series like 'The FBI' and 'McCloud', only in Spanish, and soccer. Soccer, for God's sake!

In room 734 Dylan slept deeply. He was still asleep when the maid came to the door and said it was ten o'clock. Ten o'clock! No, it couldn't be! He'd missed that plane back to Durango and it was his big scene today, where he got to throw the knife he'd been practising with!

He slung all his stuff in a carpet bag and flung himself down to the lobby, his eyes still popping like a camera shutter, just adjusting to being awake, to all these people down at reception, to the actual time it was! And then they tell him that it's okay anyway, and it's really ten at night, and he needn't have worried after all. He shook his head in relief.

There was no problem in making that plane the next Monday morning. He passed through gate four, the exit for Durango, and again nobody showed any sign of recognition. At least, they didn't ask for his autograph. But then, nobody wanted to talk much at 6.30 am, except, it seemed, Coburn and Wurlitzer, who were deep in conversation about the former's part.

Kristofferson was looking a little groggy. He'd been ill over the weekend. Probably that damned Irish whisky. He'd been smashed when he left the airport that Saturday evening. Hadn't stayed for the whole session, either.

Bobby got on the plane when they called the flight and sat down towards the back where there were a few empty seats around him. Kris and Rita were right down the other end, on the very front row.

About three-quarters of a hour out from Mexico City he saw the newspaper guy get up out of his seat, walk down to Kristofferson and crouch down to him talking.

This is part of what Kristofferson was saying. "...I was just disgusted with him. He'd start a song and then keep changing it around. He had horn players, trumpets, and they didn't know a damn thing what they had to do 'cause he couldn't make up his mind. I left about three." He said this very tiredly, then answered the question he'd been asked. "No, we haven't talked today."

Dylan saw all this, he saw the guy go back to his seat, and then he spoke to Bert Block about the newspaper he worked for.

That was when he spoke to me. I guess you could say I was startled.

Dylan talks in this light, soft voice with a husk to it, and he has this disconcerting habit of forcing you to lead the conversation.

He takes another person's sentence, chops it up in his mind, tosses it into the air and examines it when it falls, all before replying, so there are often a long couple of seconds before the answer comes; it's an unnatural limbo. It's not that he's unfriendly, but he's guarded and watchful to the point where conversation with strangers appears onerous for him.

He's also terribly shy, which he largely masks with an air of alienation he throws around him, like an enveloping cloak with a built-in burglar alarm.

It's because, beneath all the layers of the onion, there lurks a deep vulnerability that people instinctively feel protective towards him and are inspired to unsolicited loyalty, as if to say anything out of turn would not only betray a confidence, however unspoken, but would be bruising for him.

He doesn't smile too much and publicly he laughs even more rarely. His public persona never falters. Even those who could be considered friends are not privileged to many intimacies.

He may be the loneliest man in the world or he may be the happiest. There is no way of telling. Those who have known him since his early New York folk days say he has mellowed, but in so becoming he now holds the world at a distance and treats it from a detached position on his terms. All that may be fairly said is that those that count themselves among his friends, or even good acquaintances, prize their situation dearly.

Dylan talked to Playboy about his desire for anonymity back in 1966. "People have one great blessing," he said, "obscurity, and not really too many people are thankful for it. You can't take everything you don't like as a personal insult. I guess you should go where your wants are bare, where you are invisible and not needed."

Considering all this attitudinising, our conversation was prosaic enough. He did say, most interestingly, that he had been to England quite recently for a few days ("The clothes are different since last time"). We spoke for five minutes. Then I glanced out of the window briefly, turned back, and he was gone.

But disembarking from the plane, while everyone waited at tiny Durango airport for their baggage to be taken off, I found him at the bar, sipping a cup of coffee and engrossed with a camera belonging to CBS Records executive, Michael O'Mahoney, asking normal stuff like what lens it had. This was almost eight in the morning.

"It's not happening in London," I said, apropos a remark made on the plane. "New York's the place."

"That's what John Lennon says." Focusing the lens.

"I saw Eat The Document there, at the Whitney."

Pauses, returns the camera to O'Mahoney and looks directly at me. "Do you know Howard?" (Alk, the man who co-edited the film with Dylan).

"No. Was it originally like Don't Look Back before it was re-edited?"

"No, it couldn't be. We didn't have enough footage. There was 40 hours of it, but the camera was jumping around all the time. That was the only stuff we could salvage."

"Would you go black and play England ever?"

Silence. He turned three-quarters and carefully placed his cup on the counter. There was no answer. Instead, taking off at a sudden tangent, "Did you see Fly?"

"You mean the one about a fly crawling up the wall for half an hour? No." All three of us laughed, the first time I'd seen him do so.

"Did you see Hard On?" he asked suddenly.

"Huh?"

"Hard On."

"No, but I saw Rape. You know, the one with that girl being chased." He nodded.

"Andy Warhol was making movies like that years ago. The Empire State Building, all those shadows. I prefer the stuff with Morrisey, actually." I was trying not to sound smug.

He nodded again, then, "Did you see Lonesome Cowboys?"

"No, but I saw Heat..." It was getting to be quite funny. Every time he asked me, he looked so intense. "...Sylvia Miles."

"Yeah." Silence once more.

"Tell me, how can you stand it down here?"

"It's not too bad because I'm making a film. If I wasn't..." The sentence was chopped off because the producer, who was fidgeting all this time like an old hen over her chick, had come up and told him he could get into the car.

The next time I saw Dylan was on the set later that day and he was locked tight once more behind his stoniness.

I went out to El Suaz around one that afternoon, when the sun was cutting through the thinness of the desert air and the horizons were as sharp and concentrated as if focused through a lens.

This time nerves on the set were so jagged you could run a finger along their psychic edge. There was the same pregnant hush as two days ago, but it was even more intensified, as if everyone were holding in their breath in some giant expectation. It was the fascination of peering through a microscope, of seeing Dylan put through his paces in a crucial scene.

The shooting was out in the open, with six huge silver reflectors tilted on high above the scene. Peckinpah sat in his canvas director's chair by the camera. Emilio Fernandez, the famous Mexican director, was an onlooker. Before each take there was an abrupt cry of "Silenzio!", repeated twice to cut dead any lingering conversation.

As the scene was shot again and again the tension was alternately

Left: **No leopard-skinned pillbox hat, but there's more than a hint of Marc Bolan in Dylan's choice of headgear on this occasion...**

cranked up and then relaxed momentarily, so that with each successive time it became tighter and increasingly insufferable. I wanted to snap it violently, like severing a taut string, to let out all that constricted breath in a great explosion of air.

As the camera rolled Dylan was sitting on a chair surrounded by half a dozen ragged Mexican kids. He was strumming an acoustic, wearing a brown shirt, black pants and a grey top hat.

On the far right of the scene a cowboy was leaning on his horse. Billy the Kid and half a dozen of his gang were around a campfire on the left, nearest the camera.

One of this gang, Harry D Stanton, dressed in black with an old, greasy hat of the same colour, sat on a fence and shouted out, "Hey Chita, bring some beans, soup and tortillas, and be quick about it," and out from left comes this young Mexican serving wench carrying the chow, accompanied by Rita as another peasant chick. There's a lot of laughing and tomfoolery, with Kristofferson's voice striking a resonant bass note.

It's then that Dylan arrives. He's playing nervously with his knife, turning it round in his hand. The jitters seem genuine. He walks a dozen paces towards the campfire as the cowboy on the horse shouts after him, "Hey, boy, what's your name?" like he was a piece of dirt, and then he stops and faces around with the knife in his hand.

"Alias," he replies shortly. His body twitches a little. The knife taps against his leg.

"Alias *what?*" barks the horseman, the second word like the snake of a whiplash.

"Alias whatever you want," comes the rejoinder. Tough punk stuff. The gang laughs.

"They just call him Alias," says one. His interrogator grunts.

There's the sound of muttering – and then suddenly, in a flash-point that takes you by surprise, Dylan's right arms arcs back with the knife, and not the horseman but a seated outlaw gargles in the back of his throat and is knocked on his side by the force of the knife supposedly sticking through his neck. The moment still seems unexpected, even after the sixth take.

"Cut," says Peckinpah. "Aaaah!" goes all that escaping air, in relief. "Print it," grins Bert Block. The tableau of watchers and watched dissolves for another five minutes.

Print it! This is Bob Dylan, throwing a knife in a Sam Peckinpah movie, would you believe!

It's ironic. He leaves society at large as some kind of generational leader, a musical Messiah, and returns years later·as an actor playing a small role in a movie – yet already the film, before it's been finished even, sets us agog with speculation.

The questions mount. Will Dylan really turn away from music to concentrate more on films? Will he start making records again on a more regular basis now he's been drawn once more into a kind of public performance?

Could he ever return to doing concerts? The only answer that is really ascertainable is his acting ability, which will be on the line when this movie comes out some time after May. But even then there will be arguments about his performance, about its *meaning*.

He's unwavering, however, in his refusal to relinquish any part of his private self to his public, and this seems destined to continue.

You ask who is Bob Dylan? He is Alias. Alias whatever you want.

© Michael Watts / Melody Maker / IPC Syndication

Above: **A classic mid-sixties portrait of the angel-haired folk-poet hipster from Hibbing, Minnesota. Against all traditional rules of the game, his unique blend of social commentary, protest and radical politics had led to hit singles and multi-million selling albums.**

key recordings

1962	Signed to Columbia by John Hammond, *Bob Dylan* signals arrival of a unique talent
1965	Consternation in the folk world as Dylan goes electric for *Bringing It All Back Home*
1966	With help from Nashville's finest, Dylan cuts the classic *Blonde On Blonde*
1975	The results of Dylan's 1966–67 work-outs with The Band finally released as *The Basement Tapes*, while the new *Blood On The Tracks* became a multi-million seller
1976	Five weeks at No.1 in the US were fully deserved for *Desire*
1978	Still on a roll, Dylan delivers the excellent *Street Legal*
1983	Dire Straits guitar ace Mark Knopfler steps up to produce *Infidels*
1986	A feast for completists, the five-album box set *Biograph* includes 18 previously unreleased tracks from Dylan's past
1988	Dylan becomes Lucky Wilbury for *The Traveling Wilburys Vol.1*, teaming up with George Harrison, Tom Petty, Roy Orbison and Jeff Lynne
1988	A return to critical acclaim with the Daniel Lanois-produced *Oh Mercy*
1991	Even more joy for Those Who Want It All, in the shape of *The Bootleg Series Vols 1–3 (Rare and Unreleased)*
1992	*Good As I Been To You* sees Dylan back to a solo/accoustic format with a set of non-original traditional folk songs
1997	Lanois returns to produce the well-received *Time Out Of Mind*

The bullets which killed John Lennon as he made his way home in New York on December 8, 1980 did more than rob his wife, Japanese conceptual artist Yoko Ono, of a husband, and his sons, Julian and Sean, of a father. They also stilled a voice that had thrilled, provoked and entertained millions for close on 20 years, and murdered a songwriter who had helped change the way in which popular music was written and performed.

As a member of The Beatles, John Winston Lennon (born in Liverpool on October 9, 1940) became one of pop music's most influential artists and articulate spokesmen – something he could not have envisaged when he first stepped out as a teenaged member of the Quarry Men Skiffle Group in the late 1950s. Immersed as he was in the excitement of rock'n'roll music, Lennon would find a soul-mate in Paul McCartney, and the two of them created a rare chemistry that would catapult them to unimaginable heights between 1962 and 1970, when The Beatles formally disbanded.

The inevitable strain of superstardom had pushed Lennon into exploring his own artistic destiny long before that, however, and his 'discovery' of Yoko Ono's provocative art works in 1966 – and their deepening personal relationship – had helped end not only his first marriage but effectively terminated his creative partnership with McCartney.

Lennon's first collaboration with Ono was the startling Unfinished Music No.1 – Two Virgins album (with its much-banned full-frontal nude portrait of the couple) in 1968, and a year later they cemented their new union by marrying in Gibraltar, staging a week-long 'bed-in for peace' in a Montreal hotel and releasing their Life With The Lions album. Still operating under The Beatles' name, Lennon depicted all this in the hit single 'The Ballad of John and Yoko'.

As The Plastic Ono Band, Lennon and Ono enjoyed their first hit with the anthemic 'Give Peace A Chance', assembled a band and released a live album (mostly of 1950s rock classics, but including Ono's uniquely discordant first pass at the aptly-titled 'Cold Turkey'). In 1970, as

the last rites were being performed on The Beatles, The Plastic Ono Band enjoyed a trans-atlantic smash with 'Instant Karma', a single produced by Phil Spector.

Lennon's eponymous debut album in 1971 revealed a man intent on exorcising personal demons and demolishing old heroes after a term of intense psychotherapy, while Imagine – the album released later the same year – managed to blend unashamed love songs ('Oh Yoko' and 'Jealous Guy' included) with an attack on Paul McCartney ('How Do You Sleep'). The title track would become a huge hit and one of the century's most-performed anthems.

Now living in New York and fighting what would be a three-year battle to gain residential rights in the US, Lennon and Ono continued to collaborate on artistic projects that puzzled and outraged many. Rare commercially-viable undertakings included the single 'Happy Xmas (War Is Over)' in 1972, and the 1973 and 1974 albums Mind Games and Walls And Bridges.

In 1974 Lennon and Ono separated when he hit the bottle big-time and began an affair with May Pang, his former PA. Reunited, in 1975 they celebrated the arrival of a son, Sean, and Lennon began a five-year stint as a full-time house-husband. It was not until October 1980 that his double album of new songs, Double Fantasy, was released to critical acclaim and international No.1 hit status. Then, on November 8, as Lennon and Ono returned to their apartment after a recording session, he was hit by the five shots fired by 'fan' Mark Chapman.

Inevitably, John Lennon has enjoyed many posthumous hits, had his commercial output re-packaged and re-released on many occasions, and been the subject of innumerable biographies, few of which seem to come close to defining accurately his unique blend of magic, madness and majestic skill at painting pictures with words.

Previous page: **John and Yoko on stage. Yoko's experimental vocalisations left many fans bewildered and outraged. There is no doubt that his insistence on including her in all his appearances in the late 60s and early 70s alienated some who'd once thought that Lennon really was 'bigger than Jesus'.**

November 6 1971 Richard Williams

IN THE STUDIO WITH LENNON AND SPECTOR

Up on the 17th floor of the St. Regis Hotel in New York City, John Lennon is learning to type.

P...I...M...P, he types. I AM A PIMP.

"It's great," he says, "Yoko's teaching me."

John is in his bedroom, surrounded by the detritus of creation: guitars, books, notepads, nylon-tipped pens, and...a box full of Elvis Presley singles.

"I asked someone to get all his singles for me," he says, now down on his hands and knees, opening the box and spilling the bright red RCA labels over the floor.

The next ten minutes are spent sorting them out. 'My Baby Left Me', 'Hound Dog', 'One Night', and the old Sun classics are in one pile, while crap like 'Bossa Nova Baby' and 'Are You Lonesome Tonight' go on another.

"I'm gonna have a jukebox with just Elvis records on it. Isn't it great?"

In the next room, the living room, is still more tribute to the life and works of a total media freak. There are piles of Yoko's books, Grapefruit, stacks of big film cans, and a hi-fi.

His travelling record collection includes albums by Bo Diddley (three), Chuck Berry (two), Lenny Bruce (six), the Mothers (everything), Paul McCartney ('Ram' – and it's been played at least once), and Link Wray (with cover inscribed "To John and Yoko – thanks for remembering – Peace, Link Wray").

The story behind the Wray inscription is that John and Yoko were getting out of the lift at 1700 Broadway, which houses Allen Klein's office, when they were confronted by Wray, who was going up to Polydor's offices in the same building.

Wray apparently said, "Hey – John and Yoko." John didn't say anything to him, but turned to Yoko and breathed, "Yoko, that's Link Wray. Without him..." Whether it's true or merely apocryphal, it illustrates one of John's most endearing characteristics: he *remembers*.

Back in the bedroom, John's talking about the Plastic Ono Band, and his plans for going on the road early in 1972.

"I've got a lot to learn," he sighs. "It's been seven years, you know...but it's important to get the band on the road, to get tight. It's been fun just turning up at the odd gigs like Toronto and the Lyceum and the Fillmore, but I'm sick of having to sing 'Blue Suede Shoes' because we haven't rehearsed anything."

To that end, the band will have a nucleus of John (guitar and vocals), Yoko (vocals), Nicky Hopkins (piano), Klaus Voorman (bass), and Jim Keltner (drums). With luck, there'll also be Phil Spector on guitar and vocals, on stage for the first time since the Teddy Bears (which comes into the Believe-It-When-You-See-It department), and a lead guitarist. John wrote to Eric Clapton, offering him the gig, but Eric isn't too well and didn't reply.

"We'll probably get some kid who just walks in and knocks us out. D'you know anything about a guy called Roy Buchanan? He's supposed to be the greatest, but I've never heard of him. I'll have to find out. I don't want to play lead – I'm just an amateur."

But the flexibility will still be there, and other musicians will be able to come and go as they wish. The nucleus will ensure that they don't have to jam all night on old 12-bars.

John wants to make the whole thing into a travelling circus, sending Yippie leader Jerry Rubin ahead of the troupe to round up local bands and street theatre groups in whatever cities they're playing. As an illustration of the kind of people they want, John mentioned David Peel and the Lower East Side in New York, and the Pink Fairies in London.

Right: **A vintage shot of Lennon in very early 60s Hamburg was used for the cover of his 1975 Rock 'N' Roll album. Set to be produced by Phil Spector, it would ultimately be a John Lennon production after he and Spector fell out when work began on the album two years earlier.**

Left: **The two virgins: John and his wife, Yoko Ono, take some time out in their New York apartment. The couple set up home in Greenwich Village before settling into the Dakota Building complex off Central Park. It was there that Lennon was shot and killed by Mark Chapman in December 1980.**

He gets to talking about his songs, and how he pinches bits from his favourite rock and roll numbers. There's a new one about Chuck Berry and Bo Diddley, which he sings sitting on his bed, and he shows you how the middle-eight is pinched from US Bonds' 'Quarter To Three', which he heard on the radio the other day.

Then there's the song he and the Plastic Ono Band will be recording that very night, for their Christmas single. It's called 'Happy Christmas (War Is Over)', and he says that when he first played it to Spector, the producer said that the first line is a direct crib from the Paris Sisters' 'I Love How You Love Me', which Phil produced back in the pre-Crystals days.

"I like quoting from old songs," John says, "but you get into such trouble with copyrights. It's a drag."

He jams what looks like a set of earphones, with an antenna protruding from each side. It turns out to be an FM stereo radio, and within seconds he offers it to Yoko.

"Hey, listen Yoko, that's 'Get A Job', one of the old ones." She listens, and he turns, "I'm having to educate her about rock and roll, you see."

That evening, John is sitting on the fringed carpet of the Record Plant, a studio on West 44th Street. He's surrounded by five young acoustic guitarists, to whom he's teaching the chords of 'Happy Christmas'.

Why all those rhythm guitars? Listen – just remember whose producing this session, brother.

One of the guitarists is Hugh McCracken, the brilliant session musician who played on 'Ram', but John doesn't know that yet.

He asks them for their names. "Chris". "Teddy". "Stu". "Hugh". John turns to Yoko. "Hey, that Hugh looks like Ivan, doesn't he? Hugh, you look just like an old school-mate of mine."

There's a little break, and everybody gets up and walks around. Someone tells John about Hugh.

"Oh, so you were just auditioning on 'Ram' were you?" John asks. "Yeah, 'e said you were all right." Everyone grins.

They're back to learning the tune, getting the feel. "Just pretend it's Christmas," John tells them. "I'm Jewish," says one. "Well pretend it's your birthday then."

They've all got it down, so John leads them into a jam on 'Too Much Monkey Business', 'Rock Island Line' and 'Slippin' And Slidin'. It's meat and drink to him.

Suddenly there's a little flurry at the entrance. Phil Spector's arrived, in big shades, wearing a big red and white button saying "Back To Mono", which breaks everyone up. But he's serious, you know.

Immediately, the session is working. Within seconds of getting behind the huge board, Spector is thinking in terms not just of sound, but of arrangement, drama, production. It takes him about ten seconds to get a sound which transforms the guitars from a happy rabble into a brilliant cutting wash of colour, and they aren't even miked properly yet.

"Play that back to 'em," Phil tells the engineer. "Get 'em relaxed." It does just that, and during the playback Phil goes into the studio and dances around with John.

They run through the changes again, with Nicky Hopkins on piano this time. Immediately, Phil tells him: "Nicky, I'd like to hear more of that with octaves in the right hand...make it more dramatic." John leans down to the guitar mike and shouts: "Don't dictate on them yet, Phil. Let's get comfortable first."

Already, you see, Spector is into the groove, moulding and blending and transforming in the tradition of 'Be My Baby', 'Then He Kissed Me' and 'River Deep'. Right now, well ahead of everyone (even Lennon), he's hearing what it's going to sound like when it's coming out of a million transistors.

At this point, they add bass and drums. Jim Keltner settles behind his kit, and one of the rhythm guitarists is moved over to the bass because Klaus's flight from Germany has been delayed and he's going to miss the session. They can't wait.

They run it down a few times, and Keltner's expression while he's playing is like that of a man whose toes are slowly being eaten away by a shoal of piranhas. It's sounding very good, the tape is spinning all the time, and after each run they come back and listen.

John: "I like ones that sounds like records..."

"...before you've made 'em." Phil finishes the sentence for him.

Without even seeming to notice, they're doing takes. During the second or third, it really begins to lift off. Phil is sitting at the board, staring through the sound-proofed window into the studio, spitting out comments at the engineer: "More echo on the piano, Roy...more echo...more...more echo, c'mon! More! That's it!"

He stands up during the second chorus, arms wind-milling, looking at Keltner, signalling him to lay into his tom-toms, urging him to explode like Hal Blaine did almost ten years ago. Keltner strains to oblige, and the take ends in a blaze of glory with Phil shouting "F***ing great! Great!"

Now, as the overdubs start, the Spector magic is again overwhelmingly apparent. At John's suggestion, the acoustic guitars play a mandolin-like riff, strongly reminiscent of Ronnie Spector's 'Try Some, Buy Some', and all sorts of percussive effects are tried.

Above: **John shelters Yoko as they leave London's Marylebone magistrates court in November 1968. The couple had been charged with possession of cannabis and John was fined £150 (then about $450) after taking the rap.**

Nicky plays chimes and glockenspiel, which have been hastily hired, and Keltner adds a jangling four-on-a-bar on a handy pair of sleigh bells.

"How can you make a song called 'Happy Christmas' without bells?" Phil had asked, rhetorically, earlier. Now he's smiling and mutters from the corner of his mouth: "I know something about Christmas records, you know."

Instantly, minds float back to Philles LP 4005, 'A Christmas Gift To You', several months in the making back there in the Sixties, and now a rare classic to those who know it. After that, Phil probably knew more about making Christmas records than anyone in the world.

The instrumental overdubs over, time comes for the vocal track to be cut. The song itself is really in three parts: the verse, sung by John; the chorus, sung by Yoko; and a secondary chorus, sung under the lead vocal, for which they'll be getting in a bunch of kids the next day.

John says he wrote it "because I was sick of 'White Christmas'," and it could well take over as the annual Yuletide anthem. It's terrifically singable, in the tradition of 'All You Need Is Love' or 'Give Peace A Chance', and it's very pretty too. The words are simple and direct, with the chorus going, "War is over/if you want it/war is over now," while John and Yoko express appropriate good wishes to all mankind.

The pair of them enter the studio, clap on the cans, and start singing over the track. John sounds wheezy, unable to hit the high notes, and Phil shouts through the talk-back: "Yoko's out-singing you, John." He tells everyone in the booth: "He's smoking his ass off while he's singing," and shakes his head in disapproval.

John finally gets Yoko to come in at all the right places, with the aid of tactful prods in the back, and when Phil's got the right echo on the voices they finally lay it down right, and come back to listen to the rough mix.

It's right, and they start talking about what they're going to do with the strings, which they'll overdub in a couple of days. Phil has the idea of getting them to play 'Silent Night' over the fade, and after falling about they all agree that it's exactly right.

Nicky is worrying about the piano part, which he's already overdubbed, and wants to do it again. They listen back once more, tell him that it's perfectly all right as it is, and John adds: "Did you know that George wanted to redo his guitar solos on 'Gimme Some Truth' and 'How Do You Sleep'? That's the best he's ever played in his life, and he'd never get that feeling again, but he'd go on for ever if you let him."

Once again they remix what they have. By this time it's four o'clock, and after a few more listens everyone goes home. Three hours later, I wake up singing "War is over...if you want it...war is over now."

Jim Keltner is the kind of musician all too few drummers are. His experience comes from long days and nights in the studios of Los Angeles, and from years of listening to the best.

His musical interests are wide. He talks with equal pleasure of going to see Ornette Coleman years ago, when the altoist had drummer Ed

Blackwell in his band, and of living near Hal Blaine, who himself created a whole style of drumming, partly on the early Philles records.

Keltner talks softly, but wields a big talent. His playing is tight, precise, and funky, and Lennon says of him: "He's a drummer who leads you, instead of dragging, and there aren't too many of those". That's why he's in the Plastic Ono Band, instead of all the other names you could mention.

He knows a hell of a lot more about musicians than most of his contemporaries bother to learn. He particularly reveres the late Benny Benjamin, whose work gave the early-Sixties Motown records their unstoppable drive, and for tightness, he says, you can't beat Jabbo, James Brown's veteran percussionist.

Drinking orange juice on 8th Avenue just before dawn, he pricks his ears up to the sound of Diana Ross's 'Surrender' on the jukebox. It's all music – he's all music.

It's the following night, and the band is running through the song which is going to be the single's B-side, Yoko's 'Snow Is Falling', the first of her songs that she ever showed John, when they first got together five years ago. At last, she's getting a chance to record it.

But there's an argument. John and Yoko can't agree about the tempo. "I'm not gonna play on this," says John, who was picking out lines on heavy-reverb guitar. "I asked you to play the organ," says Yoko. "I've been asking you to do that all along."

John decides to go back into the booth, where Phil greets him with: "I thought this was supposed to be a light thing." It was, John agrees, but "she says 'faster' and they all get to rocking like – "

Yoko is telling Nicky to play lighter on the intro. "Pretend that it's snowing...that snow is melting your fingertips. Not that banging."

Nicky gets it right, while Klaus and Hugh McCracken (who's been invited back after his performance the previous night, and on the strength of his reputation) work out little runs and licks which turn out like early Curtis Mayfield.

They all try it, and Yoko and Klaus get into a shouting match about where the chords go at the end of the song. Klaus gets up, unstraps his bass, and appears ready to walk out. But John placates both him and Yoko, and they try it again – with successful results.

They take it, get a good one, and come back to the booth.

John: "Fantastic..."

Phil: "Great, great tape echo..."

Yoko: "How was my voice?"

Phil: "Great...lots of tape echo..."

It sounds simple and pretty, but within five minutes they're talking about adding organ, chimes, more guitar, and even sound effects.

Above: **Lennon performs his 'Yer Blues' on the set of The Rolling Stones' Rock and Roll Circus, with a little help from his friends Keith Richards (on bass for a change) and Jimi Hendrix Experience drummer Mitch Mitchell. Also in the band that night in December 1968 was Eric Clapton (left)...and Yoko Ono.**

Above: **John, George Harrison and Yoko being interviewed in the offices of Apple, The Beatles' HQ, in London.**

What they want is the sound of a celeste, but there isn't one available, so the engineers get to work to make the electric piano sound like one.

While they discuss it, Phil pronounces the name "cheleste". Everyone else starts by calling it "Seleste". But within minutes, it's "cheleste" all round. Phil is the musical heavy, you see, and if that's how he says it, that's how it is.

As the engineers work, Nicky and Hugh and Jim start to play the blues. "Oh-oh," says Phil. "They've started jamming, and we'll never get anything done. Let's put a stop to that." He moves to the connecting door.

"STOP JAMMING!" screams Yoko, nearly bursting the talk-back speakers. They stop as one man, in mid-semiquaver, leaving John to add, almost apologetically: "Well, you've got to do something while they're trying to make the piano sound like a celeste." His pronunciation has slipped back to the "s".

Yoko is obviously tense, and confides that she believes that the musicians don't take her songs as seriously as they might. But this is a very good song, no doubt about it; very attractive and extremely commercial, and by the time the overdubs have been done it sounds like a potential A-side, much stronger than her current single, 'Mrs Lennon'.

Only one thing remains, and that's to put on the sound effects. Someone digs out the effects album that all studios keep for such occasions, and they decide to open and close the track with the sound of "Feet In The Snow", superimposed on "Strong Wind".

The engineers begin splicing the tapes, and Phil asks John: "Have you heard Paul's new album?"

"No."

"It's really bad...just four musicians, and it's awful."

"Don't talk about it. It depresses me."

"Don't worry, John. 'Imagine' is number one, and this will be number one too. That's all that matters."

"No, it's not that. It's just that when anybody mentions his name, I don't think about the music – I think about all the business crap. Don't talk about him."

Splicing over, the lights are turned off for the final playback, and it's magical. "Listen...the snow is falling everywhere."

Leaving the studio, it's a shock to realise that those soft, white flakes aren't drifting down through a cold night air. Actually, it's quite warm out.

John and Yoko are being talked about as the new Burton and Taylor, but really they're closer to Douglas Fairbanks and Mary Pickford in the way that they're at the centre of an artistic maelstrom.

They've been in New York since the middle of August, and they're likely to stay there a long time. John's recent statement, in the MM, that they're not appreciated in Britain, is entirely understandable when one sees them in New York.

There, they're in a creative milieu which understands and embraces them, and, what's more, moves at their phenomenal pace. Everybody travelled to Syracuse, in upstate New York, for Yoko's recent exhibition, whereas if they'd held something similar in, say, Coventry, it would have been virtually ignored.

It's a never-ending furore, and to zone in on it even harder they've moved out of the St. Regis Hotel and into the Village, where they've bought one loft and are renting another, from ex-Spoonful drummer, Joe Butler.

Butler's loft, where they're presently living while the other is being readied, has two huge rooms with a wrought-iron spiral staircase up to a small roof garden. The walls are painted brick, the furnishing and fittings immaculate and mostly interesting antiques.

The Lennons have both bought push-bikes, which is the way to travel around the Village. John's is English, Yoko's is Japanese. Coincidence, they say, and John's has got a nice shiny chromed bell on the conservative sit-up-and-beg handlebars.

"Everybody cycles around the Village," John says. "Dylan goes about on his all the time, chaining it to the railings when he stops, and nobody ever recognises him. I can't wait to get out on mine."

But the main beauty of the Village is the company they can keep. In the next loft to the Lennons is John Cage, whom they haven't seen yet (although Yoko keeps trying to rouse him by banging on the windows), and around the corner are Dylan, Jerry Rubin and a host of other superstars.

"It's the best place in the world," John states flatly. "Every time the car leaves the Village, I feel sick. Going back to England is like going to Denmark – and I don't want to live in Denmark."

Sunday afternoon at the Record Plant, and they're starting early because the choir is there, and the choir has to be in bed soon.

The choir is 30 black kids, aged from about four to 12, with a quartet of nubile young teens whom John instantly dubs "The Supremes". A few mothers are there, too, generally shushing and finger-wagging and making sure that ribbon-bows aren't crooked.

John and Yoko teach the kids the song and the words to "Happy Christmas" from a blackboard, and after only a few tries they've got it, superimposed on the already-mixed track.

"F***ing great!" shouts Phil afterwards, leaping around, and the engineer quickly checks that the talk-back is off.

It's all finished now, apart from the strings, so the Lennons, the band, the kids, the engineers, the secretaries, Phil, and Phil's brother-in-law Joe, gather round to pose for the picture for the cover of the single.

A plastic Christmas tree, with lights, has been erected and towers above the group. The photographer is being a little slow, having trouble getting everyone into the frame, so Phil takes over: "C'mon Ian...when I shout 'ONE TWO THREE', everybody shout 'HAPPY CHRISTMAS' and you take the picture. ONE TWO THREE (HAPPY CHRISTMAS) ONE TWO THREE (HAPPY CHRISTMAS) ONE TWO THREE (HAPPY CHRISTMAS). Okay Ian, you got it."

I'll bet he even produces his breakfasts.

Above: **John and Yoko's first notorious 'bed-in',** held in Amsterdam after they'd married in Gibraltar on March 20, 1969. In May that year they'd repeat the stunt in Montreal, Canada, where the singalong chorus of 'Give Peace A Chance' was recorded by a choir that included LSD guru Dr Timothy Leary, Beat poet Allen Ginsberg...and British pop singer Petula Clark!

key recordings

1968   Release of *Unfinished Music No 1 – Two Virgins* to establish John and Yoko's intention of doing their thing, regardless of public opinion.

1969   *Unfinished Music No 2 – Life With The Lions* is continuation of *Virgins* project plus a cassette-recorded side of Ono's miscarriage labour at Queen Charlotte Hospital, London. *Give Peace A Chance* single first to use Plastic Ono Band name. Poor sales of second single, *Cold Turkey* leads Lennon to return MBE medal to Queen in protest. Release of avant-garde *The Wedding Album*.

1970   *Live Peace In Toronto 1969*, recorded at Canadian rock revival festival, gives Plastic Ono Band first US Top 10 album placing. *Cold Turkey* single peaks at US No.30. Phil Spector-produced *Instant Karma* goes Top 10 in US and UK.

1971   After intensive therapy, Lennon releases *John Lennon and The Plastic Ono Band* album, which includes hit single *Mother*. In May has US and UK hit with political *Power To The People* single, and in September leaves Britain for ever. Release of *Imagine* album in October signals most commercial post-Beatles period as album and title track top international charts. Widening rift with McCartney evidenced by inclusion of acerbic *How Do You Sleep*. Legal hassles restricts release of Spector-produced *Happy Xmas (War Is Over)* to US, where it peaks at lowly 57 in charts.

1972   Identical US chart position achieved by controversial *Woman Is The Nigger Of The World* single, a track taken from highly political double album *Some Time In New York City*, recorded with NY band Elephant's Memory and The Mothers of Invention. *Happy Xmas* reaches UK No.4 when finally released near year end.

1973   *Mind Games* album a hit, as is title track single.

1974   *Walls And Bridges* album tops US charts and lodges in Top 10 in UK. Single *Whatever Gets You Through The Night* also tops US chart.

1975   Single *No.9 Dream* is decent transatlantic hit. Lennon records *Rock 'n' Roll* album with Phil Spector and has international hit with cover of Ben E King's classic *Stand By Me*. A Greatest Hits compilation, *Shaved Fish*, helps *Imagine* (not previously released there on 45 rpm) to achieve UK hit status for first time. Lennon announces intention of quitting music business to raise his son, Sean.

1980   *Double Fantasy* album released and hits No.1 position all over world. Lennon's death signals huge sales for singles *(Just Like) Starting Over, Imagine, Give Peace A Chance, Jealous Guy, Woman* and *Happy Xmas (War Is Over)*.

1995   A home-recorded demo of Lennon's previously unreleased song *Free As A Bird* is augmented by fellow Beatles McCartney, Harrison and Starr to create the opening track (and a hit single) for first volume of *The Beatles Anthology* CD series.

A great deal of what you need to know about Paul McCartney can be gauged by where he chose to close the millennium – in December 1999 he took his new band to play not in any of the world's large stadiums but in The Cavern, the 300-capacity cellar club built on the site of the original Liverpool club he and The Beatles had last played on August 3, 1963. Just as tellingly, the album with which he chose to greet the new century, Run Devil Run, was a collection of golden oldie rock 'n' roll classics – the kind of music he cut his teeth on.

McCartney has enjoyed a curate's egg of a solo career. Parts of it have been excellent, but his innate conservatism has often led him to play it safe and, whisper it, bland. His first eponymous album (which topped charts worldwide) was a solo tour de force, with James Paul McCartney playing every instrument. Its success was due to his status as a Beatle, and even if music critics (and, later, John Lennon) were to be underwhelmed by the preponderance of slushy ballads on that and his 1971 album, Ram, McCartney's rock credentials were proved by ballsier offering like the throat-tearing 'Maybe I'm Amazed'.

By his third album, Wild Life, McCartney had the support of Wings – his wife, Linda, on keyboards, ex-Moody Blue Denny Laine on guitar, and US session drummer Denny Seiwell. Trekking across Britain and Europe, McCartney and Wings were substantially tighter for the 1973 Red Rose Speedway album (featuring the smash single 'My Love'). McCartney had also dented his goody-goody image by being busted twice for marijuana possession (in Sweden and Scotland) and having the BBC ban his 'Give Ireland Back To The Irish' single.

Asked to write the theme for the Bond movie, Live And Let Die, in August 1973 he came up with a massive, complex and thunderous opus which became another international hit, then flew Wings to Nigeria for the sessions which would result in Band On The Run, an album that sold six million copies during the two years it spent in the US and UK charts.

McCartney returned to the States in April 1974, with a five-piece Wings (guitarist Jimmy McCulloch and drummer Geoff Britton having joined). In Nashville McCartney produced sessions for Peggy Lee, but came into his own again in 1975 when Venus And Mars (which

Above: **Paul chats with Mick Jagger, one of the many Swinging Sixties figures who sat in during the live world-wide TV transmission of The Beatles' 'All You Need Is Love' on June 25, 1967. They reckon 400 million people watched The Beatles' appearance that night.**

"We couldn't think of anywhere else to do the interview. We thought we might as well come to you. For me, it takes me back ten years at least, when we used to come touting ourselves round, although this time we're not touting ourselves.

"It was the very first thing we did when we came to London. I remember going to Robert Stigwood's office, and he wouldn't see us. Never been struck on him since."

Much mirth, and a lighting of cigarettes. Glasses of Chateau Holborn Viaduct were poured, and a convivial atmosphere reigned. The last we had heard from Wings, they had been riven by splits, when drummer Denny Seiwell quit along with guitarist Henry McCulloch, just prior to the group's trip to Lagos to record. What caused all that and how were the McCartney's received in Nigeria?

"We enjoyed it eventually. We're all a bit British y'know. First thing you have to adjust, as if you were going to Spain.

"You've the different food and climate and stuff so you've got a lot of adjusting to do. It was at the end of the rainy season when we went.

"We thought it was going to be tropical, warm and fantastic. It turned out to be a torrential monsoon.

"And we got robbed while we were down there. Some guys robbed us – with a knife. We got held up walking out late at night, and you're not supposed to do that.

"They took our tape recorder and cameras and gear. So that didn't help.

"And then Fela Ransome Kuti accused us of trying to steal black African music.

"So I had to say, 'do us a favour Fella. We do all right as it is actually. We sell a couple of records here and there.'

"And he's welcome to their music. It's very nice. I love it, and wish I could do it, but he's welcome to it.

"But he does have a fantastic band out there, one of the best live bands I've ever heard. It's funky and not very sophisticated.

Right: **He plays a pretty mean bass, too. Originally one of The Beatles' three guitarists (Messrs Lennon and Harrison were the other two), Paul switched to bass only when the group's original bassist, Stuart Sutcliffe, quit in 1961 to concentrate on a promising career as a painter.**

"You saw it in Ginger Baker's film, but it didn't come off at all well in the film.

"There was one and a half weeks of pretty bad vibes. It felt a bit dangerous, and raw, and your not sure how you're going to figure.

"The press were fine, very charming. But it's funny what they pick up. They picked up that I was 'the one who introduced drugs to the Beatles.'

"It's such a long range from the source, they must have picked up stories through about fifty African countries before they got to them, and they are really garbled accounts. I think they just give everyone a hard time to see what you're made of."

What lured them to Africa?

"Sunshine," said Linda.

"We got a list off EMI of all the studios around the world. It's a big company. We checked on the availability of Lagos and it turned out it would be free for the three weeks we wanted to record.

"So we thought great – lying on the beach all day, doing nothing. Breeze in the studios and record. It didn't turn out quite like that.

"But that was why we went – it was for an adventure. We did seven tracks there and came back and did a couple of tracks and mixed here."

How did they get on with er, the insects?

"Oh not too bad. It does bother some people. We're not creepy-crawly freaks. Linda and lizards – great. She doesn't mind. But somebody else, for instance the engineer we took out, who did 'Sgt. Pepper' and 'Abbey Road,' he couldn't stand them.

"So a couple of the lads put a spider in his bed. It was all a bit like scout camp.

"The worst a lizard can do is bite you, so we're not freaked out by that, not like Ringo's wife who can't stand a fly in the room. She has all their positions charted, and if one comes near her, she freaks out."

Having just heard a portion of the album, it didn't sound at all African influenced.

"It isn't" agreed Paul. "Well, it is, but you wouldn't be able to hear it. I know it was influenced by Africa, just because of the atmosphere rather than the music. In Africa I felt like you had to come-on.

"In England you can lay it back, and be timid and you get away with it, because nobody minds. Out there, you've got to be very forward.

"And there's no way you can lay on them modern Western liberal crap. So in a way we were influenced by the challenge of the people and country.

"Linda thought I had died one night. I was recording and suddenly felt like a lung had collapsed.

"So I went outside to get some air, and there wasn't any. It was a humid, hot tropical night. So I collapsed and fainted."

Said Linda: "I laid him on the ground and his eyes were closed and I thought he was dead!"

Paul went to the doctor who advised he had been smoking too much. When the McCartneys got over their initial worries, they found Nigeria was an exciting, friendly country.

But only three of Wings made the trip. What happened to the others?

"Only Denny (Laine) was with us. You know two of them left? Denny (Seiwell) and Henry quit and Denny rang up an hour before we left from Gatwick, to say he couldn't make the album, so that was a panic time.

"Henry left over what we call 'musical differences.' And it was actually that. We were rehearsing and I asked him to play a certain bit, he was loath to play it, and kinda made an excuse about it couldn't be played.

"I, being a bit of a guitarist myself, knew it could be played, and rather than let it pass I decided to confront him with it, and we had a confrontation. He left rehearsals a bit chocked, then rang up to say he was leaving.

"I thought 'fair enough,' so it was exactly the stereotyped 'musical difference.' And Denny didn't want to come to Africa.

How did they make up the numbers?

"There was just the three of us, on the album, except for the orchestral overdubs, which we didn't play. We got Tony Visconti to help with the arrangements.

"One guy, Remi Kebaka, who is from Lagos, ironically, turned up in London for a loon, and we got him on one track playing percussion.

"He's the only other person on the entire album, except for the orchestra. I played all the drums and bass. Denny sometimes doubles on bass."

When did Paul first get into playing drums?

"For years I like suggested to Ringo a lot of what he might play and I heard drums well. I first got into it listening to 'Sweet Little Sixteen,' where there was a drum break around the kit.

"I would ask Ringo to play some variation on that. And at sessions I would climb on the drum kit and start having a go.

"And in Hamburg, one week Tony Sheridan's drummer got sick and I drummed for him, for the extra cash, for a week.

"So I've done a bit of drumming, including a couple of Beatle tracks, but nothing much that I can remember.

"We always used Ringo because he's a real drummer. There's nothing flash to the drumming on the Wings album, nothing difficult.

"But I can hold quite a good beat. Liking drums anyway, it gave me a good chance to fulfil an ambition.

Most of the songs on the album, called "Band On The Run," incidentally, were actually written in Scotland, at the McCartney retreat.

"It's a collection of songs, and I'll leave it to you to say if they are good or not. The basic idea about the band on the run is a kind of prison escape.

"At the beginning of the album the guy is stuck inside four walls, and eventually breaks out. There is a thread, but it's not a concept album."

Does the story apply to Wings escaping from the Beatles?

"Sort of – yeah. I think most bands on tour are on the run."

How much satisfaction has Wings given the couple since its inception?

"Got us on the road," said Linda. "Which is what it's all about."

"I wanted some way I could feel easy about appearing live again," explained Paul. "It was very difficult after the Beatles, because at the time, they weren't interested in going live except on really big gigs.

"I was more interested in kinda playing smallish things, and getting near audiences again. It was like the pub rock bit.

"It was selfish reasons really, I just wanted to play live! But we got a good British tour out of it, and the second half of the European tour was good.

"And we loved the University tour we did because that was really down home. So we accomplished what we set out to do, and now we are putting Wings Mark II together.

"I miss it for sure," said Linda, "because I'd never done anything like that before."

" She's a real trouper now," nodded Paul.

Do Wings have any plans for a Christmas single?

"No, not at the moment. We're just seeing how 'Helen Wheels' does. We might take something off the album.

"We like 'Helen,' it's a good boogie-rocker, and seems to be doing quite well at the moment.

"I'd like to see it move a little more. I'd like to see them all move a little more!"

Why hasn't it done so well; is there any explanation?

"Well, in America it's done well. In Britain? Dunno really. We don't have a policy on singles. We're a bit vague on all that.

"All we need is for someone to say, 'that'll make a good single,' and we bung it out. We're a bit haphazard. But they all seem to sell quite well.

"We've not had a great big hit single in Britain for a while. The British market is a bit funny at the moment. I mean "Eye Level" and next week Gary Glitter or Donny Osmond. It's quite a big teenybopper market.

"Yet Gary, and Dave Cassidy and the Osmonds don't do anything in America. And big acts here don't do well there. Bowie, for instance, doesn't do a lot in the States.

"So we're quite content at the moment just to have a number one album. That'll do me!"

What kind of market is Wings aimed at?

"General – general market really. We'll turn up at Butlin's holiday camps. Anywhere people want to listen to some music. We're not directed at any one audience."

Will Wings get heavier?

"I don't like the idea that we played 'gentle rock,' as someone said. Don't really like that, and it's not what we're trying to do. Live – it comes on much more rockin'. When we get to the records, it's been a little kinda, lightweight.

'I can't put my finger on it, we're just into stuff that we like, and it changes from time to time.

"One minute with me, I'm dead keen on ballads, and we were in a French club the other night and my favourite track played the whole night was Fred Astaire singing 'Cheek to Cheek.'

"Everybody in the club rocked like mad and we all had big beaming smiles. My musical tastes are vast you know, classical music, even Al Bowlly, and Pink Floyd in the same breath.

'The last concert we went to was Eric's at the Rainbow. I hope this thing comes off where he's going to play with a band again.

"That'll be the best thing for him. It'll make it all less precious. That's what I found in my case anyway.

"You start off with all that 'We are coming to witness a legend,' type thing, and it turns into 'We're coming to see a band,' and it's much nicer.

"By the time we did our British tour with Wings, it just felt like a working band. I do think Eric needs to play in public a lot more regularly, just to kind of ease up the pressure.

"He played fine at the Rainbow. But even that was a bit precious, when the compere came on and said: 'He's here!' Yes, we know he's here, we've come to see him.

"But we're just quietly looking around for a really nice guitarist, and drummer. I still don't know in my mind yet, exactly what I want.

"We went with Henry because I knew he was a good guitar player, and that nearly worked out. Even if we keep chopping and changing, it doesn't worry me too much.

"It would be nice to have a steady band, because the public like it, and like to get settled with a band.

"We were going to tour Australia in the New Year around January, but we've cancelled that, and we're looking around, but not desperately. We're not auditioning people.

"We just took Jimmy McCulloch from Blue, who's rehearsing with Chris Stainton, and we did a couple of tracks with Jimmy in Paris.

"We're just playing with people to get the feel of what we want and what they like.

"We had one track of Linda's which we tried to include in our albums but it never seemed to fit. So what we're going to do is a bit like Derek and the Dominoes. We're doing a thing with Linda, not like 'I am Linda McCartney, come and listen to me, I'm going to be a big star,' and all this big hype.

"That she doesn't want, and I don't fancy either because it's too pompous. She's not ready for it, she's still an apprentice, which is cool because she doesn't mind.

"It's the right position for her. So we're doing this thing called Suzie and the Red Stripes. And she is Suzie! Plus Jimmy McCulloch and myself and Denny Laine. Red Stripe is a beer in Jamaica."

"I'd rather have a Red Stripe," sang Linda.

"It looks like we'll be doing an album from Suzie and the Red Stripes. So Linda will have an album, but not plugged hugely as Linda's album.

"We're not trying to hide the fact that it's her, but it'll be like Derek and the Dominoes, a slight anonymity."

"I've written a few songs," said Linda, so we'll put out an album and have a bit of fun. The sessions were very relaxed and turned out great.

"We had one track that was supposed to be a B side and it kept going for eleven minutes. No one could stop.'

There was a feeling abroad (and at home for that matter), that the rock scene had become too industrialised. Was there a movement back to the roots, and casual simplicity?

"There's a feeling that it's industrialised," said Paul, grabbing a cigarette. "But it has got to be a big business, naturally, because there's so much money involved.

"In the days when a singer would be fobbed off with an E-type Jaguar for it all, as in the case of Jimi, then there's plenty of opportunity for...stealing'.

"And I think the rock scene has become much more intellectualised than ever it was.

"But with every movement in that direction, there's a counter movement, like the pub rock bands. That counteracts the big-deal.

Above: **Paul and Linda share a mike. Like John Lennon, Paul would be criticised for including his wife in his post-Beatles band, Wings. Like his former partner, Paul simply shrugged and did it his way.**

"I know Eric Clapton had an idea of going out with just a caravan, setting up a tent and playing. And our university tour, when we just turned up and played, was very well received, although we weren't the greatest band when we did it.

"We were there playing and it wasn't a big deal, and nobody had to queue for hours.

"But then I wouldn't like to see the Stones play a pub in Streatham, because that would be ridiculous."

Paul began to recall the great days of the discotheques, when raving was the nightly routing and stars flocked together. Did he miss those days?

"I feel, yes, a lot of the community spirit in rock has gone, but it's changed. You meet people for dinner a bit more. We went out for dinner with Elton John the other night, and I see people around studios and they ring up.

"Rod Stewart asked me to do a song on what's supposed to be his last solo album...wink. I don't think it will be...but!

"So I did a song for him and apparently it's really great, although I haven't heard the track yet. It's called 'Mine For Me.'

It's a custom made song for him. Those are the kind of ways you meet people now.

"You don't seem to meet anyone down at clubs, although if you happen to be at Tramps on the right night you might see Gary Glitter, Rod Stewart, Keith Richard and myself, looning around. Or Mick – Mick 'n' Bianca.

"Yes, so I just wrote a song for Rod when he rang up. He's cheeky but a nice lad. And being a hack, I'll write a song for anyone.

"I always have seen myself as a hack. That's why I did the Bond theme, it only has to appeal for me, and I'll do it. I don't like to be 'a major influence on the music scene,' I don't believe that and it would be unsafe if ever I did.

"But I must say, I still love the scene. We were even thinking of opening a club. We stayed up one night in Scotland, and designed it and everything.

"It would have been a fantastic place. And I must say, hearing the discussion on the 'Old Grey Whistle' the other night, about pub rock, I thought everyone was wet, except the one with the fly-away collar from Melody Maker. He seemed actually to know what was going on.

"Kilburn and the Highroads were on and I got the feeling the cameras were putting them off and they hadn't been filmed a lot. The singer was trying to get it on despite the BBC film team and big lights.

"I imagine a lot of gutsy, raw music will come out of that scene. I'd like to have the freedom to play in a pub. I'd still like to play to say 56,000 people and then the next night – go play a pub.

"Obviously though if you are big, you get into difficulties tying to play a small place. The one lousy thing with being 'big' is the feeling that you have to be big, no matter what.

"And of course – no one's all big. I don't care if it's Jagger, Rod or Bowie. They've all got a pub rock band inside them.

"And why else would Led Zeppelin wanna go and do the Marquee that time? Or David? Gigging is the whole trip."

But when an artist achieves fame and success, isn't there always the danger of a total reaction against the scene – of not wanting to do anything or speak to anybody? Didn't this happen to Paul?

Above: **Mr and Mrs McCartney share a cuppa at home. Linda's death in 1998 stunned Paul and it would be more than a year before he returned to performing in public.**

Above: **Paul's departure from The Beatles in 1970 saw him retreat to the peace and tranquillity of his farm in Scotland, a sustained period of solo songwriting…and the cultivation of a fine beard.**

"Well, immediately after the break-up of the Beatles, and not because of any of the other reasons, but just because a good band had broken up, I felt, what am I going to do? I needed at least a month to think a bit.

"I went into a period of what everyone called being a recluse, a hermit in isolation. All sorts of little snide articles appeared saying: 'He's sitting up in Scotland, looking into his mirror, admiring his image.'

"It was not at all true, I was just planting trees. I was just getting normal again, and giving myself time to think."

Did you feel – abnormal?

"Yeah. I'm sure about the time Eric was being called God, I'm sure it got to him. You can't help it, you do have a reaction, like George Best, against the pressures, y'know what I mean?

"I never used to understand when they used to say, 'What are you going to do when the bubble bursts?' A joke question, and we always used to say ha, ha, we'll burst with it. I never once took that question in.

"What did they mean, 'bubble burst?' And the pressures – what about the pressures?

"Whilst I could see there were pressures, I couldn't feel them. I was just a rocker, doing my business.

"But if something dramatic, like the Beatles breaking up happens, that's when you can begin to feel pressures.

"I don't know if that's the problem with Eric, but he should just play and not give a damn. It doesn't matter anyway.

"Then you can start to come out with music and enjoy things. That's the way I feel now, so that's why I'm not sweating about turning Wings into an almighty super group.

"One chapter is finished now, we just want to take it easy, still do music, still play live."

Hasn't Paul now created his own environment, which he can control more than the old Beatle-Apple set-up?

"No, that's just journalese. We were always pretty in control as the Beatles. People used to say we were manipulated. We were never manipulated, I don't think.

"Maybe subtly, and certainly in the business sense because we just didn't know anything about business.

"Brian Epstein came to us once and said: 'I'm going to sell you to Bernard Delfont' although he put it nicer than that.

"We said, 'right man, if you do that, we'll never play another note. 'We'll just play 'God Save The Queen' on every record, and see how you like that.'

"That was an instance of attempted manipulation.

"That was a long time ago, about halfway through the Beatles. We were getting big and it was getting a bit too much for Brian.

"So he thought: 'I'll sell out,' and put us with a good pro agency, which they still are. But we just didn't like the idea of being sold.

"Eventually we got Apple, and then gave it all away, as Roger Daltry says."

Did Paul read Richard DiLello's The Longest Cocktail Party, about Apple?

"Yeah, but he didn't know. It's entertaining and good, and it's about what went on in the press office.

"In fact the book's almost about Derek Taylor really, because it's Derek's whole personality, that Apple office. 'Oh Paul can't make it. Tell 'em we'll give 'em Ringo.'

"Actually it was only half of the truth. In the other room, there was all other stuff going on.

"It's a long weird, and involved story, and if anyone ever gets it down, it will be very interesting."

Is Paul completely in control of his own affairs now?

"Not completely, but beginning to be, and I advise anyone who's going to sign up with any agency to take a look if there's a possibility they can own it. Because there always is, and no one ever know it.

"Particularly with songs. If you write a good song, I maintain, you should own it totally. But no publisher will let you own the copyright.

"I'm always harping on about 'Yesterday,' because it is a big song of mine, and probably the only big song I did on my own.

"Well, I don't own the copyright of that, that's been sold and lost in the mists of time.

"Lew Grade owns it. No fault of his, he's a good businessman and heard it was up for sale. But that's why I say to anyone new coming into the business, check it out with an accountant or lawyer.

"I'd always trust rockers with my money, rather than sharks. George for instance, just gives a lot of it away because he actually has got morals.

"Whereas certain people tried to put the Bangladesh concert money straight into their pocket.

"During two years, none of the Beatles took anything out of Apple except business expenses. All the money had to go into the company.

"At least some of the newer ones are hip to all this, and I think Paul Simon owns 'Bridge Over Troubled Water,' and that's fair enough.

"The old trick is to say, 'we'll set up your own company,' and they set one up that gives you small rights, and not knowing anything about companies, you think you have your own company, and they let you name it after yourself, you know Macka Production or something, and you think of course, I've got my own little office, my own little secretary, but if you ever check into it, the actual money isn't coming your way, and you'll be getting like five per cent."

Meanwhile Stella was growing impatient and bored with the MM conference room. She let out a petulant yell.

"Stop that!" warned dad. "Do you want to go to bed? That's the ultimate deterrent y'know."

Paul, Linda and Stella decided it was time to end what had been a fascinating and surprising interview. But not before a tea lady had burst in, ostensibly looking for cups, but actually taking the opportunity to embrace the couple.

"Thanks for all the pleasure you've given us," she said.

"Well," smiled Paul through his last egg sandwich, "we must come and do this again."

© **Chris Welch / Melody Maker / IPC Syndication**

Above: **A triumphant peace sign to fans at the end of another two-hour show. More than two million of them saw his 13-month world tour in 1975–76.**

key recordings

1970	Paul becomes first Beatle to break away with self-produced *Paul McCartney*, a No.1 album worldwide
1971	Critics savage first Wings album, *Wildlife*, but millions of fans disagree
1973	*My Love* becomes Paul's newest international hit as the album *Red Rose Speedway* continues his roll of international chart domination...
1974	...a fact confirmed by the six million sales of *Band On The Run*, his best yet
1976	As Paul and Wings hit American stages for the first time, *Wings At The Speed Of Sound* gives him another US chart-topper
1982	Stevie Wonder, Ringo Starr and veteran Carl Perkins lend a hand to make *Tug Of War* a smash, along with the McCartney-Wonder duet single *Ebony and Ivory*
1983	Michael Jackson comes aboard for *Pipes of Peace*, and shares vocals to make *Say Say Say* another McCartney multi million-seller
1989	Elvis Costello becomes Paul's first songwriting partner since John Lennon, with fine *Flowers In The Dirt* the result
1992	Classical composer Carl Davis, diva Kiri Te Kinawa and Liverpool Philharmonic help to realise Paul's evocative *A Liverpool Oratorio* project
1999	Paul ends his first twenty years as a solo superstar with a back-to-basics rock'n'roll tribute, *Run Devil Run*

If it's true, as many eminent critics suggest, that The Rolling Stones have not made a truly great album since 1972's Exile On Main Street, it is difficult to explain why – close on twenty years later – they were still able to sell out, without any recent hits, the vast stadiums they played in the US and Europe in 1989 and 1999, and still attract the kind of sponsorship deals bands 30 years their junior would die to have underwriting their live work. The answer is, of course, that The Rolling Stones long ago ceased to be a rock band and became An Institution.

Formed in 1962 when singer Mick Jagger and guitarist Keith Richards linked up with pianist Ian Stewart and guitarist Brian Jones, The Stones solidified their first classic line-up early in 1963 by the addition of bassist Bill Wyman and drummer Charlie Watts, at which time (thanks to their manager Andrew Oldham) Stewart became a studio-only member and their full-time tour manager.

Initially a full-blooded R&B group and promoted by Oldham as the 'bad boys' of rock, by 1965 they had ceased covering US material to give them hits on both sides of the Atlantic and had begun recording songs written by Jagger and Richards – their first US No.1 coming from the self-penned '(I Can't Get No) Satisfaction'. Later that same year they would score their first US album chart-topper (Out Of Our Heads) to cement their challenge to The Beatles.

International hit albums and singles followed in close succession and the band's switch to full-blown rock band came with the entirely Jagger-Richards penned Aftermath in 1966. In 1967 the duo (later to be nicknamed 'The Glimmer Twins') were arrested, along with Marianne Faithfull, charged with possession of various drugs and sentenced to terms of imprisonment. After an unprecedented public outcry, both were released pending appeals which were successful. Brian Jones, however, was finding refuge in drugs as his artistic role in the band diminished, and by the end of 1968 – when their classic Beggars Banquet album was released – he had become a serious liability. Officially fired in early

1969, Jones died in a late-night swimming accident in July, only days before The Stones played their well-documented gig in Hyde Park, with new guitarist Mick Taylor.

Touring the US for the first time in two years, in December '69 The Stones' continued ability to enmesh themselves in controversy was confirmed when Hell's Angels security guards killed a black fan while the band played a free concert in California. Their continued ability to make great music, however, was confirmed by their late '69 album Let It Bleed. Their stage performances also became bigger and better, and the addition of guests like guitarist Ry Cooder, sax players Jim Price and Bobby Keyes, and pianist Jack Nitzsche during the 1971 tour to promote their Sticky Fingers album (the first for their newly-founded label) signalled an intention to experiment more. Now based, for tax reasons, in the South of France, it was there in 1971–72 that the double album Exile On Main Street was recorded.

In 1974 Mick Taylor departed, his place being taken by former-Faces guitarist Ronnie Wood, and while his arrival coincided with a gradual drop-off in worldwide record sales (no more automatic chart-toppers and very few new classic songs) The Stones' increased pulling power as a live act was an undisputed phenomenon.

With Jagger, Watts, Wood and Wyman peeling off for occasional solo projects, and Richards and Woods coming under legal scrutiny and punishment for drug possession, in 1980 The Stones revived their recording fortunes with the dance-oriented Emotional Rescue, which topped both the US and UK album charts, and Tattoo You, which did the same in 1981. Bill Wyman quit the band in 1982.

But it would not be until 1985, when he teamed up with David Bowie to record 'Dancing In The Street' for Live Aid, that Jagger could celebrate an unqualified smash in his own right, his earlier solo album (She's The Boss) surprisingly proving no more than a qualified success. Increasingly devoting more time to a putative film acting career begun in 1969 with the startling Performance and dire Ned Kelly, Jagger spent some years at arm's length from Richards, both personally and artistically.

Whether it was financial pragmatism or true blood-brotherhood which made them settle their differences in the late '80s, the 1989 Steel Wheels album was the closest The Rolling Stones (now a vast rock 'n' roll circus on wheels, with staging and special effects often overwhelming the music) have come to re-capturing the full majesty of their work in the late sixties and early seventies.

What's most important, perhaps, is the fact that their fans – old and new – continue to help them break box-office records all around the world every time they turn up the volume. It may only be rock 'n' roll, but they sure do like it.

4 6

December 23 1974 Michael Watts

EXILES ON MAIN STREET

For ten years now it has been an incredible fact, the partnership between this replete feline with his bumpy, giblet lips, as Tom Wolfe described him, and the lean and hollowed axe-man, features like a funky wasteland, image that of a hoodlum-like bike-boy from 'Scorpio Rising'.

A decade is a long time in the brittle world of rock and roll, whatever it might have been to Rodgers and Hart or Kern and Hammerstein. Fissures appear in the superstructure, psychological scars open and bleed again, there are pressures, both vague and tangible.

And all this time there's this accretion of myth, building, billowing out, obscuring until finally the whole edifice collapses and crushes the individual under its weight.

They say that's what happened to Brian. As a rhythm and blues band was swallowed up by pop mania, he couldn't adjust to the whole myth which developed, to the fact that the singer was now getting all the attention – and he, Brian, had started the whole show, had been the leader, the one who collected the two pounds ten or whatever after those early gigs! The innate paranoias mushroomed. It was insidious at first, and then crushing.

But for Mick and Keith it may have been a good thing. After that the air was cleared. The balance neatly tipped between them. No hang-ups.

They grew into their roles, and though the mythology of hothouse exotica increased even – the whole fin de siecle, prince of darkness, decadence syndrome – they became secure in handling, even manipulating, it. It's like the guitarist in the studio. What's played in the room doesn't necessarily come out on the final tape, nor is that always desired. Distortion!

The dichotomy between reality and public fantasy is often baffling. Truman Capote, who toured America this year with the Stones, could find no illuminating spark. In the end he gave up his attempt to write a story and simply dismissed them as "unisexual zombies".

Left: **The Rolling Stones doing what they do best – live, loud and arrogant as they leave another stadium-full of fans hoarse from screaming.**

Chuck Berry, says Jagger, is a great example of a confusing myth: "He can destroy what you want, what you thought of him, but on the other hand, the next time you meet him he can make up for it."

Unisex. Zombies. Satanists. Kenneth Anger calls Keith Richard his "right hand man".

In fact they are so different, even from each other, Mick and Keith.

The one is nearly as much a socialite and movie star celebrity as he is a rock singer. Photographed entering Max's Kansas City and leaving it. In Andy Warhol's Interview magazine. On the fashion pages. Top of the ten best-dressed men league. The group's press agent, most willing to talk to reporters. The original rock androgynous.

And the other, pure one hundred per cent musician. Apostle of raunch. Equally as fascinating, perhaps more so, in his gaunt and wasted pose. He still best represents the politics of delinquency and the spurious glamour of the drug culture. The establishment's whipping boy, yet he continues to ride it out with just a contemptuous glance over his shoulder.

Mick is fidgety, a coil of strung-out energy, his body always posturing, his hands beating at something...the flat of his thighs, a table-top, picking things up compulsively. Keith is slow-motion, almost abstract. Even gentle. A cloak of world-weariness on his shoulders. The answers seem to come from far away, as if the questions have long been considered and debated within.

Close-to he's less raunchy. When he shakes hands, his is soft and boneless.

IT is five days to Keith's 29th birthday and he is sitting at a table more than three thousand miles away from London. Jagger appears off and on.

We are speaking of England. Keith talks about its tremendous capacity for absorbing attitudes, "like a big piece of wet cotton wool."

"It doesn't matter what it is he's saying, it will just absorb it until it's part of the establishment. That's England's big trick. After all, didn't they do it to the Beatles? Slap a medal on them. They could never pin an MBE on the Stones, but still, all those things they put them through...

"You only have to listen to the BBC. Once every day to be completely in touch with what is going on in England."

It's not the most prolific place in the world, he admits, but he dislikes not being able to live there, for tax reasons.. There are far worse places, like Switzerland, where he's been living for most of the past four months since the American tour ended. There they've sacrificed everything creative for their feeling of security – financial, physical and everything else.

He's seen the kids in Switzerland: "They come up to me in the street and say, 'hey, you're a Rolling Stone! I'm in a band. How do we get to be really big and earn lots of money? What do you have to do to make a good group?'

"And I say, 'well, look, why don't you try starving?' They can't even comprehend that, man, they're so rich. I mean, have you ever heard of a good Swiss musician, a good Swiss painter or writer?

"England gets fooled by the newspapers and TV that if it doesn't have the best standard of living in the world, at least it's got the second best. England doesn't even know, man! They're being fooled all along the line! People in Switzerland, France and Germany live twice as good as anybody in England. They're twice as bourgeois, twice as rich."

He sighs. He's still searching for THE place, but he can only find the answer by moving around. He prefers now not to live anywhere, but just to travel between places he knows and a few he doesn't.

This Christmas he's rented a house with Jagger in Jamaica. He'll move in Anita and the kid. He hesitates. "It's a drag not to be able to go and see me mum," he says obliquely. "Just because of some stupid tax."

And then there was France, of course. What made him unhappy about France? And he replies, well, really, it was a question of what made them unhappy about him.

Before he'd even known what drugs were everybody had believed they were out of their heads. They had come up to them in Richmond and Ealing with that sidelong look that people had in those days, when it was very taboo and mysterioso exotic, and they'd whisper, "what are you on?" And he'd reply, well, actually, he'd just had a brown and mild.

Keith doesn't think musicians are necessarily attracted to a drug lifestyle. They just come into contact with it more than most people because...look, a cat plays a club, and that's where the local pusher hangs out to supply the kids; the guy naturally gets into contact with the musicians playing there.

That's the only connection he can think of in the first place. There may be a whole culture on the West Coast devoted to drugs, but it

Above: **Smiles of relief all round in July 1967 as Mick and Keith leave court. Their earlier convictions on drug charges had been overturned on appeal and The Glimmer Twins were free to begin plotting the next phase of The Stones' careers. Stage One would be the creation of the masterpiece album Beggars Banquet in 1968.**

hasn't sustained anything musically. He doesn't think drugs have added anything to music, let's put it that way.

"They might have flashed the inspiration for a couple of good songs, but I don't think there's anything fantastic been written under the influence of drugs that couldn't have been written without. But you f ind out what it's like because it's there."

It's like the desire to climb Everest, to attempt it because it challenges the experimental instincts. But dangerous, too. The newspaper headlines stand out vividly. "Hendrix, Morrison, Joplin – victims of the drug culture."

Because they died, because they died, he repeats. Before they weren't seen as that. With Hendrix, people either just dug him or they thought he was some evil, nasty drug-taking black man, which was the other half of his image to moms and dads across the land. But once you were dead, you were the "victim of the drug culture."

He casts an ironic eye. They have all died because they had 'J' and 'I' in their name, who knows? Brian Jones, Jim Morrison, Janis Joplin, Jimi Hendrix...Mick Jagger!

"Somebody tried to lay a hex on us last year because of that. There was some incredible scheme worked out by somebody in America about letters 'I' and 'J'. Apparently, Mick was the next.

"And the cat has got some incredible story about a painting by Franz Hals who was a Dutch warlock who painted a picture in the 16th, 17th century, of a guy playing the lute, called 'The Minstrel', or some-thing like that – the cat looks just like Mick!

"So the guy worked on these two coincidences to the point where everybody was walking around..." He does an eyeball-rolling impression of an acid freak.

"It was really amazing. I mean, his date came and went and nothing happened, but I got a copy of the painting, just to see. It's incredibly like Mick, an incredible likeness. It looks just like Jagger. Same haircut, same mouth."

But Jagger looks like several people.

"Exactly, exactly. If you put a frame around the face and paint it black it'd look like Hendrix, too. A wig, it'd be Janis Joplin." Faint smile. "A pair of spots and it'd look like Carly Simon."

Below: **Mick and Keith in conversation with Hell's Angels security guards at The Rolling Stones' concert in London's Hyde Park. The first gig to feature guitarist Mick Taylor, it was held only two days after the death of founder-member Brian Jones, on July 3, 1969.**

5 0

He stares into a Vodka Collins that's been laid before him. His current favourite drink. Tequila Sunrise was the American tour.

The death of rock stars. It's got a romantic tinge to it, but actually it's very sordid.

"It's always sad when somebody really good and obviously still into it suddenly just...(he snaps his fingers abruptly) just like that. I mean, some people do die young and that's all here is to it.

"Some people have said it all by the time they're 22 or 25, but I don't get that feeling with Hendrix or Janis Joplin. I don't think that they were finished, or that it was their time to go."

The sense of death and decadence, Edgar Allan Poe. There are always people drawn to the Stones because they think they see the aura of decadence. It's never just the Palm Court Orchestra in town to play for the night. You can't divorce the music entirely from the scene that it's all built on. It's all part of "the Stones are the Stones, warts and all." The daily media's horror of rock groups seems to begin and end with them. They don't get excited about anybody else's excesses as much.

A shrug of resignation.

"I know," he says, "I know. I guess you can only have one bad boy at a time, really, and we're it. There's not really much you can do about it. They can print what they like about us because people believe it anyway.

"It amuses me personally, but on another level it's kind of frightening – the generalisations they can make without anybody apparently having to take any responsibility for it."

Did he feel this incredible pressure from the establishment weighing upon him?

"God, no! If I felt it, man, I'd just give up and go away! I'm not uncon-scious of it, but...I don't feel there's any kind of weight. It seems that the press turn you into what they want you to be, and as far as the people are concerned, that's what you are."

Someone else at the table, from another paper, says, "We'll say you're nice."

"We don't give a –" comes the short reply.

It's Jagger leaning into the conversation. He's been making long hops between this table and the telephone. Bianca, in London, stricken with 'flu. There's a solid impression that Mick is...keeping an eye on the talk, on Keith. The PR man. There's something protective there.

Above: **A shot from the photo session for Through The Past Darkly (Big Hits Volume 2), released in September 1969 and dedicated to the memory of Brian Jones (second left).**

Anyway, the Stones versus the establishment, and Mick is saying it's all political, and that on his side he likes to live outside the legality, to do what he likes, and other side's there's this...well, not exactly conspiracy, but it does become that.

"Once you plant some idea in people's minds, there doesn't have to be. The conspiratorial element is there. Once you've got the idea underlying they can re-use it, and that is a conspiracy.

"For us it's a big drag. No one quite throws their hands up in horror at us anymore, but we do object to the politics of it. We feel that our right to be able to play where we want to and when we want to is being interfered with.

"No one else gets the hassles we get and we don't do anything no one else doesn't do."

Poor Mick. But times do change. Take the American tour. It was their must successful yet, musically and financially. And there was no trouble, no cop crushed, no deaths. America has changed since the last time, in '69. The atmosphere less intense, the audiences more into just having a good evening.

Above: **Lean on me…
Mick gets close to
Ronnie Wood, the
former Faces guitarist
who replaced Mick
Taylor in 1975. Originally
slated to be a Rolling
Stone solely on gigs,
he would soon win a
full-time place in the
band.**

In '69 they were coming to watch…messiahs. This time it was no longer ominous. The campuses were quiet.

There's a different generation in there who obviously don't give a cuss for getting beaten on the head, teargassed and maced, which the previous generation seemed to have a capacity for taking.

Has anything really happened? Or have we gone the full 360 degrees, back to the beginning?

There's always a surge forward and then a slump, says Keith, until it seems nothing has happened at all, but in actual fact lessons have been learned.

"America has changed, believe me, quite considerably in the last ten years, but it doesn't appear to if you look at the country.

"Take the FBI. It still pokes its nose in, but not only does it now have another chief, it's lost the guy who started the whole shebang, who was the FBI. Ten years ago, America was just a big put-on. It was exactly what every English person thought it to be, except much more so, with dating rings, holding hands, hamburgers and teenage heaven – it was all there! In '63, '64. Ugh! Would you kiss her on your first date? That was the burning question then."

"…Only if she's got bad breath," mutters Jagger. And now? The crafty look of the pusher. "Oh, it's 'Want some acid, man, want some acid?' You know."

The drug culture, with its fantastic grip on the American young.

Sociologists ask why. Is it because America has refused to face up to the problem, like England has, which is just to give people who want smack? Give it to 'em and then it's cool.

"In England there hasn't been that enormous increase in junkies, and also they don't go around thieving, stealing and mugging to get bread for their next fix, which is what happens in America. For a nation that can put a man on the moon, it isn't that much of a problem to find a cure for heroin addiction, not if they really wanted to.

"You know, during the war the number of junkies in America dropped to almost zero because they just policed the f–ing ports properly. In wartime everything just snaps into action, right? You can't get anything into that country unless they want it in.

"Which means they can do it if they want to, if they really wanted to stop it. But you can make more money out of heroin than out of anything else."

Drugs, money, politics – revolution! There's lots of causes but no revolution, Jagger is saying.

"There are charities, there's people in jail who need money, there's people who don't have anything to eat that need money, there's all these people – but there isn't a revolutionary movement."

Fifteen hundred miles away, in New York's East Village, 'The Trials of Oz' is just opening to celebrities from the theatre and movie world: the media. Music by Mick Jagger.

Mick and Keith, the most famous and enduring partnership of them all! Capote's unisexual zombies! Five days away from Keith's birthday. For Mick's 29th, Ahmet Ertegun threw a huge party in New York with Zsa Zsa Gabor and all those socialites.

Keith: "It's probably because the newspapers ain't as interested in me as Jagger." A faint, wry smile. "All you care about me is when the warrants are out.

"Another Vodka Collins, please."

© **Michael Watts / Melody Maker / IPC Syndication**

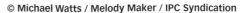

Above: **Keith gets down 'n' dirty as Bill Wyman keeps it solid. In 1986, while inducting Chuck Berry at the first annual Rock 'n' Roll Hall of Fame ceremony in New York, Keith admitted: "I lifted every lick he ever played."**

key recordings

1964 After two years spent creating a formidable live reputation in Britain, the Stones manage to dislodge 'With The Beatles' from the top of the UK album chart with *The Rolling Stones*, thanks to 100,000 advance sales orders

1965 Recorded in the US, *Out Of Our Heads* confirms band as unmatched makers of white R&B music

1966 Now an international phenomenon, release of *Aftermath* is first Stones album to consist entirely of Jagger-Richards compositions

1968 After a year of drug busts and jailings, the Stones get down 'n' dirty for the blues-laden *Beggars Banquet*

1969 With guitarist Mick Taylor on board and the band back in the US, *Let It Bleed* is justly hailed as an all-time classic

1971 Now boasting their own label (via Atlantic) and an Andy Warhol-designed jacket, *Sticky Fingers* sees The Stones in continued fine fettle

1972 Stuck in France to avoid UK taxes, the band create the brilliant *Exile On Main Street* and carry out record-breaking US-European tour

1980 The Stones flirt successfully with dance music for *Emotional Rescue*

1989 Proving they can still rock with the best, *Steel Wheels* provides the soundtrack for another over-the-top world tour

1995 Recorded in a London club during the 'Steel Wheels' tour, *Stripped* reveals that the Stones remain a formidable live band with no need of silly staging and expensive effects

In November 1999, David Bowie admitted to 'huge gaps' in his memories of the 1970s, thanks to his enthusiastic use of recreational drugs during that decade. What follows, then, is a public service announcement which may help the man born David Jones in 1947 and who has re-invented himself so many times that his partial amnesia is understandable.

Born in the Brixton district of south-west London, in 1964 Bowie formed The King Bees, an R&B band, followed by outfits called Manish Boys and The Lower Third. When these failed to click he went solo and won a short-lived (and commercially unproductive) recording deal with British Decca's new-wave label, Deram, in 1967.

In August that year Bowie (he'd changed his name to avoid confusion with Monkee Davy Jones) met and began studying under the fringe theatrical performer Lindsay Kemp. Equally important was his first meeting with record producer Tony Visconti at a BBC radio session.

Chart success first arrived in 1969 when 'Space Oddity', a song released around the first US moon landing, became a Top 10 hit. Unable to follow its success, Bowie and Visconti concentrated on producing two fine but only marginally successful albums, David Bowie and The Man Who Sold The World, for Philips Records.

Seizing the opportunity offered by the surprise hit, in 1971, of Peter Noone's version of his 'Oh You Pretty Thing', Bowie signed a long-term deal with RCA. Throwing all his theatrical skills into the mix, Bowie produced two breakthrough albums, Hunky Dory and Ziggy Stardust and The Spiders From Mars. The second, which was supported by a ball-breaking touring schedule and the emergence of Bowie's stalwart right-hand man, guitarist Mick Ronson, also produced the Top 10 single 'Starman' and led to the re-release, in 1973, of 'Space Oddity', this time a UK No.1.

Bowie was Ziggy for the next 18 months, and while he buried that character at the end of 1973, there can be no doubt that Ziggy helped provide a template for the glam-rockers who then dominated the British pop scene.

The US did not take Bowie to its heart until 1975, when the funky styling of his Young Americans and Station to Station albums found the audience he craved there. He also scored his first US chart-topper with the single 'Fame', a number he'd written with John Lennon.

Now juggling careers as a rock performer and movie actor (he'd made his big screen debut in 1975 with The Man Who Fell To Earth and was destined to appear in such others as Just A Gigolo, The Hunger, Labyrinth, Merry Christmas Mr Lawrence and Absolute Beginners down the years) - Bowie began working with producer Brian Eno. Together, they created the Low, Heroes and Lodger, albums, heavy on synthesised sounds but catchy enough to produce more hit singles.

It wasn't until Bowie teamed up with Queen in 1981 to record 'Under Pressure' that he found himself with another US hit. His 1983 smash album, Let's Dance (produced by Nile Rodgers) was the inspiration for his worldwide Serious Moonlight tour and two more big hits - 'China Girl' and 'Modern Love'. The 1985 Live Aid event saw Bowie and Mick Jagger teaming up to revive the Motown classic 'Dancing In The Street', which lodged itself at the top of the UK charts for nine weeks.

Four years later Bowie emerged as the singer in a hard rock quartet called Tin Machine, but within a year was headlining a world tour dedicated entirely to performances of his own back-catalogue. In 1990, to prove that he hadn't done yet, Bowie released his Sound and Vision album, its design winning the Best Album Package trophy at the 32nd annual Grammy Awards.

Married to the supermodel Iman in 1992, Bowie spent the 1990s in selective mode. His 1993 album Black Tie White Noise gave him another No.1 in Britain, and two years later he was back on the road to promote his patchy Outside album. In 1996 David Bowie was inducted to the Rock and Roll Hall of Fame in Cleveland and won a Lifetime Achievement citation at the annual Brits Awards in London.

Bowie continues to come up with surprises so it's possible that he will adopt another guise for the new millennium. He can still ring dramatic ch-ch-changes to his music and people's perceptions of him. Whoever he chooses to be.

January 22 1972 Michael Watts

OH YOU PRETTY THING

Even though he wasn't wearing silken gowns right out of Liberty's, and his long blond hair no longer fell wavily past his shoulders, David Bowie was looking yummy.

He'd slipped into an elegant-patterned type of combat suit, very tight around the legs, with the shirt unbuttoned to reveal a full expanse of white torso. The trousers were turned up at the calves to allow a better glimpse of a huge pair of red plastic boots with at least three-inch rubber soles; and the hair was Vidal Sasooned into such impeccable shape that one held one's breath in case the slight breeze from the open window dared to ruffle it. I wish you could have been there to varda him; he was so super.

David uses words like 'varda' and 'super' quite a lot. He's gay, he says. Mmmmmm. A few months back, when he played Hampstead's Country Club, a small, greasy club in north London which has seen quite a lot of exciting occasions, about half the gay population of the city turned up to see him in his massive floppy velvet hat, which he twirled around at the end of each number.

According to Stuart Lyon, the club's manager, a little gay brother sat right up close to the stage throughout the whole evening, absolutely spellbound with admiration.

As it happens, David doesn't have much time for Gay Liberation, however. That's a particular movement he doesn't want to lead. He despises all these tribal qualifications. Flower power he enjoyed, but it's

Left: **Bowie and his main-man, guitarist Mick Ronson, harmonise on stage. One of the most flamboyant performers of his generation, Ronson would Lead Bowie's band for many years and provide a perfect foil for the singer's more outrageous stage moves.**

individuality that he's really trying to preserve. The paradox is that he still has what he describes as "a good relationship" with his wife. And his baby son, Zowie. He supposes he's what people call bisexual.

They call David a lot of things. In the States he's referred to as the English Bob Dylan and an avant garde outrage, all roll up together. The New York Times talks of his "coherent and brilliant vision". They like him a lot there. Back home, in the very stiff upper lip UK, where people are outraged by Alice Cooper even, there ain't too many who have picked up on him. His last but one album, 'The Man Who Sold The World', cleared 50,000 copies in the States; here it sold about five copies, and Bowie bought them.

Yes, but before this year is out those of you who puked up on Alice are going to be focusing your attention on Mr. Bowie, and those who know where it's at will be thrilling to a voice that seemingly undergoes brilliant metamorphosis from song to song, a songwriting ability that will enslave the heart, and a sense of theatrics that will make the ablest thespians gnaw on their sticks of eyeliner in envy. All this, and an amazingly accomplished band, featuring super-lead guitarist Mick Ronson, that can smack you round the skull with their heaviness and soothe the savage breast with their delicacy. Oh, to be young again.

The reason is Bowie's new album, 'Hunky Dory', which combines a gift for irresistible melody lines with lyrics that work on several levels - as straight-forward narrative, philosophy or allegory, depending how deep you wish to plumb the depths. He has a knack of suffusing strong, simple pop melodies with words and arrangements full of mystery and darkling hints.

Thus, 'Oh! You Pretty Thing', the Peter Noone hit, is on one strata, particularly the chorus, about the feelings of a father-to-be; on a deeper level it concerns Bowie's belief in a superhuman race - homo superior - to which he refers obliquely: "I think about a world to come/Where the books were found by the Golden Ones/Written in pain, written in awe/By a puzzled man who questioned what we are here for/Oh, the Strangers came today, and it looks as if they're here to stay." The idea of Peter Noone singing such a heavy number fills me with amusement. That's truly outrageous, as David says himself.

But then Bowie has an instinct for incongruities. On 'The Man' album there's a bit at the end of 'Black Country Folk' where he superbly parodies his friend Marc Bolan's vibrato warblings. On 'Hunky Dory' he devotes a track called 'Queen Bitch' to the Velvets, wherein he takes off to a tee the Lou Reed vocal and arrangement, as well as parodying, with a storyline about the singer's boyfriend being seduced by another queen, the whole Velvet Underground genre.

5 9

Then again, at various times on his albums he resorts to a very broad Cockney accent, as on 'Saviour Machine' ('The Man') and here with 'The Bewley Brothers'. He says he copped it off Tony Newley, because he was mad about 'Stop The World' and 'Gurney Slade': "He used to make his points with this broad Cockney accent and I decided that I'd use that now and again to drive a point home."

The fact that David Bowie has an acute ear for parody doubtless stems from an innate sense of theatre. He says he's more of an actor and entertainer than a musician; that he may, in fact, only be an actor and nothing else: "Inside this invincible frame there might be an invincible man." You kidding? "Not at all. I'm not particularly taken with life. I'd probably be very good just as an astral spirit."

Bowie is talking in an office at Gem Music, from where his management operates. A tape machine is playing his next album, 'The Rise And Fall of Ziggy Stardust And The Spiders From Mars', which is about this fictitious pop group. The music has got a very hard-edged sound, like 'The Man Who Sold The World'. They're releasing it shortly, even though 'Hunky Dory' has only just come out.

Everyone knows that David is going to be a lollapalooza of a superstar throughout the entire world this year, David more than most. His songs are always ten years ahead of their time, he says, but this year he has anticipated the trends: "I'm going to be huge, and it's quite frightening

Above: **I can see clearly now...Bowie attempts a Lindsay Kemp mime pose. Maybe one he picked up while studying with Kemp's theatre group during the Summer of Love – 1967.**

in a way," he says, his big red boots stabbing the air in time with the music. "Because I know that when I reach my peak and it's time for me to be brought down it will be with a bump."

The man who's sold the world this prediction has had a winner before, of course. Remember 'Space Oddity', which chronicled Major Tom's dilemma, aside from boosting the sales of the stylophone? That was a top ten hit in '68, but since then Bowie has hardly performed at all in public. He appeared for a while at an arts lab he co-founded in Beckenham, Kent, where he lives, but when he realised that people were going there on a Friday night to see Bowie the hit singer working out, rather than for an idea of experimental art, he seems to have

Left: **The cosmic gladiator look, circa 1973. Bowie's constant shift of image and musical style have often obscured the fact that he is a consummate song writer and brilliant performer who maybe didn't need to go to extreme lengths in costume design.**

Opposite page: **Bowie stripped down to funky basics during his Heroes period, in the mid-late Seventies.**

become disillusioned. That project foundered, and he wasn't up to going out on one-nighters throughout the country at that particular time.

So, in the past three years he has devoted his time to the production of three albums, 'David Bowie' (which contains 'Space Oddity') and 'The Man' for Philips, and 'Hunky Dory' for RCA. His first album, 'Love You Till Tuesday', was released in 1968 on the new Deram label, but it didn't sell outstandingly and Decca, it seems, lost interest in him.

It all began for him, though, when he was 15 and his brother gave him a copy of 'The Subterraneans' by Jack Kerouac; when he decided he wanted to play an instrument he took up sax because that was the main instrument featured in the book (Gerry Mulligan, right?). So, in '63 he was playing tenor in a London R&B band before going on to found a semi-pro progressive blues group, called David Jones and The Lower Third (later changing his name in '66 when Davy Jones of The Monkees became famous). He left this band in 1967 and became a performer in the folk clubs.

Since he was 14, however, he had been interested in Buddhism and Tibet, and after the failure of his first LP he dropped out of music completely and devoted his time to the Tibet Society, whose aim was to help the lamas driven out of that country in the Tibetan/Chinese war. He was instrumental in setting up the Scottish monastery in Dumfries in this period. He says, in fact, hat he would have liked to have been a Tibetan monk, and would have done if he hadn't met Lindsay Kemp, who ran a mime company in London: "It was as magical as Buddhism, and I completely sold out and became a city creature. I suppose that's when my interest in my image really blossomed."

David's present image is to come on like a swishy queen, and gorgeously effeminate boy. He's as camp as a row of tents, with his limp hand and his trolling vocabulary. "I'm gay," he says, "and always have been, even when I was David Jones." But there's a sly jollity about how he says it, a secret smile at the corners of his mouth. He knows that in these times it's permissible to act like a male tart, and that to shock and outrage, which pop has always striven to do throughout its history, is a balls-breaking process.

And if he's not an outrage, he is, at the least, an amusement. The expression of his sexual ambivalence establishes a fascinating game; is he, or isn't he? In a period of conflicting sexual identity he shrewdly exploits the confusion surrounding the male and female roles. "Why aren't you wearing your girl's dress today?" I said to him (he has no monopoly on tongue-in-cheek humour). "Oh dear," he replied, "you must understand that it's not a woman's. It's a man's dress."

He began wearing dresses, of whatever gender, two years ago, but he says he had done outrageous things before that were just not

accepted by society. It's just so happened, he remarks, that there are bisexuals in the world - "and - horrible fact - homosexuals." He smiles, enjoying his piece of addenda.

"The important thing is that I don't have to drag up. I want to go on like this for long after the fashion has finished. I'm just a cosmic yob, I suppose. I've always worn my own style of clothes. I design them. I designed this." He broke off to indicate with his arm what he was wearing. "I just don't like the clothes that you buy in shops. I don't wear dresses all the time, either. I change every day. I'm not outrageous. I'm David Bowie."

How does dear Alice go down with him, I asked, and he shook his head disdainfully: "Not at all. I bought his first album, but it didn't excite me or shock me. I think he's trying to be outrageous. You can see him, poor dear, with his red eyes sticking out and his temples straining. He tries too hard. That bit he does with the boa constrictor, a friend of mine, Rudy Valentino, was doing ages before. The next thing I see is Miss C with her boa. I find him very demeaning. It's very premeditated, but quite fitting with our era. He's probably more successful than I am at present, but I've invented a new category of artist, with my chiffon and taff. They call it pantomime rock in the States."

Left: **More a rocker than a glam star in this shot, Bowie was strongly influenced by the Beat poets, jazz and the rock'n'roll of the 1950s.**

Despite his flouncing, however, it would be sadly amiss to think of David merely as a kind of glorious drag act. An image, once strained and stretched unnaturally, will ultimately diminish an artist. And Bowie is just that. He foresees this potential dilemma, too, when he says he doesn't want to emphasise his external self much more. He has enough image. This year he is devoting most of his time to stage work and records. As he says, that's what counts at the death. He will stand or fall on his music.

As a songwriter he doesn't strike me as an intellectual, as he does some. Rather, his ability to express a theme from all aspects seems intuitive. His songs are less carefully structured thoughts than the outpourings of the unconscious. He says he rarely tries to communicate with himself, to think an idea out.

"If I see a star and it's red I wouldn't try to say why it's red. I would think how shall I best describe to X that that star is such a colour? I don't question much; I just relate. I see my answers in other people's writings. My own work can be compared to talking to a psychoanalyst. My act is my couch."

It's because his music is rooted in this lack of consciousness that he admires Syd Barrett so much. He believes that Syd's freewheeling approach to lyrics opened the gates for him; both of them, he thinks, are the creation of their own songs. And if Barrett made that initial breakthrough, it's Lou Reed and Iggy Pop who have since kept him going and helped him expand his unconsciousness.

He and Lou and Iggy, he says, are going to take over the whole world. They're the songwriters he admires.

His other great inspiration is mythology. He has a great need to believe in the legends of the past, particularly those of Atlantis; and for the same need he has created a myth of the future, a belief in an imminent race of supermen called homo superior. It's his only glimpse of hope, he says - "all the things that we can't do, they will."

It's a belief created out of resignation with the way society in general has moved. He's not very hopeful about the future of the world. A year ago he was saying that he gave mankind another 40 years. A track on his next album, outlining this conviction, is called 'Five Years'. He's a fatalist, a confirmed pessimist, as you can see.

'Pretty Thing', that breezy Herman song, links this fatalistic attitude with the glimmer of hope that he sees in the birth of his son, a sort of poetic equation of homo superior. "I think," he says, "that we have created a new kind of person in a way. We have created a child who will be so exposed to the media that he will be lost to his parents by the time he is twelve."

That's exactly the sort of technological vision that Stanley Kubrick foresees for the near future in 'A Clockwork Orange'. Strong stuff. And a long, long way from camp carry-ons.

Don't dismiss David Bowie as a serious musician just because he likes to put us all on a little.

© **Michael Watts / Melody Maker / IPC Syndication**

Above: **Maybe the feather boa was Bowie's answer to the real snake Alice Cooper liked to drape around his neck. And Bowie thought that was 'very premeditated'!**

key recordings

1971 After many false starts, Bowie becomes Ziggy and launches his alter ego on the world with *Hunky Dory* and the classic *Ziggy Stardust and The Spiders From Mars*. Ecce homo superior...

1975 With Ziggy buried, Bowie hits the US for six with *Young Americans* and *Station To Station*, and has No.1 single with *Fame*, co-written with John Lennon

1983 Bowie (with help from producer Nile Rodgers) becomes a disco dude for *Let's Dance* and returns to singles charts with *China Girl* and *Modern Love*

1993 *Black Tie White Noise* proves The Thin White Duke's staying power as it hits No.1 in UK album charts

lou   reed

Considering his significant influence on many other writers and singers during the past three decades, Lou Reed has enjoyed a remarkably patchy track record where his own career is concerned. That said, anyone wanting to buy tickets for any Reed gig is advised to book early – he still packs 'em in with monotonous regularity and remains a mesmerising stage performer.

Born Louis Firbank in 1942, his parents' dismay at Reed's determination to shuck off his Long Island middle-class raising (using rock'n'roll as his outlet) led to an enforced course of electro-therapy in a psychiatric hospital when he was 18. His future as musician and writer was set at university, however, when he first met Sterling Morrison – later to be a member of The Velvet Underground – and became influenced by the work of poet Delmore Schwarz.

Finding work as a songwriter for 'soundalike' bands, it was while with such a group, The Primitives, that he first met John Cale. Reed and Cale's decision to form The Velvet Underground in 1965 proved momentous and they soon became the darlings of the New York pop-art set, thanks to their close association with Andy Warhol.

In 1970 Reed left the Velvets and did not re-appear until two years later, when he released his eponymous debut album, produced in London by Richard Robinson. Flawed by unsympathetic backing by members of Yes, it nevertheless confirmed Reed as an intriguing writer, a fact reinforced by the release later that year of the David Bowie-produced Transformer. That became a Top 20 hit in Britain, aided hugely by the single 'Walk On The Wild Side', which also made the US Top 20.

Reed's homeland did not take to his 1973 album, Berlin, a dark collection of songs dealing with drug addiction (on which he spoke with the authority of bitter experience) and its inevitable toll on a relationship. It did make the UK Top 10, but flopped back home. A live album (Rock 'n' Roll Animal) in 1974 returned Reed to favour in the US, but few fans could fathom the barrage of electronics and feedback that was his 1975 album Metal Machine Music. A second concert album (Lou Reed Live) limited the damage that it did to his career.

but it would not be until his 1976 Coney Island Baby that Reed's credibility was restored.

His love of early rock and his period with the Velvets was reflected in his next two albums, Rock 'n' Roll Heart (1976) and Street Hassle (1978), by which time Reed had established his reputation as a fascinating, if not always intelligible or reliable, live performer. This would be captured on his 1978 double album, Take No Prisoners.

While Reed has continued to release new albums every year or so, few could be described as consistently good or interesting. Exceptions to that generalisation are his 1989 album New York – which saw him return to the stripped down two-guitars, bass and drums format he knows and does so well – and the haunting Songs For Drella, the tribute to Andy Warhol he and John Cale released in 1990.

But until he hangs up his guitar for good, it's only a fool who'd say his hit-making days are over. Lou Reed remains capable of springing any amount of surprises.

May 13 1978 Allan Jones

DON'T MAKE ME CRY – THERE'S ONLY ONE LOU REED

Carmine flipped a quarter into the juke-box and swayed unsteadily beneath the dull neon glow of the Miller High Life sign. He looked as ripped as hell; eyeballs spinning deep inside bruised sockets, like the principal dancers in a kinetic ballet, nerve ends jangling like hysterical air-raid sirens.

You could catch his panic like a hot, impatient breath on the back of your neck. He was shaking so furiously that he might have been grooving to some demon beat pounding a dangerous rhythm in his brain, like wardrums on the horizon.

His nervous shuffle brought him to the bar; he smacked at its scarred, polished surface with the flat of his hand, forcing through his cracked teeth a colourful obscenity. He hung back a beer with a hungry gulp and listened with vague attention to the cowboy lament (some romantic pap by Michael Murphy) on the Wurlitzer. He swore at the barman, who ignored him and continued to pick meanly at the coins left as tips along the counter. Carmine bit his lip and scrambled frantically up the bar towards us, cursing his own bad luck and demanding conversation.

"Some real bad s– gone down tonight," he complained fiercely, his voice a blurred speedfreak whine. "Real bad, you know. Like...uh, those b–, man, they really screwed me, you know...Like, we wuz in the car, man...I had an ounce of grass man...real quality grass...an', uh, you know, I was, like, rolling some J's for the gig, man...I had like five, six on the back seat, rolled, man...

"And, uh, these guys I wuz with, man...these assholes...like, they couldn't wait, man. I had, like, one more to roll...it was in my hand, man...and these idiots get outta the goddam car...and I'm going', like, 'Ferchrissakes, get back in the car, we'll get busted, man!'

"But these assholes, they wouldn't lissen...assholes...and the cops are, like, cruisin' down the block, man...and they see these three guys standin' outside this car, and the doors is, like open...so, what are they gonna think? It's like, New Jersey on a Saturday night, man. They think these guys is rippin' off the goddam car!

"An' I'm sitting there in the back, man, with, like, five loose J's an'a ounce of grass. Christ, the assholes...I'm gonna wring their f– necks, man...an' the cops, man, they stop and they come over to us...and their start shinin' these lights through the windows, man, and it's like Christmas with all these lights, you know, an' I'm sittin' there like a turkey, man. Jesus. Those assholes.

Carmine hurled back another bullet of beer with angry zeal.

"So...they took the grass, man...an OUNCE of really incredible grass...the mothers. They wuz gonna pull me down to the station house, but I wasn't into that...I showed 'em my discharge papers, man...Like, I was in the Marines, man. I got papers, an'a citation. The MARINES, man. Crazy mothers. I was in Nam, man.

"So...they just took all my grass. An' I just, like wanted ONE J, man...Cuz, like, after the gig, man, I wuz just gonna go home, take my German Shepherd an' go sit on the cliffs an' look at the sea an' blow this, man...that's so cool, man...But, I still got these..."

He fumbled in his overall pockets and emerged with a phial of rather dubious looking pills. "Black Beauties, man. I'm gonna hit these, man, an' then I'm gonna go lookin' for those guys I wuz with...an' believe me, man...I'm gonna be in the mood to KILL."

I wanted no part of impending massacre; let's not form a bloody posse, I thought squeamishly (I panic quickly, especially when confronted by a potential homicidal maniac in an anonymous bar in New Jersey – "they're all animals in Jersey," I remember Jim telling me). I told Carmine that I sympathised with his predicament, and that I was sure it would all work out for the best in the end.

Then we split as if our tails were on fire and God was serving free beer in the bar of the Capitol Theatre, just across the road in downtown Passaic.

"See you again, man," said Carmine, wrestling with my thumb.

Yes, we're in Passaic, New Jersey. To see Lou Reed, of course; Arista, Louis' record company, having coughed up enough crackers to wing across the Atlantic a quartet of European correspondents (two from Blighty, one from France and another from Germany).

Louis, you see, after more than five years spent suffering the indifference and hostility of Yankee critics, has come close to blowing them away with his most recent tortured opus, "Street Hassle". The carefully orchestrated jeers of the yahoos has now surrendered to a chorus of applause; "Street Hassle" has been cheered onto the racks and Louis is in the unusual position of having his new album being declared a masterpiece, a brilliant vindication of those wilderness years on the vicious borderline of defeat and squalid neglect.

Right: **The rock gunslinger hits town. Lou Reed is one of the world's best stage performers on a good night. On others he can bemuse and confuse in equal measure.**

Previous page: **The true rock'n'roll animal, Lou Reed passes comment on something that deserved nothing more than a Bronx cheer.**

Above: **A quiet moment for the man who's lived his life at 100 miles an hour, apparently unaware that there is a brake pedal available. Or maybe that's only for wimps?**

And his present ocean-to-ocean American tour is, similarly, driving the hacks to their typewriters, filing superlatives to the probable confusion and surprise of their editors who'd had Lou typed as a terminal loser, long bereft of his original talent and now merely wasting everybody's time waiting for obscurity's under takers to take him on the final, cruel drive into history's footnotes.

Blah, to them: Louis is back on the case with a venomous urgency.

And we're here to wave the flag for the resurrection.

The Europeans made their initial connection with Louis in Philadelphia. A three-hour drive out of New York City, with Elvis Costello's "Pump It Up" screaming across the airwaves, the Jack Daniels and Blue Nun bottles rolling empty on the Cadillac floor before we were off the New Jersey turnpike and the moon coming down like a day-glo yo-yo, wearing the clouds like shades...and, eventually we're burning rubber a half block down from the Tower Theatre...

Louis is sprawled out in this grubby armpit of a dressing room, backstage at the Tower, still flashed on the energy he'd been pumping out minutes earlier as his set had climaxed with a two-pronged encore of "Sweet Jane" and "Rock 'n' Roll", seminal monsters that will forever hang about his neck.

I had last seen him a year ago, after a night of hysterical chaos in Gottenburg in Sweden (I really must tell you about that sometime – you'll love the bit where we sank all the remote control boats in the seafood restaurant), flat out drunk on the wall-to-wall of his hotel room.

We'd destroyed a case of brandy and – a last ditch effort, this – quarrelled over a bottle of Schnapps. The latter did it for us both. I had to be carried to bed as dawn laughed through the windows; Lou was unconscious when I left him. There were no coherent alibis.

I stroll into the dressing room. He greets me politely.

"Jesus God!" he smirks. "It's the faggot dwarf. You grew. What happened? We thought you were dead. You look well. What happened...you get religion? Your head's still too big for your body.

"You still drink? Have a beer. Jesus. Last time we saw you, man, you looked worse than anybody I've ever seen, except myself. You still working for Melody Maker, trying to influence the diseased minds of the cretins?

"Say hi to the band, faggot...isn't this a great band? Weren't we great tonight? Weren't we the best rock 'n' roll band you saw in your life?

"God above, we aren't a rock 'n' roll band. We're a f– orchestra! And did you ever hear anyone play guitar like I did tonight? Wasn't I just great? No. Save your superlatives for the article...

"Oh, man, I got this guitar now (it's the Roland Guitar, freaks!)...man, with THIS, I sound like the Dante of the rock 'n' roll guitar. THIS is the sound I've been after for years.

"I was playing like this all the time...you know that...I just had to wait for all those stupid, pallid imitators to die off. I was just waiting for the cretins to get the tickets, so's I could take over man...this is where it really starts to hurt."

I was relieved that Louis had lost none of his overwhelming modesty in the year since we'd last met.

"Oh...oh, I still KNOW I'm the BEST, man. Who else is there? Kansas? Mel Torme? come ON, I'm Dante with a beat, man. When I get onstage with this f– monster (the Roland Guitar Synthesizer, fans) I'm like...like, Bach, Bartok and Little Richard. I'm so hot at the moment, I burn myself every time I touch a guitar...

"What did you think of 'Street Hassle' tonight? Great, uh? That gets spooky, man like, I thought tonight they'd have to carry me off screaming...that's ME on the line out there. Like Dante, man. It gets really close in there...but, f– it...

"If they put ME in purgatory, man, I'd be the landlord...hey, why didn't you come see us the last time we were in Europe?"

You didn't play England, I explain (Lou did a Continental trek late last summer after his last London concerts in May).

"That's an excuse, NOT an answer. We'll let it pass. You're right. We played places like Germany. Hell. You gotta be careful there, man. The hotels are like concentration camps. All Dobermans and suspect showers...'You wanna shower?' 'Uh...no thanks, man...uh, yeah...okay...but easy on the Zyklon B...' Who needs it?"

A friend worked on that tour; he told me several horror stories about Lou holding to ransom Continental promoters.

Like, at one place he's said to have stalked off stage in the middle of his set and threatened the promoter with a switchblade, and demanded more money for the gig. He got it, too...

"You're well informed for an idiot," he replies cheerfully when I confront him with this piece of scurrilous gossip. "But it wasn't a blade...it was a can opener...I didn't have my blade with me.

"It was upstairs in the dressing room...what was I gonna DO? Say, 'Look, I'm threatening you, but I don't have my blade...could you just stay there a minute looking scared while I go get my knife? I just used whatever came to hand.

"If I hadn't found the can opener, I'd have used the leg of a chair. I was so angry...Like, I don't stand for being pissed around, man. On this tour we had a sound guy who had no brains. Right? So I came out one night and said, 'Hey...let's talk. There was no talking. So he kicked his monitors off stage and I sacked the mentally retarded cripple...I don't f– about."

Louis is still bitching about this incident two days later when we meet him in New York; we'd been talking about his audience, his attitude to them, whether he thought of his performances as entertainment and how he felt about them constantly barracking him from the stalls.

"F– it," he says succinctly. "I'm not one of those people who NEEDS applause. I know what those people in the audience are like. I can do without it. I only need my own applause.

"But, listen...I don't insult my audience. I respond to them in their own way. And they know what I'm saying. They're just not used to anybody onstage taking them seriously enough to have a dialogue with them... I'm that serious. All my songs are that serious. This is MY life on the LINE.

"'Street Hassle' is that serious. It's ME on the Line. And I'm talking to them one to one. And it gets very intense out there. I realise that...like, 'Street Hassle', I realise I did myself a hell of a good speech in that. And it's scary 'cos it looks like I'm making myself too vulnerable, at least from the audience point of view.

"It's scary when an artist does that, 'cos it would be so easy to get him, that is, me. Anybody who's like a Bob Hope or a Don Rickles – it isn't going to be so easy to get HIM.

"But here's a guy who's gonna be a songwriter and perform songs like THAT...and you can heckle him or throw beer cans at him...He IS vulnerable. And,...like, what reason can a guy have for doing that? It would be easier not to do it. Obviously. So I must be serious about my audience and what I'm doing to bring attention to it...

"But I don't want to leave them with a part of me, or change the way they think...Oh, no...On the other hand; I'm not beyond entertainment. It's just that I'm a very rare and exquisite kind of entertainment...if you want to call it entertainment.

"On an entertainment level, I think I function pretty well. If you're looking for that, I'm pretty good.

"I wouldn't recommend me as entertainment, though. If I was going out, I'm not the person I'd go to see...then again, if I wanted to take a chance – I might.

"No. I don't get upset when they yell at me. Why should I? They're at a rock 'n' roll show. Not in a museum. Like I told that mixer who was f– me around, I said, 'This ain't a seminary in here, man, crank it up...they don't get little booklets with the lyrics. Turn the thing up!' And he said. 'But they can't hear every golden word!'

"And I said, 'They're not supposed to...if they wanna hear the words they can go home and listen to the records.'"

Meanwhile: backstage here at the Tower Theatre, Philadelphia, Louis wants to know what's happening in England. Someone spouts some facts 'n' info about Rotten's latest plans..."Johnny Rotten," sez Louis benevolently, "should stick a safety pin in the end of his p– and shove it through his nose..."

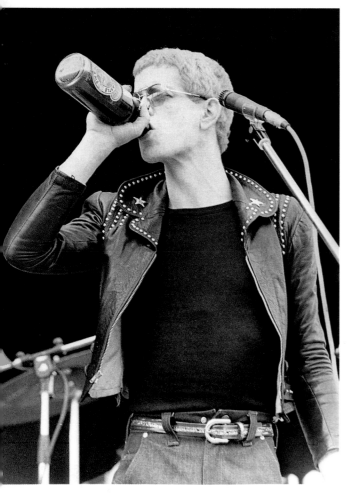

Left: **Blondes, they say, have more fun. Lou Reed tests the theory, with a little help from a bottle of Newcastle Brown Ale.**

Mention is made of the current rumours of a joint enterprise involving ex-Pistols Steve Jones and Paul Cook and former NY Dolls Heartbreakers' guitarist, Johnny Thunders.

"Johnny Thunders," laughs Louis. "Don't make me cry...there's only one Lou Reed."

He starts talking about his band again; yes, they were great, we agree.

"I'm gonna call them New York," he tells us, "what do you think?" We-eee-ell, I hesitate, I think it sounds a little precious.

"Oh...oh!" squeals Louis. "The dwarf thinks it's precious...okay, faggot, we'll call the band MUTTON, how does that feel?"

Uncomfortable, I think; I switch the subject...He and Bowie are currently carving across the States on tours. When was the last time you saw David Bowie, Lou?

"Well..." he stalls, and then in a flash, "I looked in the mirror this morning and he looked fine...ah! But why are we talking about 'me' when we could be talking about ME."

Good point; let's get back to the gig.

Ian Dury and the Blockheads are chasing the applause to the end of their set at the Tower Theatre, Philadelphia, when The Europeans arrive.

("Ian's great," Lou will say later. "But his act needs subtitles. Can you understand him? First time I heard him I thought he was Rumanian. Call that English? It sounds like a tongue disease. I know, by the way, why he calls the band the Blockheads...I spoke to one of them for the first time, yesterday.")

Ian, backstage, is talking to an American girl. She wants to know who he likes, who his influences might be.

"Ever 'eard of Syd Barret?" he ventures. She smiles vaguely. "Worrabhat Cyd Charise, then?"

Louis stalks out on to the stage of the Tower in Philadelphia like a man looking for revenge. He's whipped off his shades before he hits the mike; and he stands there for a second zeroing in on the audience, prepared to decimate every last excuse for these last years of flabby alibis, confused embarrassment and idiot posing.

He's looking for revenge; both upon himself and the more fickle amongst us in tonight's audience, for these last squandered years.

"KER-BLOODY-THWAAACKKK!" he hits the mike. A straight arm chop from the waist. I didn't even see it coming and the band are lobbing hand-grenades in the specific direction of "Gimmie Some Good Times", which also opens the "Street Hassle" album...

"Gimmiegimmie some gooooooodtimes, gimmie gimmie gimmie some PAIN," yowls Lou, "dontcha know things always looook ugly – to me they always look the SAME..." And the band takes care of the rest.

From the last time he appeared in London, he's retained on keyboards the dazzling Michael Fonfara, on saxophones Marty Fogel, and on drums, the assbashing Michael Suchorsky, who has all the violent kick and simultaneous sensitivity of former Roxy Music drummer Paul Thompson.

Stuart Heinrich is on guitar (such blissfully evil sounds he concocts!). "This is a guitarist," Lou will say in New Jersey, "that can make Hunter and Wagner eat s–!"

Ellard "Moose" Bowles, a monstrous black bass player, lays the boisterous foundations for the evening's success alongside Suchorsky. Two foxy dames, Angela Howard and Christine Wiltshire, are at hand to provide back-up and harmony vocals.

"Satellite Of Love" follows; a radical exercise in reorganisation, it lacks entirely the slight charm of the original on "Transformer", as Louis

Above: **Preaching to the converted. "Oh, I still know I'm the best, man. Who else is there?"**

peels away its initial insignificance to reveal a dark perspective on hatred and betrayal.

It leaves me suddenly breathless as he goes into the originally burlesque routine of "I've been told that you've been bold with Harry, Mark and John..." which he here reels off with real hurt, confronting a lover with her betrayal.

And, God, this is beginning to hurt; he's pulling no more punches, he's getting right down there in the grime and deceit of it all and he's still snarling and biting.

When he did this in Passaic, New Jersey, accentuating every muscle of every syllable, almost bleeding with venom, I began to wish I was taking my chances with Carmine on the prowl for his buddies; especially when Lou straps on his Perspex guitar and winds up for a solo that sounds as if he's stringing together every moment of pain he's felt during the last whenever.

His guitar growls and bites and staggers back on itself; and it's over, this solo, before you're really locked onto it. He doesn't play it for inspection or applause. He hits you with it, like a challenge.

I could've done with maybe a walk around the parking lot to clear my head, but Louis, smashing out a riff so obsessive that it clearly needs psychoanalysis, urges the band into "Leave Me Alone"; a frightening/ frightened plea, whose power I barely recognised on "Street Hassle".

This version unwinds with a power so annihilating it would demand an apology from disaster; Louis rants with shivering rage as the band chant the title line behind his aggressive, taunting lead.

Heinrich knocks out phrases that send shivers through the theatre and Fogel's saxophone screams like it's having its toenails pulled out.

My God, I thought, they're going to have to arrest these people before they do us some serious damage!

Then Lou calms it down with that touching epistle about racial harmony, "I Wanna Be Black", the sheer bad taste of which elevates it to levels few others would ever have considered.

I was choking with laughter, but a few of those weirdo college students there in the audience clearly thought this was taking it all a little too far.

"Walk On The Wild Side" – inevitably part of the repertoire – fills the next space. A version full of conceit – Reed stops in the middle of the first verse, lights a Marlboro, takes one drag and throws it at someone in the front row of the stalls. "Hey, BITCH, let's take a walkonth'wild siiide," he drawls, hitting the mike with another of those righthand smacks that bolts you upright.

This, however, has so far been a preliminary skirmish; the real warfare is just now cruising around the corner and into view.

It starts with Lou standing in a blue spotlight crooning to himself, distracted, almost; concentrating upon nothing but his memories and his anger and pain..."Let's hear it for the Excellents," he mumbles. "They did it first...I stole it from them and it's called 'Coney Island Baby'."

There's a waver of applause, but no one seems to know what the hell he's talking about (it transpires that a group called the Excellents recorded in about 1965 a song that inspired his own painful sage – oh: you knew; well it was news to me, too). The music begins to drift past us, followed by Lou's monologue.

"When I was a young man in high school, I wanted to play football for the coach...and all those other guys, they said he was mean and cruel, but you know, I wanted to play football for the coach.

"They said I was a little lightweight to play lineback, but I gotta play football for the coach...You know something, man, you gotta stand up straight, or else you're gonna fall...and then you're gonna DIE..."

Heinrich's guitar creeps in here, carrying its own pack of Kleenex to wipe away the tears.

"You know," Lou continues, laying it all on the line, "when you're all alone and lonely in your midnight hour and you find your soul's been up for sale, and you begin to think about all the things you've done and you begin to hate just about EVERYTHING...and all your two-bit friends.

"You got any two-bit friends?" he asks Philadelphia, "or are they all dollar 50 friends like mine, who sold you for a SUBWAY RIDE? And then started talking behind your back saying, 'Hey, Lou Reed – there ain't no way you're ever gonna be no human being..."

The blue spot hits him again and he begins to scratch at the melody, playing a fractured guitar phrase..."I'm sending this out one more time to Lou and...uh...Rachel. I'm just a f– up Coney Island Baby..."

He stands away from the microphone, his voice dying away as the singers repeat and phrase behind them in a vocal dive that carries with it an extraordinary anguish. And then I realise that Lou is really bringing it all back home this time with a vengeance. This is musical autobiography with the chapter headings written in painful self-examination.

"This song's called 'Dirt'," he announces; and we spend the next ten minutes eating. The band lurch into the kind of superheavy riff that even Zeppelin would've left in the closet. It doesn't hit you so much as smother you. This is for real, pop-pickers; none of that fashionable, stylised menace passing for venom.

Then he performs "Street Hassle," and if God had any tears left to cry the audience would drown.

"Street Hassle" isn't just another song about degenerate street rats; it's a tragedy about lust, betrayal, disappointment, death and despair on a universal scale that is challenged by few contemporary examples of rock songwriting.

It derives its enormous strength and impact from those specific qualities Lou Reed was thought to have long since lost.

His immaculate sense of observation and ear for dialogue serves him brilliantly, especially in the second of the three fragments where he recounts the conversation of two of the protagonists in the drama, one of whose old lady has OD'd to the minor discomfort of the other who decides that the best solution would be to drag her body down onto the street, wait for a car to slam over it and claim her death "as just another hit and run".

And nowhere has his powerful poetic gift been better displayed than in the final passage, where he sings with authentic passion, "Love has gone away/Took the rings off my fingers/And now there's nothing left to say..."

This final elegy is performed with an understated elegance that culminates in a display of dreadful and overwhelming poignancy and desperate longing for all that has been lost and can never be replaced. The final echo of the hypnotic central theme that holds together the three segments (carried by Fonfara's discreet use of the synthesizer), whispers into the wings, followed by Reed and the band.

And it's all over, but for the encores, "Sweet Jane" and "Rock 'n' Roll" (in New Jersey he will perform a 15-minute arrangement of "Sister Ray", but only after making his audience wait for over ten minutes while he recovered from the emotional outpouring of "Street Hassle").

Yes. The wasted years have almost entirely been vindicated; but he won't let us forget how much they cost him...

Sunday morning in New York City. The police sirens are screaming like renegade banshees through Central Park. The Europeans are waiting for Lou Reed in the bar of the Essex House hotel. He shows up an hour late and demands an Irish coffee from the barman. "I'll just send for an Irishman to make it," he wisecracks.

Louis is not amused. "Hey," he snaps. "If I'd wanted a comedian, I'd have called room service. Just fix the drink. Make it a double."

"What you want? TWO Irish coffees?"

"No. I want a doubleshot. And don't miss the glass. I don't want to have to lick the bar again." The drink is served. The cream is whipped into a sickly curl. Lou looks at it with distaste.

The incident annoys him. He decides to return to his room. We follow at a safe distance (no use upsetting him at this stage).

Lou Reed's room looks like a warehouse after a four-day aerial bombardment. Amplifiers, guitars, synthesizers, video games, stacks of disco cassettes, trailing miles of wires and cables cover the carpets and every other available surface. Clothes and boots are strewn everywhere. Trays of drinks, bottletops, glasses crack underfoot. Now, I could hardly be described as Miss Tidy 1978; but this is ridiculous.

Lou is sitting amid this rubble, revealing no visible concern for the outrageous clutter. I fling half-a-ton of debris from the bed and collapse upon it. Lou is fiddling about with the Roland Guitar Synthesizer.

"Isn't this the greatest? I'd tell you about it, but you just wouldn't understand. Anyway, it doesn't come with an information booklet and I haven't figured it out yet myself...(he starts whacking out some Hendrix-derived riff).

"Hear that? I used to take acid too, you know. This is marvellous. Delusions of grandeur. That's always been my style, anyway.

"This is the greatest guitar ever built by human people. It makes every other guitar look tragic. This thing is the invention of the age. I haven't been this excited since the first record I made...you gotta realise, the Virgin Thrill has long gone." He points to the video patterns

Above: **The young Louis Firbank as a member of Velvet Underground, the band he quit in 1970 to pursue what has been an always-eventful solo career.**

of the television screen. "Isn't that impressive? No? Then f– you.

"This is the sound I heard in my head at the time of 'Sister Ray,' I've done nothing but track this one sound down. It's been frustrating, 'cos I always approached the guitar as if it was an orchestra – am I not the king of flash? That's what distortion was all about.

"But I didn't know what I was doing then. I just had, like a Vox Super Beetle…but, oh look, man. Who can remember back then? Who can remember what we were doing…"

His attention is caught once more by the video patterns. "See that? That's what we're gonna be using as a backdrop. Can you imagine it? That as a backdrop, with six little figures at the bottom. Six little dots, man."

Hey, Lou – you don't really see yourself as a dot, do you?

"Why not, I'd rather look at that than me. What kinda question is that? That's such a loaded question."

I just thought you'd want the audience to know that they were watching Lou Reed, not just a dot.

'But how could they doubt it for a minute?" he responds with a marvellous gesture. "So who else would do that? We've already established what I LOOK like. Now we can go past it. All this time, it's just been like saying 'hello.' Now that's settled. So just look at this."

Listen, a word of advice. You don't interview Lou Reed, you sit there and he talks to you and you're damn lucky if you can squeeze a word in sideways.

"My life can't be caught up in other people's conversation," he says at one point. "I don't talk to that many people. I do most of the talking because I deserve to. If somebody's faster and smarter than me I'd shut up and listen. It doesn't happen too often, though."

So we sit here, this French journalist and me, and we listen to Lou and we agree with him when he tells us how great he is; and it becomes increasingly clear that he's in quite a dislocated mood.

His conversation follows no convenient logic; so we just dig and try to ride out the cresting waves of high speed raps and try to make sense of his more, uh, abstract flights.

I try to force him to focus on these last confused years, and to explain his survival when almost everyone had given him up for lost.

"I'm, uh, very legitimate on a number of levels," he begins, piecing together a coherent statement. "And that's the only reason I think I'm still here…Like, people think on many levels that I'm a vicious and conniving this and that, who doesn't do the right thing, who's self-destructive, who can't be trusted.

"The thing is, it was always like, LOU REED…he was always doing it. I'm the only honest commodity around. I always was. I mean, even if I was an asshole, I was an asshole on my own terms. It's not like I'm dumb and I didn't know.

"Even when I was an asshole, I was a literate lunatic. Even my bull was head and shoulders above everyone else's. It's always been honest and personal, you know…When you buy a Lou Reed record you gotta expect LOU REED. 'Metal Machine' took care of that…"

When, in your career do you think you were the biggest asshole, I ask.

"Hey…you're really pushing it aren't you…I don't think I WAS an asshole."

I was using your own words.

"Yeah…yeah, I know," he says wearily. "But I think an asshole is somebody who wastes time. It's not a question of good or bad. It's just that during this period I hadn't reached a conclusion about things. I

didn't CARE. I was having a little dialogue with myself, about life, the world, my vocation, what I wanted to do.

"No, I wasn't looking for an identity. I had an identity. I was a lot of people, I'm a pretty expansive creature. I can be one thing and then another. No one of them is any more me than the other. But they're all parts. I mean, it's not that hard…In novels no one would think twice about it. It's just that rock 'n' roll has been treated as such a mutant, idiot child medium…

"But that," he says, winging off at a tangent, "made it easier for anyone with even half a mind to walk in and just dominate that end of it. The trick was not to become intellectual flash…On the other hand, I didn't HAVE to worry about that because I didn't CARE…

"I always assumed that I was great. I never doubted it. People's opinion of me don't matter. I know my opinion is the one that's right. It took me a long time to learn that.

"The only mistake I ever made over the years was listening to other people. 'Hey, Lou,' I finally said, 'can't you understand that you're right, that you've always been right? Why do you insist on bringing in all these other people?'

"Now I don't. But, it's frightening if you're always right and you're never having to work for it."

Why are you so convinced, Lou, that you're always so right?

"Because I can do it right in front of you like THAT (he snaps his fingers for emphasis and almost falls off his chair). It's not very hard for me. Apparently, it is for other people.

"But now I MADE my decision, and I'm looking out at the world and, like, it's 'Jesus Christ, Lou – you really are a very rare commodity!'

"I've only known a few people I thought were that good. Delmore Schwarz, Warhol…I mean, I get tons of publicity. I don't go looking for it. I always assumed that I'd get it. And I DO.

"There are some people who get press agents…but they wouldn't be able to stay in the same room as me. It'd be hopeless. The thing is – I'm convinced I'm right.

"And I am, for me…I ended up in rock 'n' roll, 'cos there was a working machine that was just sitting there that needed overhauling and somebody to pay attention to it. And I realised that I could do that very well, 'cos I was doing it anyway. And since I was doing it I thought I might as well do it in the open market place.

"And if you look back at the Velvet Underground, in retrospect it's remarkable. If you look at other areas, there's nothing. The Velvet Underground is legitimate. It can hold its own. I mean, I didn't write Death Of A Salesman. But then, I didn't find that an interesting play, anyway.

"Even now I don't think there's anyone in rock 'n' roll who's writing lyrics that mean anything, other than ME. You can listen to me and actually hear a voice. These other people are MORONS. They really are."

Oh come on, Lou, I exclaim, exasperated. What about Bowie? Dylan? Neil Young? These people aren't exactly compiling shopping lists.

"Oh…uh " yeah. I was wondering about that the other day. I was thinking 'Who the f– is there around, who was, like, with me, from the year one who's still viable?' David hasn't been around as long as I have.

"And David is gaining and losing ground at the same time. He's managed to scuttle as much of one part of his audience as possible, and tried to go for another and they aren't there yet. I think he lacks people around him who might challenge him. He's in danger of becoming a guru…"

But, counters my charming French companion, you – Lou – have been a guru to a lot of people.

"And you might've been a German Shepherd to a lot of people," Lou responds lightheartedly. "That has nothing to do with me. I know that that exists, and I make room for that.

"Like, I went through that very early. Like people said, 'I took heroin because of you.' I don't wanna KNOW...It's so AWFUL to have that kind of power over these poor sick savages. Please, leave me out of it.

"At least I like to think I told them about it gently – ah! I don't get involved in that kind of tedious dialogue. I don't bother even thinking about it. It's bulls-thinking. It has nothing to do with me. I just always have that power over people. It's up to me whether I want to live with it."

I still want an answer to his outrageous dismissal of his contemporaries. And I'm in the mood to pester him until I get it.

"Right...right...David's right there. But he's getting more and more isolated. I listened to that last album, man. It's scary. I don't relate to it. It's interesting and I admire it; the technique, the craft, the use of language and the acting involved in it. But it's not something I identify with.

"Dylan? Dylan's not around any more. Of course, he was NEVER around for me. But he did have a nice flair for words that didn't mean anything. And he knew it. They were just marijuana throwaways. But they loved him for it. But he became dull. Then, he was dull anyway.

"He did write some nice stuff, though, that I don't think maybe he appreciates...But he's never made a rock 'n' roll record. Of course he hasn't. Can you imagine what it was like where he was...on the other hand, isn't it a shame that he's such a loser. Sure I think he's a loser. He's not strong. I know I'M strong.

"If I couldn't handle this thing. I'd remove myself. I'm a sensible guy."

New York has its own resident symphony orchestra; the sirens of the police cars that chase each other through the city. Right now the solo violinist is screeching past the open window of Lou Reed's hotel room on Central Park South.

Above: **Poetry in motion. A blur of light and movement as Lou Reed does his thing.**

Right: **No longer the whip-thin style icon of his youth, as this recent picture proves, Lou Reed can still work the old magic with an audience which never tires of waiting for their man.**

Left: **The man in black
breaks with the habit
of a lifetime and adds
a touch of cowboy
trimming to his outfit.
It was only a phase…**

Above: **...as he proves in this shot, taken during another back-stage reverie.**

"You know," he says, "it's like, war right from the top. The minute you wake up in THEIR world and you tune into the fact that you gotta get out, it's war. And they'll do anything to stop you.

"I usually have a commonsense view of it all, but I know that right down on the bottom line, it's absolute warfare from the very first. No question about it.

"I claim that THEY are poisoning us from the start, and that we don't stand a chance. I really believe there's a war, and that we're on one side and they're on the other. And I think that rock 'n' roll is terribly, terribly political and subversive and that they're absolutely right to be afraid of it.

"And right across the board there are a lot of albums with words like mine. I'm just more of a threat because of what I represent. I am an enticement to THEIR children. I'm still banned on the radio, not because of what I look like, but because I represent certain ideas.

"I mean, I don't have long hair, I don't wear earrings or glitter. Maybe they just don't like Jewish faggots. How seriously can you take it? So they don't play me on the radio? What's the radio? Who's the radio run by? Who's it played for?

"They should take me very seriously...they do. They wanna keep me locked away. I'm dangerous.

"They're afraid of that. And they really should be because a lot of us really aren't kidding, and we just keep going. And they can't stop us, man.

I spoke to Lou after the Philadelphia concert and caught in the euphoria of that success he proceeded to trash all the albums that had preceded "Street Hassle"; I remind him of this statement. He'd like to clarify.

"'Street Hassle' is the best album I've done. "Coney Island Baby' was good, but I was, like, under siege 'Berlin' was 'Berlin'. 'Rock 'n' Roll Heart' is good – compared to the rest of the s– that's around. As opposed to 'Street Hassle,' they're babies. 'Coney Island Baby' is a very shaky album, in a lot of respects; because it's a very bare Lou Reed you've got there. It may not sound vulnerable to whoever's listening to it. But you were getting a photo after the fact."

But do you think you've achieved as much as you should or could have over the last four or five years?

"That's another unanswerable question," he says flatly. "I achieved as much as I could have, by definition. There's a school of thought that says it's incredible that I'm still here at all, right here with this one.

"The ending's the only thing that counts in my life. I've lived through people saying, 'Oh, Lou. That's the best thing you ever did...Like beat "Heroin"...beat "Sister Ray"...' Well, people are beginning to realise that that's exactly what I'm doing.

"I've just been out of work for a long time, you know. I didn't care about all those albums. They were the best I could've done at the time. No one asked me to do my best. I was told not to, man.

"I thought that I was lucky to be making records at all after 'Metal Machine'. Like I know a lot of people who aren't even allowed to make a noise in the house. I just thought I was lucky.

"But really I want to be able to listen to my own records, and at one point it was not exciting, because I was the only one there and no one was interested in what I wanted to hear and or say...But I didn't take any easy options. It was a situation of no choice.

"I don't look back, though. I think people who look back are making a mistake. They're wasting time. I coped with whatever I was coping with. And I assume I did the best I could, because I always do, you know. No doubt about it. If somebody doesn't like it or think that I could've done better – fine. That's just the way I did it.

"I know when I'm good and when I'm bad. And I'm NEVER bad, sometimes I just don't bother. And for a long time I didn't bother...But like Andy ways, "If you complete one thing, even if you don't know what you're talking about, you're miles ahead of everyone else'. So shut up and DO IT.

"If you have an idea, start it and finish it. And I started it when I put 'Heroin' out. I started it with the Velvet Underground. That's when it started. Then I left it for two years.

"But I decided that I hadn't finished what I started. But I had to really think about coming back and finishing it, about involving myself with all these people in this business.

"Because you're talking about people who're not creative people. Because there are very few creative people – and most of them are lunatics.

"If you wanna make adult rock records you gotta take care of all these people along the way. And it's not child's play. You're talking about managers, accountants. You're talking about the lowest level of human beings.

"You're talking about lighting people tacking on an extra 200 dollars a night AFTER kickbacks. You're talking about road managers selling cut cocaine to musicians. You're talking about people who're putting down on a corporation payroll 50 people who don't even exist.

"You're talking about people who won't file your taxes, an officer of the corporation who doesn't pay your holding tax, so you find yourself owing to the government and in contempt of court, and heading for jail, money that's going out for drugs is going down on YOUR tab.

"You're talking about a situation where the artist wonders where all his money went, and he's in litigation with his record company and his manager and he doesn't have any money to defend himself, so no lawyer will even touch him.

"But the people who stole the money can defend themselves with the money they stole, which is his. But no one will touch him, because in a pop medium your lifespan as a moneymaker is two to three years at the most. And there's no known case of a manager losing to an artist, and the record companies know that so they'll back the manager.

"And maybe they're right to do that, because the act maybe is not that bright and/or f– up and doesn't even have the strength or stamina to get out of the situation, anyway. 'Cos when you decide to get hot'n'heavy with these people it's no use saying, 'Oh, man – I just play the guitar.'

"Musicians protect thyself 'cos the heavens are coming down. That's when it comes down to, 'Do I even want to make a record?' Given the way people are generally, given the trouble you have to go through just to get the lyrics on there – I was told THREE times to ditch 'Street Hassle'…I never thought that these people knew what they were talking about, but inevitably they made me feel very insecure.

"My only problem, then was that at that point, I assumed that was it. There was nobody I met who I wasn't disappointed with or found out was a sleaze…but I'd decided to come back and finish it.

"What else was I gonna do? Walk away and leave it? But I don't want all those people who've put their faith in me thinking that I turned out to be a total sham, like everyone else they ever believed in.

"I want to keep the illusion.

I am of a mood these days," says Lou Reed, "that tells me that I'm a right wing fascist liberal. I cover all bases. I cover it all from all points of view, and you know there's something to be said for all of them, given the lay of the land.

"I don't think of people as sheep. I think of them as dogs. There's not much you can do for them except treat them as people. Most of them aren't civilised. They live in their houses and they read their newspapers and they agree with what's in there.

"Why shouldn't they? They don't travel a whole lot. Nobody ever told them anything. They've got no psychological difficulties with their religions or their schools.

"It's amazing that people aren't at war 24 hours a day. I'm surprised more people aren't shooting each other in the street…I just don't know how it all got set up this way.

"I can go to Japan and they got highways that look like the ones in Nebraska. Jesus. It's like a primitive attempt at logic. Like 'We all go this way on the highway and we'll be there in an hour.' Wow. They're really trying, aren't they? It's pretty sophisticated, uh? They all move at roughly the same pace. Except the blacks in Africa and I guess they're pretty f– anyway."

We have been talking now for close on two hours. Even Lou's sounding tired of his own voice. He started chain-smoking, about 90 minutes ago. He'd start one and leave it in the ashtray. Then he'd light another one. To save embarrassment, I started smoking his. Then he started smoking mine and pretty soon it was like musical chairs with nicotine. We've ended up juggling a pack and a half between us…

"What it's all about," he's saying, "is doing it on you own terms. Reasonably. Without getting killed by somebody or shot on the street. But you still gotta satisfy your own standards. It would be easy to satisfy THEIR standards.

"It would be difficult for me now, 'cos I've started manipulating people again. "Street Hassle' proved that people listened if I shouted loud enough. I can't manage to get through on THEIR standards anymore. But I admire people who can.

"It's a talent to be consistently mediocre. But it's usually real pap. Like Jacqueline-Susann-type pap. But that is a talent. But it's not Dostoevsky…but, like, how many Dostoevskys are there?"

God, Lou, you don't want to be the Dostoevsky of rock 'n' roll, do you?

"No…I don't wanna be Dostoevsky…I don't wanna be Jacqueline Susann, either. I don't see why I can't be both. And STILL be brilliant. Because I'M the ONLY ONE. There's nobody even coming up behind me. I'm still there, man.

"And even when they tried to stop me making records they couldn't stop me. Lou Reed was always there. They couldn't change me. Like, 'Sally Can't Dance'…with all that junk in there, it's still Lou Reed. I sound terrible, but I was singing about the worst s– in the world.

"They said, 'Oh – Lou's parodying himself.' But I was doing better than that. I was right down there. That WASN'T a parody. That was what was happening. All my records are for real, man. I don't know HOW to kid around. They're all REAL close to home.

"'Berlin' was REAL close to home. People would say, 'Lou – is that autobiographical?' And I'd say 'Mmmmmmm – not bad.' Jesus. Autobiographical? If only they KNEW!

"Like, during the recording session my old lady – who was an asshole, but I needed to have a female asshole around to bolster me up: I needed a sycophant who I could bounce around and she fit the bill…but she called it love, ha! – anyway, my old lady, during a recording session, she tried to commit suicide in the bathtub in the hotel…Cut her wrists…She lived…

"But we had to leave a roadie with her from then on. It's funny, another girlfriend of mine told her. 'Look – if you're doing it for real, slice THIS way – not THAT way, darling.' Anyway, she lived, so it's a bulls-scam…ON THE OTHER HAND…one rock star's wife DID commit suicide during an album recording. So these things DO happen.

"But why, my dear, should it frighten me…? What do you want me to do? Hide in the closet? There are car accidents outside. Muggings. TYPHOID. There's cancer. We're all gonna die and have heart attacks. So, what would you like me to do? Feel sad? Get upset? Get religion? Act better?

"I'd just like to have some FUN. As long as I'm going through with this thing, I would like to have fun. You know it's garbage from top to bottom – so why not?

"I'm gonna have fun…It's the only thing you can do…And you gotta hold out until they end it or they kill you…or you get away with it."

©Allan Jones / Melody Maker / IPC Syndication

7 8

Above: **Louis goes walkabout as security staff persuade over-eager fans at London's Crystal Palace Bowl to stay in the water. Damned hippies…**

key recordings

1972 First solo album since leaving The Velvet Underground, *Lou Reed* produced in London by Richard Robinson. David Bowie steps in to produce *Transformer*, including the hit single *Walk On The Wild Side*

1973 Reed's darkest album, *Berlin*, still makes fascinating listening

1974 The live set *Rock 'n' Roll Animal* gives Reed his first major US hit

1978 Reed at his moody best for the brilliant *Take No Prisoners* – which didn't

1990 Reunited with John Cale, Reed recalled their mentor, Andy Warhol, on the hauntingly evocative *Songs For Drella*

The fact that James Jewel Osterburg has made it into the new millennium more or less in one piece is astonishing enough. That he should have done so still able to perform with most of his infamous ferocity and energy intact is nothing short of miraculous, for the wild man better known as Iggy Pop spent the best part of thirty-something years doing his best to ensure that he would not survive to do any of the above.

Born in Michigan in April 1947, Iggy first played in Ann Arbor high school rock bands, mostly as a drummer and most notably with The Iguanas (with whom he acquired his nickname) and, in 1965, with the Denver-based Prime Movers blues band. Dropping out of university to study drums with long-time Howlin' Wolf sideman Sam Lay, he'd become singer-guitarist Iggy Stooge by the time he and the brothers Asheton (bassist Ron and drummer Scott) and formed The Psychedelic Stooges. Aptly, they made their live debut on Halloween Night, 1967.

With Dave Alexander joining as bassist (leaving Iggy himself free to concentrate on the vocals when Ron Asheton switched to guitar), they dropped the 'Psychedlic' part of their name and signed to Elektra in 1968. John Cale produced their first eponymous album, and while neither of their two Elektra releases sold well at the time, they have since been hailed as classics.

While The Stooges underwent a number of personnel changes during the next two years, heroin addiction wreaked the greatest change on Iggy himself. Now liable to indulge in bloody self-mutilation of his skinny torso during the course of frenetic free-fall live appearances, he was headed for oblivion by 1972 when long-time fan David Bowie brought him to England to record the powerful Raw Power album. A 1974 live album (Metallic KO, initially released only in France) saw The Stooges making a farewell bow. Two members – Steve MacKay and Dave Alexander – would later die of substance abuse, while Ron Asheton eventually formed Destroy All Monsters.

Iggy proved a formidable role model for many punk bands and in 1977 David Bowie produced two new seminal albums, The Idiot and Lust For Life, containing such classics as 'The Passenger', 'Night Clubbin'' and 'China Girl' – the latter track co-written with and destined to be a hit for Bowie. Iggy repaid Bowie by providing backing vocals on his hit album Low.

Signed to Arista in the late 70s, Iggy was unable to produce any notable or commercial work and in 1982 – after publishing his brutally honest autobiography and releasing the Chris Stein-produced Zombie Birdhouse, underwent a lengthy and ultimately successful drug cure and married. He also branched out into acting, appearing in such movies as Sid And Nancy, Hardware and The Color Of Money, as well as the TV series Miami Vice.

Re-united with Bowie in 1986, Iggy released the fine Blah Blah Blah, an album which produced his first-ever British hit single, 'Real Wild Child'. Guns N'Roses guitarist Slash co-wrote four of the songs and was heavily featured on Iggy's 1990 album Brick By Brick.

Working through the 90s at a slower pace, Iggy closed the decade with Avenue B (Explicit), an album which – with its ballads and often-spoken narrative – was something of a departure. Dealing with life, death and the frailty of human relationships, Iggy proved that he'd emerged from all the madness wiser and saner than anyone could have imagined.

13 August 1977 John Orme

IGGY'S LUST WORDS

Iggy Pop had been out swimming near San Francisco, he confessed. "Last night a few people came round and we had some sushi, which is a Japanese dish of raw fish wrapped in seaweed. There was a little saki around, and well, you know the way it goes. So I just went for a swim in the ocean this morning and that is why there is a little water in the ear that I am speaking to you through."

Organised chaos. That is how it seems with Iggy, even though he is a few thousand miles away at the other end of a telephone.

There is plenty on his mind at the moment. A new album, "Lust for Life," is ready for release next week, and Iggy was in London only three weeks ago doing the UK master for the record. His tour is finalised, and he is spending a little time in America away from his hometown of Berlin as he gets ready for the road.

His enthusiasm for the new record positively vibrates down the phone lines. "We did it quick, this record. The entire thing was done in just two weeks, including the mixing. The music is hard, and fast, and stiff, the direct opponent of 'The Idiot.'

"I am singing with my full range instead of just deepdown low, like I did on that album. We worked so fast that almost everything was done in one take with only a couple of vocal overdubs necessary because of my unusual microphone technique, and one lead guitar thing, or whatever you call it when the guitar players start doodling around with their instruments."

Iggy is naturally of the firm opinion that this new record – performed with David Bowie at the piano and masterminding the production behind the songwriter's table is the best thing he has done.

Answering a question about whether he feels the need to move into new directions like films, he replies: "No, I don't fancy dressing up in a monkey suit nine hours a day on an Avengers set.

"I am more concerned with mastering this aspect of my craft: music, then perhaps I will do something else."

Is that mastery close? "Yup, with this record I think it is. This is a hot one. Even a cab driver in Naples liked it when I played the tape."

For those who like to spice their music with a few facts, Iggy's crew on the new album is much as before.

Above: **Proving that they did come out in the daylight, Iggy and The Stooges covet a neighbour's cactus in this late-60s publicity shot.**

Previous page: **Classic Iggy Pop, on stage in the 70s when he often crossed the fine line between sheer madness and total mayhem.**

Right: **A healthier looking Iggy in the 80s, after he'd cleared his body of the drugs that nearly claimed his life. But it was touch and go for a while…**

"Let's see now. Bud Sales is on drums, Tony Sales on bass, Rocky Gardiner and Carlos Alomar are on guitars, and David Bowie is on piano. Three of the songs, 'Some Weird Sin', 'Tonight' and 'Turn Blue,' were written while we were rehearsing for the last tour, and they were performed if that's what you'd call it, during the last tour.

"The best of the stuff was written in about one-and-a-half days.

"That was the way I wanted to work on the album. To achieve the immediate effect that I wanted I had to work very hard, much harder than everybody else in the band.

"A six-to-eight hour session involves, say, 12 hours work for them, but I was taking the tapes home with me and just kept going working. I had to be one step ahead of my band."

He chuckles at the mention of a possible theme in the new album.

"Well, I suppose you could say there is a lot of thematic material. It is about love, love, love – hypnotising chickens, that sort of thing. It is about a person someone anonymous that I know, and I put her in different settings. That, I suppose, is what the album is about."

Would the casual observer passing Berlin's Hansa studios (where "Lust For Life" was recorded) have seen the wild-man Iggy conform to the austere surrounding of acoustic booths and mike leads?

"Well, I just can't help but get physical, I guess, when I am singing. You can tell from the album that the band is excited, and as the music goes on it really starts to shake.

"That happened because when they are playing they are hearing

Left: **"It really makes me feel like a man when I'm onstage." The blonde Iggy delivers another of his vein-busting performances.**

my singing and vocals for the first time. The result we achieved in the studio is similar to my effect on people when I present an evening on-stage."

The Berlin studios, where Iggy recorded "The Idiot" and Bowie "Low," were a natural choice. " I live in Berlin now, and have done for a year or so.

"I like the studios, I like the place, I like the people, and I speak German very well. David Bowie first exposed me to the city, but now he is living in Switzerland."

Although the redoubtable Mr Bowie still measures strongly in his musical life, Iggy has sensed a role-change in their effect on each other.

"During the preparation and recording of the album it would appear that I was having a stronger effect on David than him on me – I think that is valid.

"He wanted nothing more than to be involved in one of my 'brash albums,' as he called them, and I think that is a good description. But I don't want to underplay his effect. He co-wrote most of the songs and had a great deal to do with the record.

"We worked very quickly together, but I don't want you to think it was all togetherness and walking hand-in-hand or anything like that. We had a lot of friction between us, and I think that is why we have done some pretty good work. There was a lot of clash going on."

When Iggy tours Britain at the end of September, he hopes to bring virtual the same band as played on the album with him, and that includes Bowie. "I may have to make just one or two changes. It is too early to say whether David will be free, but I would say it is highly likely he will come."

The idea of the British tour appeals to Iggy. "I have never seen England properly, but I love Newcastle very much, those houses with the peat roofs and the people around there. I like the look on the faces of the people there. It will be nice to show up at some of the same places as we played last time."

During his recent London visit for the mastering of the UK pressings of the album – "I did that myself, my own quality control, because I wanted to make sure that you guys in England get a decent pressing for once. And anyway, it makes me feel good to see something through from start to finish." Iggy did himself a little shopping.

"I went into a record store and was served by this really nice guy who looked like Richard Hell, or rather the way all Englishmen who try to look like Richard Hell look. He was a real gentleman.

"I bought the Clash album, which I hadn't heard and 'Pretty Vacant' and 'No Fun.'" The latter is, of course, an Iggy composition. "I certainly appreciate the Sex Pistols' performance of it."

He also heard the Damned album, which did not poleaxe him with delight; he appreciated the Clash. "There are some of those things that Joe Strummer play that sound like the way I look, really – plaintive, pretty little things. The only thing with the Clash is that I find the things that come out of the mouth not as nice as what comes out of the guitar."

He still has no real idea of a planned set for his English dates. "I have not worked out a performance as such, I will just pick some songs and we will do them.

"The way I do a song does not alter very much from the way I write and first perform it. I do not care to tamper with material, but that is not to say I won't step out of things if I feel like it at any time.

"After making a record like this, to get up onstage is really the final part. There is no manager to hassle you when you are up there. It is like being a baby Jesus in your swaddling clothes, with no need of anyone to fan you to keep you cool. It really makes me feel like a man when I get up onstage."

Er, yes…well…Maybe he had better get back to sleep now.

"Ah no, I think I well get into a little riot for the rest of the day. I have all these things here that I can use. Paints, acrylics, poster paints, cassettes, a Teac tape deck, a turntable, a lovely pair of JBC speakers, a Telecaster, a Fender Rhodes, a video…"

© John Orme / Melody Maker / IPC Syndicates

Right: **Mad, bad and dangerous to know. Iggy Pop, the rock star who once seemed destined to die young, shows that he is a true survivor.**

key recordings

1965	Elektra unleash *The Stooges* on an unsuspecting world
1972	David Bowie produces the now-solo Iggy's *Raw Power*
1977	Back with Bowie, Iggy releases two of his finest, *The Idiot* and *Lust For Life*, and scores with first hit singles T*he Passenger, Night Clubbin'* and C*hina Girl*
1986	Iggy-Bowie partnership triumphs again, *Blah Blah Blah*
1990	Songwriting and guitar playing of Slash help elevate *Brick By Brick* to great heights
1999	Older and apparently wiser, the happily married Iggy gets reflective for *Avenue B* (*Explicit*)

It may be a cliché to harken back to the outbreak of London graffiti which proclaimed 'Clapton Is God' in the mid-sixties, but the fact is that no other British guitarist has come close to commanding the respect, adulation, love that the man born Eric Clapp in 1945 has for almost thirty years. Despite many personal ups and downs during that time (many of the downs self-induced), Clapton enters the new millennium with his reputation and worldwide status intact. More importantly, so are his unique talent and complete command of his instrument.

Dropping out of art school in 1963 to turn pro, Clapton's arrival in The Yardbirds at the end of that year coincided with the release of their first two singles and a huge hike in their popularity. Deciding, in 1965, that their chart success with 'For Your Love' meant imminent commercial sell-out, Clapton quit to return to his musical roots as a member of John Mayall's Bluesbreakers, a band which included bassist Jack Bruce. Finding in him a soul-mate who also wanted to push back the boundaries of modern music, in 1967 Clapton, Bruce and drummer Ginger Baker left Mayall (with whom they had recorded some outstanding blues and played many stunning gigs) to form Cream.

An immediate international sensation when they were launched, Cream's four albums (Fresh Cream, Disraeli Gears, Wheels Of Fire and Goodbye) brought Clapton to the attention of a vast new audience. A trio beset with mounting personal and musical differences, Cream would break up in late 1968 and Clapton – enamoured of the white southern soul styling of Delaney and Bonnie, with whom he guested – would change his own playing style when he began recording solo albums in 1970, after the abortive Blind Faith, the mis-guided new 'supergroup' he assayed with Baker, Steve Winwood and Ric Grech.

If Eric Clapton's old fans were dismayed by the lack of extended blistering solos on his laid-back eponymously-titled 1970 solo album, they were mollified by some of the Layla And Other Assorted Love Songs set released under the alias 'Derek and The Dominoes' later that year, not least on the lengthy title track which would become a huge hit when it was released as a single in 1971. By then the Dominoes project had, inevitably, juddered to a halt and Clapton had begun what would be a three-year lay-off as his heroin addiction took its hold, although Pete Townshend was instrumental in persuading him out of hiding for a 1973 appearance at London's Rainbow Theatre, a star-studded event that was released on vinyl.

Now cleared of drug addiction (but still nursing an alcohol problem that would take more time to solve) Clapton, producer Tom Dowd and the band who'd play on his next four albums headed for Miami in April 1974 to record his come-back 461 Ocean Boulevard, an album which included the version of Bob Marley's 'I Shot The Sheriff' which topped the US charts. The rest of the seventies saw Clapton's work sell well, if not spectacularly, and his live performances draw even bigger audiences.

The 1980s witnessed more of the same, though Clapton was now branching out into supplying haunting, atmospheric musical soundtracks for TV and films (including Mel Gibson's Lethal Weapon series) with collaborator Michael Kamen – projects which saw his still-fluid and distinctive playing set against full orchestral scores.

In 1986 a four-CD box set retrospective, Crossroads topped the US charts while 1989 saw his superb Journeyman album – with US bluesman Robert Cray guesting – give him another smash. Now established as one of the world's most popular concert artists, in 1990 and 1991 Clapton sold out London's 9,000-seater Royal Albert Hall for unprecedented runs of 18, then consecutive 24 nights – the second series of gigs released as the best-selling and aptly-titled 24 Nights.

Tragedy struck in March 1991 when Clapton's four-year old son, Conor, died after falling out of a window in a 53rd-floor New York apartment. Clapton's output of new material has been spasmodic and patchy since then, but the re-release and repackaging of his illustrious past recording – especially sixties and early seventies blues – has given his completist fans some 15 compilations and box sets to acquire.

To them, it seems, that old graffiti still has the ring of truth. Eric Clapton is still God.

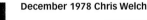

December 1978 Chris Welch

PORTRAIT OF THE ARTIST AS A WORKING MAN

Eric Clapton, whose remarks in support of Enoch Powell two years ago gave the initial impetus to the formation of Rock Against Racism, this week spoke to the MM about his political beliefs – and repeated his praise for the controversial MP's stance on immigration.

Echoing his famous impromptu speech at a Birmingham concert in the summer of 1976, Clapton said: "I think Enoch is a prophet. He's not a racist – I don't think he cares about colour of any kind."

Clapton continued: "I think his whole idea is for us to stop being unfair to immigrants, because it's getting out of hand. The Government is being incredibly unfair to people abroad to lure them to the promised land where there is actually no work.

"The racist business starts when white guys see immigrants getting jobs and they're not.

"That whole thing about me talking about Enoch was that it occurred to me that he was the only bloke who was telling the truth, for the good of he country."

Asked how he responded to the heavy criticism of his original statement, Clapton replied: "I don't mind. I believe Enoch is a very religious man. And you can't be religious and racist at the same time. The two things are incompatible."

RAR commented: "Before Eric Clapton opens his mouth he should not only understand the facts, but also the political climate in which he makes his statements – and, as a popular musician, he should exercise that responsibility.

"He obviously doesn't know what he's talking about. Powell has never said anything with the welfare of the ethnic minorities in mind – the result of his 'Rivers of Blood' speech and subsequent racist outbursts in fact made racism respectable and racist violence the norm. The only difference between Powell and the Nazis is that Powell would ask the blacks to go back and the National Front would tell them."

IT has often been said that one of Eric Clapton's major problems over the years has been to find his own identity, one in which he can be comfortable and assured. He has been through the most historically important groups of our time, undergone the pressures of an extraordinary fame, been himself up to all the excesses of the rock 'n' roll lifestyle, been close to death, known misery and oblivion, and come out of it with his talent and sanity intact.

Eric has appeared in many guises: the eager, flippant art school kid of the Yardbirds, the macho blues man with John Mayall, even a psychedelic hippie with Cream in the era of pink boots and frizzy hair. With his old pal Jeffrey (George Harrison to you), he became drawn for a while to matters spiritual.

But now he has settled down to the role of a kind of musical labourer as he seeks security and stability in the English working class ethics and manners. His speech has that inbred authority of a saloon-bar host who divides the world into two groups of people – beer drinkers, and non-beer drinkers.

He may not be 100 per cent the real Eric Clapton, but it's a good solid base to work from, and it makes life less complicated – although, even here, I suspect that taking a stand on one lifestyle is not always easy.

While Eric enjoys talking about football to strangers in the bar, the commitment to being English and working class requires entrenched, conservative attitudes.

A few years ago, at Birmingham during a gig, Eric made a few remarks that seemed to support Enoch Powell's views on repatriation. As a direct result of this, Rock Against Racism was born. The left rose to fight what they feared might be popular support for the right.

But Eric is non-political and can hardly be called a racist. He has long idolised black music and musicians. Nevertheless he seems to feel that unchecked immigration is still an issue, and it was one of the matters we touch on during a long conversation at Southampton's Polygon Hotel on Saturday afternoon. At first it seemed that Eric might well be lured off to a football match; but to start at the beginning…

The day dawned wet and miserable at Waterloo Station. Adrian Boot, hero of the Grateful Dead's Egyptian campaign, appeared clutching his trunk load of cameras and reported that Jona Lewis of Stiff Tour fame was in the coffee shop.

Jona, a smartly dressed gent, clutching a piano accordion, was intrigued to hear of the expedition to see Clapton. He was on his way to a spot of promotion himself, down in Portsmouth, and remembered that the last time he saw Clapton was when Jona was in Brett Marvin and the

Above: **Clapton and Ginger Baker mull over some possibilities during a Cream soundcheck in America.**

Thunderbolts. "We did a tour with Derek & The Dominoes back in 1970. I remember Eric as a very thin man. He's bloomed out a bit since then."

Andy Murray, one of Stiff's hierarchy, recalled that he had seen Eric play a secret holiday camp gig at Hayling Island. "He played 'Layla' for all these mums, dads and kids, and nobody seemed to recognise it, but when he played 'I Shot The Sheriff' they knew it was a hit. He was going to play at another Butlin's but they had 7,000 applications for tickets. They panicked and cancelled the show."

Another show that had to be cancelled more recently was the ill-fated Cream reunion, when Ginger Baker wanted to bring Eric and Jack Bruce together again at his polo club. Unfortunately word was leaked to the national press and the polo fraternity also panicked, expecting an invasion of fans.

Andy laid Jona's album on me, apologised for blagging at 9.30 a.m. on Waterloo Station, and we went our separate ways.

At Southampton, an hour away, football fans were already streaming into town for the afternoon's match. But at the Polygon Hotel, most of the Clapton camp were still sound asleep after a night of merriment following their gig at the Gaumont.

Roger Forrester, Eric's manager, was awake, however, bleary-eyed and clad in a dressing gown, but keen that the long-delayed interview would take place.

"You know what I had to do to get Eric to agree to an interview?" he demanded, ordering coffee from room service. "I had to go on stage last night and announce the group. I was terrified. But once Eric gets an idea into his head he keeps on and on about it. So as I had to go on stage, he's GOT to do the interview."

Not for another couple of hours was it deemed sensible to start knocking on Eric's door. He had not been to bed until 5 a.m., having been out dancing at the local discotheque. Rumour was that the local girls had not been impressed by Eric's John Travolta-style routine, and had refused to join him on the floor, so in the end he had put a bandanna round his head and danced alone.

It seemed odd that after years of avoiding publicity and trying to shake off his fame Eric was now approaching that state known to many a rock star in their 30s, when the younger generation fails to recognise them.

It seemed the height of irony when two girls sitting in the hotel bar (where we eventually found Eric, surrounded by football fans) revealed they had not the faintest idea who he was. Their favourite band was Showaddywaddy. They'd never heard of Cream or Bob Dylan, for that matter.

Eric has cut back on drinking considerably, but he felt that a glass or two of brandy might help ease us into the interview and was most affable and amenable. There was a moment when I tried to draw him away from the subject of football, and back to more pressing matters like Rock Against Racism, when he chided: "Never mind what we were talking about. Now be courteous!"

What Eric had been saying about immigration was really just saloon-bar talk, and stemmed from a remark shouted at him the night before.

"Someone shouted out 'Enoch Powell' last night. And I had to spend half-an-hour after the gig explaining to Carl Radle that he wasn't the George Wallace of England. But I think Enoch is a prophet, see? His diplomacy is wrong, and he's got no idea how to present things. His ideas are right. You go to Heathrow any day, mate, and you'll see thousands of Indian people sitting there waiting to know whether or not they can come into the country. And you go to Jamaica and there's adverts on TV saying 'Come to lovely England,' and pictures of double-decker buses."

But didn't Eric think that Enoch was a racist?

"No, he's not," said Eric firmly. "I don't think he cares about colour of any kind. I think his whole idea is for us to stop being unfair to immigrants it's getting out of order. A husband comes over, lives off the dole to try and save enough to bring his wife and six kids over. It's splitting up families, and I think the Government is being incredibly unfair to people abroad to lure them to the promised land where there is actually no work.

"The racist business starts when white guys see immigrants getting jobs and they're not. Enoch said six years ago, stop it, given 'em a grand, and tell 'em to go home.

"That whole thing about me talking about Enoch was that it occurred to me that he was the only bloke who was telling the truth, for the good of the country. I mean there's all sorts of things going on, smuggling routes....you can get as many people in this country as you like. And it's their families that suffer because they're left behind. I saw an Indian woman being grilled at Heathrow and it was the most anguishing scene you've ever seen in your life."

"The woman has completely broken down, because she can hardly speak English, and she's come here expecting to be greeted by her husband and go to a new house. Next minute, she's back on the 'plane."

Eric got a lot of stick for his previous outburst.

"Yeah, I did. But I don't mind. So did Enoch. They shoved him into Ireland. But he can do as much good there as he can anywhere. I believe he is a very religious man. And you can't be religious and racist at the same time. The two things are incompatible."

But people might think that you are being racist yourself?

"Yeah, yeah. That was the original mistake."

Meanwhile the dialogue between Eric and his new-found mates, the football fans, went something like this:

1st Football fan: "Wodger work – five nights a week?"

Eric: "Nah, I couldn't 'andle that. I'm getting old mate."

1st Football fan: "You must be, because when I was a kid you were still going." (Shouts of laughter from all the company.)

Eric: "THANK you."

2nd Football fan: "Oh yeah, was it with Cream of summink?"

Eric: "All right, none of that..."

1st Football fan: "'Ee was going afore that..."

Eric hastily changes the subject and looks across at the two rather beautiful girls sitting across the lounge. He leans towards me in conspiratorial fashion. "'Ere, go across and ask 'em how old they are." What – those chicks? "Yeah, the grumble. Well it's company, isn't it."

At this point Roger Forrester appears in his manager's cap to borrow a couple of quid.

"Here you are, son, now go and enjoy yourself," says Eric enjoying the situation, and producing a tenner.

"Oh Eric, I don't want all that, do I? That's very nice of you..."

The fans chuckle in good humour, throw back their beers, and – having failed to seduce Eric to the match – set off to watch Southampton beat Birmingham.

The two girls come over to join us for drinks, with bright, nervous smiles. They sense that somehow Eric is the centre of attraction, but reveal a charming ignorance.

Above: **The only trouble with fame is that it can go to your head. One of Eric Clapton's least attractive hairstyles in the 60s did nothing to halt his progress.**

quartet. I was scared shitless of the idea, but it ended up him telling me not to worry. His attitude was fantastic.

"The first gig was a walkover, probably as good as any of the others. In fact it's easier with a four-piece. 'Cos when we had the girls and George, I was always looking from one side of the stage to the other to check out what was going on, and like two of the girls would be redundant a lot of the time, just sitting in chairs. That saps your energy and I don't think it was good for anybody. Wasn't good for them – or me.

"Trouble is – I can't fire people. Yvonne left because she wanted to pursue a solo career, and that was like saying 'Can I go?'

"The Dominoes was a four-piece band and I enjoyed that. It's the whole thing about having a Booker T-type feel. One guitar, keyboards, drums and bass. I have to work more, it's true, and that's what I really enjoy doing. Everybody has to work. We started out this tour trying too hard. Over-compensating. Now it's a lot more simplified. Booker T was your complete unit. You could add horns to it, and singers as you wanted."

So Eric would stay with this band for a while?

"I think so. We've already done nine months' work...'

And how was he shaping up, physically?

"I'm tired, man, really tired.

"We went to a disco last night, and there were some really ugly birds there. There were about 20 bouncers to every fella. I spent most of my time chatting up the bouncers – so I wouldn't get hit! And there's no place to go to in London any more. The only club I go to is Rags. But that's a man's club. You never see women in there ever. They've got a pool table, backgammon and cards. You go in there and drink until everyone's fed up with it, or you play pool and that's it. There's no chance of pulling anything! London's no place to go. I never go there unless I can help it. Only on business.

"I was going to have a dance competition last night. I was all wound up and going to give it plenty, but no chance. None of the girls wanted to dance. I've always been a dancer. I've been a dancer all me life. Do you remember the Scene Club? You could just dance on your own there. And there was some place in Archer Street, the only one in England they called a discotheque."

Eric was with the right label (RSO) for discos. How did he feel about the fantastic success of his old manager from the days of Cream, Robert Stigwood?

"I saw him recently and he doesn't know what's going on. He's transcended it completely. He's got more money than he knows what to do with. Billionaire – I should think. And yet he's exactly the same. He's still the same great bloke. He's a GREAT bloke. All he cares about is maintaining friendships, money can get in the way of that, rapidly. In business all he has to say is yey or nay.

"Sometimes he comes up with great ideas, other times he just gives his consent. Sgt. Pepper was one idea that died, though. It really died. He offered me a part in it. I was supposed to play a weather vane or something. Billy Preston ended up doing it."

Eric, who recently re-signed to the Stigwood organisation, stipulated in his contract that he would NOT be offered any film scripts. Apparently his experience in Tommy was enough, although he is keen to complete his own film documentary of the Clapton band on the road.

He had seemingly fought shy of the media in recent years, rarely giving interviews, and those around him often complained vociferously of the treatment meted out to him in reviews and articles.

"What do you work at?" asks one.

"Musician," he responds, as if he were saying "bricklayer" or "industrial cleaning contractor."

"What sort?"

"A rock 'n' roll musician."

The girls persist with their probing questions. What was he doing here in Southampton, they'd like to know.

"I've come here to do a gig, haven't I," says Eric. "We played the Gaumont. Last night." He begins to sound testy. We wonder who has been doing the promotion.

"Roger!" says Eric. "He stands outside and offers people money to go in. I've been geeing Roger up, because he showed me last week's Melody Maker, and I wanted to know how much he paid to get us on the front page. How much was it, Chris?" Eric seems quite convinced that jiggery-pokery had been afoot.

"I mean, you don't like me," he added.

I hastened to point out that quite a lot of water had rolled under the bridge. Past knocks had stemmed from duff gigs, but the band up in Glasgow the week before had been great.

"It was good fun, wasn't it?" said Eric quietly. "Last night was a gas! Not many. Dear o Lor'. It steamed along. The band is incredibly tight."

Was he happy working as a four-piece?

"It was the original deal. But it took us four years to get around to it. The original plan was that Carl would bring Dick Sims and Jamie Oldaker to Miami. Only they arrived late – being Tulsa people – and George Terry was already around, so he joined. It was a stitch-up if you ask me! No he hasn't quit. I just called him up and said that we were going out as a

Above: **We know you're in there, Eric! Not even a beard, shaggy hair and shades can disguise on of the most instantly recognisable figures in rock music.**

Australia was one place the Clapton camp vowed they would not return to again because of hounding by national newspaper reporters, who camped outside the door and ran stories about him and Patti Boyd. One paper had run a picture captions "Ex-drug addict." But Eric seemed genuinely surprised at the heat this aroused in his friends and compatriots. For example, he wondered if I had been winding up Jamie Oldaker, who sprang to Eric's defence in last week's episode of the Clapton Saga.

"It sounded like he'd lost his temper. Did you wind him up or something? I didn't realise he cared so much. It's amazing, ennit?"

Had it been an accurate portrayal of how Eric felt about the press?

"Hmmm…" he thought for a moment. "No…the press is fine. But I don't think the press ever gets anything right. Reporting-wise, I mean. I don't think anyone has ever pulled that off. I don't think it can be done. Do you?"

My response was to refer to the hypothetical accident and the four hypothetical witnesses who all give different accounts. I referred back to the early days of Eric's comeback, when one got the impression that he didn't want to project himself too much, and his playing seemed listless.

"Yeah, well everyone likes to be lazy sometimes…"

The girls momentarily distracted Eric. Why was he talking to me all the time?

"Because I'm doing a bleeding interview," explained E.C.

One of Eric's happier memories of the past year was working with Bob Dylan on his historic European tour, and Eric's album title, "Backless," was a kind of in-joke about working for Bob Dylan's back, as the master had a habit of turning round and giving a fairly serious stare if the band were not entirely pulling their weight, a technique he may have borrowed from Benny Goodman, the jazz clarinettist also noted for "the ray."

"It was an inspiration working for Bob. Sometimes he'd turn round and it would be like 'Okay, you're not listening' and he knew all the time if you were paying attention or not. He knew what everyone was doing behind him.

"The best gig we did was in Nuremberg. It was the place where Adolf used to hold the rallies. The place where he used to come out and stand on his podium was directly opposite us. It was a black doorway. And he'd come out to an incredible atmosphere. The atmosphere was there again but this time it was for a Jewish songwriter. And Bob didn't even know."

Eric had known and worked with Dylan over a number of years. What was he like as a…

Eric interrupted me, his attention again engaged by the girls.

"She doesn't even know who Bob Dylan is, do you realise that? I do get on with Bob very well, though. I love him, he's a fantastic guy. And I still love The Soul Band. My soul brother is Richard Manuel, who plays the piano.

"The first time I worked with Bob was when I was with John Mayall. He came to London, and liked John who had made a record called 'Life Is Like A Slow Train Crawling Up A Hill,' and Bob was very freaked out by this. After calling up the Zoo and asking if he could have a giraffe delivered to his room, he called up John and we did a session at Chappell's in Bond Street. Tom Wilson was the producer and there was a huge entourage.

"Thousands of people were telling me, 'Don't play country style, play city, go electric, don't play acoustic.' It was all this. And Bob gets on the piano and starts playing. The next thing you know, there's nothing happening.

"And I said, 'what's happening, where's he gone?' And he'd gone to Madrid.

"This was back in '65. It's never been a serious friendship. We just jive. It's like working with Muddy, you know. We don't talk seriously. That's forbidden. It's an unwritten law. You don't say anything like 'I've always liked your music.'

I can't watch Muddy. It drains me completely. When he does that song 'I'm A Man,' I have to scream. I didn't want Muddy on tour to begin with."

This seemed an astonishing statement, but he explained: "I thought it would be beyond my capabilities to follow Muddy. I just couldn't handle the idea of following Muddy on stage. Originally we tried to get the Paul Butterfield Band, because Paul and I are very much the same kind of characters. There's no big deal there, and he's a harp player. But at the last minute Paul couldn't get his band together."

I thought Eric was playing more powerful guitar.

"Well I've GOT to. Coming on after Muddy Waters, you've gotta do something, and it's gotta be right. Nah, I don't practice. I get it from the band. That's where it comes from. They're the source.

"If I'm on my own in a room, who have I got to play for? I'll write a song maybe, if it's there to write. I like to play for other people. It's always for someone else. You don't do anything for your own pleasure, do you? There is a point where you've got something almost right, and

Below: **Yes, white men can sing the blues – and Eric Clapton's voice has matured beyond measure as the years have passed.**

you don't want to present it to anybody unless it's absolutely right. But no. I am not a perfectionist. Unskilled labour. Hard work. That's all it is."

Did Eric feel a sense of disorientation after his illness and cure from addiction?

"I was worried. I just didn't know where I was going. I didn't know whether I should carry on, or whether I should pack it in altogether.

"And then a song came along. It was 'Dear Lord, Give Me Strength.' It just kept coming through, like a dream. It kept coming back to me. I thought if I didn't do something, then I would be letting people down. That gave me the strength to carry on being a musician."

But there were practical considerations, too.

"I couldn't knock it on the head, anyway. Businesswise I was in breach of contract, because I hadn't done anything for three years. My contract said I had to make at least two albums a year and go on the road. So I HAD to and I knew that. It was in the back of my mind as well. It was really a matter of loyalty and word of honour. Robert Stigwood would never have come down on me, but I had given my word, whether it was written on paper or a handshake. That was a strong factor in pulling me through. Now I'm enjoying playing and there's nothing in the way."

What did he think of the audience, and the kids who came to see him today?

"I don't take any notice. Do you know what I look at? The exit signs. I can just about see the kids coming in and going out. At one gig the kids started shouting at me, 'Duane Allman'."

Eric started shouting at the top of his voice, causing the hotel fittings and fixtures to reverberate.

"Duane Allman!" he bellowed. "Jack Bruce!" Eric shook his head.

"They actually stand up and shout. It's a roar. They don't even seem to realise that Duane has been dead for about four years. So I just showed them the back of my guitar and walked off, after doing my allotted time, of course."

Does Eric feel that the past hangs over him like a cloud?

"It doesn't hang over me, I can handle it, but I feel for the band. Christ almighty, this is the LONGEST I've ever been with a band. And if they can't show some kind of appreciation for them...

"I mean, Jack has got his own life to lead, and so have I, and there are three other people playing on stage with me that are going to get hurt by all this. That incenses me, it really does." He paused to reflect.

"But then you don't always KNOW. How can you tell what's going through that guy's mind, when he shouts for Duane Allman? He might be meaning well. He might be saying 'Great, do you remember Duane Allman?' But I mean the Cream, with Jack and Ginger, was ten years ago. And I've been back on the road, now, longer than I was off it. For four-and-a-half years."

Eric insisted his 81-year-old grandmother knew more about the rock business than most kids. "She can tell me exactly what position the record is in the chart. She's a great songwriter too and I'm going to do a couple of her songs. Rose, she's a born musician.

"Ahh, knock it on the 'ead, you're driving me round the bend."

I thought for a moment this was an abrupt termination of our interview, but realised that Eric was addressing his remarks to Adrian Boot, who was beavering away with his flashgun. But Eric relented and requested a picture of himself dancing.

"Did you know," he said, sounding like Michael Caine, "that John Travolta couldn't dance before he made that movie?"

I hazarded that he looked like one of Devo.

"The best dancer in the world is Bob Marley," said Clapton.

As far as Eric's current musical tastes go, his favourite is Elton John.

"I've been playing his album for the last three weeks. Every day. It's the greatest thing I've heard this year. It's gotta be the record of the year."

One of the girls decided to ask a question we had all overlooked.

"What do you do in the group?" she asked sweetly.

"I play guitar and sing," said Eric pleasantly.

"And the only person who asks me to do sessions these days," he said, returning to the official interview, "is George. And he's just finished a magnificent album but it won't be out until January because he's got held up over the cover. He probably can't make up his mind what to call it. He suggested that my next album should be called 'The Sound Of One Man Clapton'. He's much happier and looser now. He's got a kid, as you know, and it's given him a new lease of life."

Has Eric thought of starting a family?

"I've tried, mate, I've tried. The first couple of kids I ever started to have were aborted because it was a bit dicey. But not having a family doesn't concern me really because I'm still a road musician and I can't see that going on forever. I'm a wanderer, a gypo. I get three days off, I go home and I have a row with everybody. I wander about and complain about things. Get back on the road, and I'm as happy as a sandboy."

That's good, I observed.

"It's NOT," corrected Eric. "No it isn't, mate."

Well, it was good for Eric Clapton fans surely?

"Well I'm not one to put down roots, but Jamie has just got married again and he and his wife need to be close together, so he's got this incredible turmoil going on. He doesn't know whether to throw in the road and stick to a home life, or take her with him, and she doesn't like travelling. And I don't want that kind of problem.

"I've been on the road too long man, I can't give it up."

And how much further did he feel he could stay on the road?"

"Until I drop, mate. 'Til I drop."

Why had he always worked with American musicians, since the demise of Blind Faith back in '69?

"Well, they're the best. I think they play better than most British musicians. The only two I've ever met who can come anywhere near Jamie and Carl are Dave Markee and Henry Spinetti. I think they're fine. But they're sessions musicians, studio men. The Americans understand more about the music that has influenced me.

"It's like asking these girls about Howlin' Wolf. A blank, right? But the Americans, they know what I'm talking about, and with Carl it goes back to Louis Jordan. They know where it's all coming from."

Eric started off the whole British rock guitar hero thing. What does he think about his successors, and the development of the heavy rock guitar which could be traced from the Yardbirds, via Cream, Led Zeppelin, etc. to the present wave of heavy metal?

I think it's great," said Eric unexpectedly (I thought he might disown the whole movement). "And the best person who is doing it is Brian May with Queen. I think that group is fantastic. And he is the only guitarist here who really knocks me out. Obviously there are lots more, but he's the one who comes straight to me head, because I love the way he plays."

But Eric's own guitar style over the years has remained free of flashy effects and all the inhuman sounds that technology can now unleash.

"I don't see how you can do all that and play at the same time. I

mean, you've got to stop and think about what button you're going to press, and then you stop playing. That only applies to me. Probably there are other people who can do three things at once, what comes out of the guitar is the most important thing. I can still blow myself away. I can still do that, you know."

But for a long while Eric seemed to want to get away from the limelight, as a lead guitar player with a unique, universal appeal.

"Yeah, I was fed up with being dominated, all the time. It was just getting on my *nerves*. How can you live with that on your back? You can't. It's best just to be A Musician.

"Unskilled labour, that's what it's all about. And if you pull it out of the bag, all well and good. If you don't – it doesn't make any difference. If you are being WATCHED and EXAMINED, to see whether or not you can pull it off, and you blow it, Christ it comes down on you. I comes down hard, I tell you. People expect so much from you."

What does Eric think of his old mates, the guitar heroes of an earlier generation, now?

"Jeff Beck is my favourite. I think he's gotta be my favourite guitarist of all. He's mingling with the greats today, isn't he?

"And Peter Green, he came and stayed with me when he was having a really bad time, for about two weeks. And the first week, nothing. Not a chord. And every now and then he'd complain – Why are you doing this? Why are you listening to that? Why are you playing that way? And then one sunny day I caught him outside in the garden, dancing his head off, and laughing. It was so good to see him enjoying himself at last. And then we had a play, and he had it all there, it was exactly the same. I know where he's at.

"He's got it there, and he's just decided he's not going to use it, until he feels like it."

They were remarkable days in the Sixties that produced the likes of Clapton, Hendrix, Beck and Green.

What does he think of the British scene now? Is the talent still there?

Above: **There can be no doubt that Eric Clapton is happiest with a guitar in hand and a receptive audience at his command.**

"I don't think I'm the right person to ask. I'm looking at it from an older person's point of view. I'd be too critical."

Mention of Sid Vicious reminded Eric of an unpleasant but salutary experience from his younger days: "I once spent the night in jail in America. A County jail. I was busted for being in a place where smoke was being used. It was with Buffalo Springfield and they all got done. Neil Young had a fit, because he's had a history of epilepsy. He may be cured now.

"But in jail we had to take all our clothes off and line up for mug shots, and then they hosed us down and sprayed us with insecticide and took our clothes away. While they're doing all this, Neil just went 'wh-o-o-a!' and they took him out of the room, and it was the last I saw of him. I spent the night in a cell with three Black Panthers, and I had to convince them that I was a blues guitarist.

"When I look back, it was a good experience. I'll know never to get busted. No way. One night of that was hell. Because there was no word to the outside world. It's a good idea when they take young offenders to a prison and show them what it's like, because it's not like joining the army. And I had PINK boots on! And I had me frizzed-out hairstyle, and I was wearing all my psychedelic gear.

"They took all me bracelets and chains away from me and I got blue denims with LA County Jail written all over them. But they left me in the pink boots and threw me in the cell with three Black Panthers.

"It was like I was a punk, y'know? I just had to keep talking and tell them I was English and didn't really understand what was going on, but I played blues guitar and dug Willie Dixon and Muddy Waters, and Bo Diddley and Chuck Berry. It worked. It cooled them out – just about.

"I think they had been in for about three or four years. Eventually I applied for bail. There was one guy there who had been applying for bail every day for seven years, but nobody had put the money up for him."

What is the driving force that keeps a musician like Eric on the road after a lifetime in bands, despite all the hassles?

A deathly silence greeted this, and he signalled with his eyes towards the girls sitting across the room.

"Robbie Robertson is asked by Ronnie Hawkins to join The Band in The Last Waltz, and Robbie asks: 'How much does it pay?' And Ronnie says: 'It don't pay nuthin' but you get more pussy than Frank Sinatra.'

"And that's it, y'know. I play poker and I love winning money at poker, but I love women more."

Isn't money a motive?

"No, no. I've earned a lot of money, but I've lost a lot too. I've been frivolous, not generous. And Cream only broke even, you know. Most of the money we made from Cream went towards financing the Bee Gees.

"We joined up with Robert (Stigwood), went out on the road for six months at a time and made an incredible amount of money which went straight back into the company so that he could bring the Bee Gees back from Australia, and start them. But it balanced out. It was all in the company and it was like a family deal and it still is.

"The last year has been very tough because Robert hasn't been putting himself about much, he's got so many things in the pot. I've watched people losing their jobs without even knowing why, RSO people who have been in the family for as long as I've been with the label. They've been told to clear their desks and be out by Monday. And they don't even know why.

"My contract was up, and I wondered, should I stay with this lot if they're going to get this cold? But I did re-sign because I don't think there is anybody else that I trust or love as much as Robert. When the contract came up, he said: 'You can write your own ticket.' so I signed.

"But there were clauses in the contract. One was that I didn't appear in any film unless it was under my own name. But I wouldn't mind making a guest spot in a film, as long as it was under my own name. Like those old jazz films which had Cab Calloway appearing as himself, not playing a role.

"Next year I'll probably make another album, go to America and tour for two or three months. That's the plan so far. And then I'll probably have a good time off, maybe six or seven months."

Would he start making model airplanes again?

"Ooch, no, not on your *Nellie*. That was only when I was really ill. That was the only thing that kept me alive. It was therapy. My eyes got so bad during that time, I ended up using magnifying glasses and old people's spectacles, just so I could paint the finest bits, like the eyes on a pilot."

What's his view of the "casualty" aspect of rock 'n' roll?

"A lot of people go down on the road, but you can't tell when it's going to happen. If a musician quits the road, it doesn't mean he ain't gonna get run over by a bus.

"Like when I had that accident right outside my house. I didn't know where I was for two weeks afterwards. I was in a Ferrari and had probably reached about 90 mph in a very short space of time, when a laundry van appeared. That was the last thing I can remember. All I know is I hit him and turned his van over. My skid marks were in a straight line and they found me with my head hanging through a side window. You only need to do that sort of thing once."

After his rehabilitation from drugs, he seemed to allow excessive drinking to replace one stairway to oblivion with another. Now he seems much more careful.

"I don't get legless much any more. When I'm at home and I've got nothing to do, then I'll have a drink. If I get one over the eight, I only have to look at Jamie, Dickie or Carl and I can see the disapproval straight away. They are depending on me to keep my end up. If I blow it, why should they bother?"

Now Eric has the responsibility of being a band leader.

"I'm not a very good one yet but I'm learning every day. I never wanted to be a leader and I still don't really enjoy it. As you were saying earlier, I always worshipped The Band. That was because there was no apparent bandleader. It turned out there was one – Robbie Robertson. But he was very much behind the scenes.

"Carl is mostly our leader. He's The Rock. He's The Elder. If ever I'm in any doubt about anything, he'll put me straight. I'm not talking about the running order at gigs. I mean he can be a philosophical guide

Below: **Unplugged and unshaven once more, Clapton gets lost in music. It's the story of his life.**

towards what is happening in your life. He's go all the answers you need. But he's not the closest to me. We're all pretty close. Some of us drift away for a day or two, then come back."

It was good to see E.C. back. Down in the lobby suitcases and bags began to pile up, and people began to ask each other who was in their room and who was ready to go.

Clapton was on the road once more, this time heading for Brighton, ready to play some guitar, sing a little and stomp with his friends. Let's hope we see him again soon.

"Well," said Eric, "you'll get a Christmas card from me this year. And I'll draw it myself."

© Chris Welch / Melody Maker / IPC Syndication

Above: **Clapton captured on camera by top lensman Chuck Boyd during the US leg of his 1974 'comeback' tour promoting the 461 Ocean Boulevard album.**

key recordings

1967 Clapton, Baker and Bruce create first supergroup as Cream and release classic albums *Fresh Cream* and *Disraeli Gears* to let US fans in on Clapton's magic

1970 A laid-back approach for Eric Clapton, his first solo album

1971 Pyrotechnics return for Derek and The Dominoes' *Layla And Other Assorted Love Songs*

1974 His mind and body cleaned by rehab, Clapton returns with US chart-topping *461 Oceon Boulevard* and hit single *I Shot The Sheriff*

1986 The 4-CD box set *Crossroads* breaks all kind of records as Clapton's old sixties blues catalogue tops the US charts

1989 With Robert Cray as guest, Clapton's *Journeyman* gives him another international multi-million seller

1991 The three sides of *Clapton – bluesmaster, rock star and film score writer – captured on 24 Nights*, a record of his three week residency at Royal Albert Hall

It's a measure of the impact The Sex Pistols had on the 1970s – especially in Britain and Europe – that that decade still tends to be delineated as either pre- or post-Pistols. A reaction against the assembly line productions of 'glam-rock' artists dominating the UK pop scene, The Sex Pistols were a message from the real world that Something Had To Change.

Through the so-called UK 'pub rock' movement, many hostelries had begun playing host to a new, less respectful and more anarchic breed of youngsters. The man who would identify and exploit this new 'punk' movement was Malcolm McLaren, and the vehicle he would use to help solidify its image was The Sex Pistols.

McLaren had been managing a group called The Swankers (Steve Jones, vocals, Paul Cook, drums, and Wally Nightingale, guitar) since 1973 when Glen Matlock, a sales assistant at McLaren's trendy Chelsea fashion store, 'Too Fast To Live, Too Young To Die', joined them as bassist. McLaren fired Nightingale, switched Jones to guitar and settled for the 18-year-old John Lydon, duly re-christened Johnny Rotten, as vocalist. There was a name change, to The Sex Pistols, while McLaren's emporium was re-named 'Sex'.

Gathering a large following with their violent, under-rehearsed brand of aural mayhem, The Pistols had the distinction of being banned from almost as many London clubs as they managed to play. As Britain's music papers picked up on this vibrant sub-culture and the first fanzines appeared, The Sex Pistols' onstage antics made them great copy. By October 1976 Rotten had become something of a punk figurehead and Britain's major record labels finally caught up on the plot.

EMI Records offered McLaren £40,000 (then about $100,000) and he took it. On October 8 the Pistols recorded 'Anarchy In The UK' with producer Chris Thomas and McLaren's 'outrage at all costs' PR campaign (inspired by early Rolling Stones 'bad-boy' coverage) went into action, climaxing when the band loosened a barrage of four-letter abuse at TV presenter Bill Grundy on his live early-evening news magazine show.

The ensuing outcry led to all but three of the 19 theatres the Pistols were due to play on their first UK tour cancelling their dates, and in January 1977 EMI dropped the band. But the Pistols held on to that £40,000 advance and in February added a new member – long-time fan John Beverley, now known as Sid Vicious – to replace Glen Matlock on bass.

In March 1977 McLaren signed The Sex Pistols to A&M Records (non-returnable sign-on fee: £75,000) at a photocall outside Buckingham Palace. Six days later they were again without a label after an outcry by other A&M acts forced the company to cancel the deal and rue the 25,000 copies of the Pistols' new single, 'God Save The Queen', they'd already pressed. In May the band finally found a home, at Virgin Records, whose £15,000 advance was quickly recouped from the 150,000 copies of 'God Save The Queen' they sold in the first five days, despite a daytime ban of the single by BBC Radio and the refusal of many stores to stock a record bearing a picture of the queen with a safety pin through her nose.

Rotten and Cook were injured by outraged citizens. But the hits had started coming. In July, 'Pretty Vacant' made the UK Top 10, and in October 'Holidays In The Sun' reached No.8. Meanwhile, the Pistols assumed a number of aliases (Acne Rabble, The Hamsters, The Tax Exiles and Special Guest included) to play an 'undercover' British tour.

November saw Never Mind The Bollocks – Here's The Sex Pistols race to the top of the UK charts and McLaren signing a US deal with Warner Bros. Early in December, Vicious and his American girlfriend, Nancy Spungen, were released without charge after being arrested on suspicion of possessing drugs, the band toured Holland and Britain, making their last UK appearance in Huddersfield on Christmas Day to raise funds for a children's charity.

After their US debut at the Great Southeast Music Hall in Atlanta, Georgia on January 5, 1978, the Pistols played only five more dates before Rotten stormed out. Sid Vicious over-dosed in New York and was hospitalised, McLaren returned to London and Jones and Cook flew to Rio de Janeiro to hang out with Ronnie Biggs, the former Great Train Robber.

By year end The Sex Pistols were nothing more than a remarkable footnote in rock history. Johnny Rotten had reverted to being John Lydon and formed Public Image Ltd (PiL). Vicious had recorded a number of astonishing tracks (he couldn't sing any better than he could play bass), killed Nancy Spungen and died of a heroin overdose in New York. There would be posthumous hits (see discography), a couple of movies, some videos – and a lengthy lawsuit which did not end until 1986 and resulted in McLaren reaching an out-of-court settlement with Lydon, Jones, Cook and Sid Vicious' mother. The four were also awarded £1 million by the official appointed to wind up The Sex Pistols' business affairs.

There was a brief and exploitative reunion in the mid-90s, but The Sex Pistols left us with an abiding memory of how far so little can be spread if you've only got the chutzpah to do it. And someone like Malcolm McLaren to make it work.

Previous page: **Lights, camera, action! The Sex Pistols tear into another riotous set at the 100 Club. The message on Sid's button says it all...**

June 4 1977 Allan Jones

ROTTEN!

John Rotten stands with his arms casually outstretched in a sardonic parody of the crucifixion, a look of languid hatred flickering for a moment across his pallid features before giving away to an expression of petulant contempt.

A policeman searches Rotten's pockets and frisks his scrawny frame with dedicated efficiency.

He finds nothing.

John lowers his arms and curls his lips around a can of lager, taking a defiant swig as the police constable who has stopped him in the fierce sunlight along Westbourne Grove in Notting Hill diverts his attention toward Sid Vicious.

Sid smiles malevolently as he turns out his pockets and P.C. B510 takes out his notebook to scribble down a few pertinent details.

Imagine the conversation:

"Name?"

"Sid Vicious."

Above: **Despite Malcolm McLaren's promotion of them as the Baddest Boys in Rock, The Sex Pistols did not take themselves too seriously, as this all-smiles publicity shot of the band proves.**

"V-I-C-I-O-U-S?"

"S'pose so."

"Address?"

"Here and there."

"Date of birth?"

"How should I know?"

Rotten looks on in disgust: he and Sid had been walking along the street after a photo session for the Melody Maker when the Old Bill appeared suddenly and turned them over.

"We look different, see, and it frightens them," he says in that sarcastic intonation he so effectively employs. "I can understand it, though. This is called living in England in 1977. If they ask for violence, then we'll give them violence. What else can they expect if they treat people like this?"

A guy from Pistols manager Malcolm McLaren's office has the temerity to ask the officer why, precisely, he stopped John and Sid.

"Turn out your pockets," the officer replies to our disbelief.

"Arrest him, officer," Sid thoughtfully advises our friend P.C. B510. "He's a Nazi..."

Above: **Messrs Jones, Matlock, Lydon and Cook spray one for the camera. Legend has it their departure from EMI was precipitated by a mass shake-up and spraying of Coke cans in an executive's office...**

"And you're a big mouth," responds B510. "And if you don't move along I'll book you."

"It happens all the time," says John Rotten as he, Sid, Paul Cook and Steve Jones collapse into the interview room at Virgin Records' offices just off the Portobello Road. "All the time. Everywhere I go. Wherever I go. Every time I walk down a street. If it ain't a copper, it's some big fat ignorant turd. It happened yesterday. In Highgate. I was just walking along…"

"On your way to the f– pub," interrupts Sid.

"Nah, acourse not," John replies wearily. "They've banned me from all the pubs up there. I can't even get a drink in Highgate anymore."

This bright Tuesday afternoon is the first time that all four members of the Sex Pistols have visited the offices of their new record company, with whom they signed only three weeks ago (for £45,000, according to McLaren; "for an unspecified amount of money," according to Virgin; "for no advance at all," according to Rotten).

Now, for all its enterprise, Virgin has never had to deal with a pack of maverick delinquents like the Sex Pistols in its entire history.

And here they are with a group whose capacity for outrage has antagonised over the last year the entire nation and provoked their enforced departure from two major record companies. No, Virgin has always been more closely associated with the Woolly Hat Brigade (Gong, and various compatible hippy combos) and rather serious European ensembles rather than the rock and roll defiance expressed by the Pistols.

The shock waves of the signing seem to be reverberating still through the company; and you should have seen the concerned and apprehensive expressions decorating the bemused faces at Vernon's Yard last week when the Pistols staggered, like the Wild Bunch swaggering defiantly into Ague Verda for their final stand in Peckinpah's movie (I rather fancifully thought), down the cobblestone alley and into the reception area at Virgin.

"Where's old Branson-pickle, who's that c–, and where can I get something to f– eat?" demanded Sid Vicious as he dropped in a loose-limbed pile of rags and leather onto a couch.

"More to the point," countered John Rotten, "where can I get a bleedin' drink?"

Steve Jones, looking burly and aggressive, and Paul Cook (as ever quite amiable), wandered about clocking the premises, amused at the confusion they were causing. We were joined by the staff of the Virgin press office and drinks and sandwiches were promised to appease John and Sid, who complained constantly of being a dying man.

"I'm so f– ill I'm going to puke," he observed colourfully.

"You've just got a big spot on the end of your nose," he was rebuffed by Jones.

"I know, it's because of all that f– pressure I'm under. I'm too f sensitive to have to put up with all this," Sid commented weakly.

"Where's that booze?" asked John irritably.

"Give us some free albums," Sid, reviving suddenly, demanded of Virgin PR. Al Clark. The request was politely declined. "If you don't give us them we'll steal them," Sid warned.

It was immediately clear that his recent illness had not blunted young Sid's rapier-like wit.

"Stand a bit closer," he subsequently ordered a photographer. "I can't gob that far in my present state."

I first saw the Sex Pistols in April, 1975, at the Nashville in London

when they supported Joe Strummer's 101'ers.

John Rotten stumbled to the front of the stage, held together with safety pins and wild conceit, his blond hair spiky and greasy, his dark eyes alive with venom. "I bet," he screamed at the bewildered audience, few of whom were at all familiar with the group or its nascent attitude, "that YOU don't hate US as much as WE hate YOU!"

He was quite mistaken; the audience responded to Rotten's jeering abuse with extrovert disdain and made clear their instinctive dislike for the Pistols' leering aggression and crude music.

I went away that evening and wrote a review of the band that concluded with the profound hope that no more would be heard of them. Some hope.

By the end of the year they had become the most notorious group in the country; controversy, disaster and constant publicity elevated them from obscurity to international disrepute in a blur of months of persistent outrage.

Their history – as short as it is – reads like a series of reports from a battlefront, so full of incident has it so far been. They precipitated a whole new wave of bands cast in a similarly aggressive stance: the Clash, the Damned, the Buzzcocks, Generation X, Chelsea, the Slits…all of them owe a debt to the Sex Pistols.

The media, faced with the explosive anger and rebellion expressed by these bands, reeled in confusion The music press was split in arguments over the respective merits of these young groups; their admirers congratulated them for the energy and passion of their music and applauded the violence with which they had disturbed the complacency

Above: **Sid Vicious takes up Classic Rock Star Pose 14, with the addition of The Presley Sneer adopted so successfully by Billy Idol, to prove that it's all been done before.**

Above: **London fans go wild as Sid, Paul, John and Steve give it their best shot.**

that had recently settled on the rock establishment.

Their critics conversely condemned them for their inarticulate anarchy, their apparent nihilism and their musical incompetence. Those of us in this latter category floundered in our attempts to place these groups in any correct perspective and may even have felt slightly threatened by the collective aggression and determined disregard for convention displayed so arrogantly by these new wave renegades with their punk toughness and volatile outbursts.

We may even have wished, despite our increasing fascination with the movement, that they'd all just shut up and make some music or disappear up the slipstream of their own invective...

"You were probably right when you wrote that rave review," John rotten comments sarcastically as he tugs on another lager. "We were probably really bad then. Don't f– apologise. The point is that we were just starting. We just sent out and we DID IT. We formed when music was becoming too serious.

"Rock and roll is supposed to be FUN. You remember fun, dontcha? You're supposed to enjoy it. It's not supposed to be about critics, or about spending 100 f– years learning a million chords on the guitar. It's the spirit. It's what you say that's important."

There is something to be said, I ventured, for a certain musical eloquence; you can't survive indefinitely on undiluted energy and passion.

"Yeah," Rotten replies, his voice undulating in that particular sarcastic rhythm of his, "I understand that, and we are concerned about the quality of what we play...but, like, when you criticised us we were just starting. We just went out and we done it in front of the public. We didn't stay in a rehearsal studio until we were so perfect we were boring.

"The whole idea was to get out and have some fun and we hoped that someone out there would see us and have fun, too. We just wanted

to get out and play and we hoped that some people would see us and go away and form their own bands. We wanted to make a new scene."

"We f– did," comments Steve Jones, and then adds with a curious sense of disenchantment, "and for a while it was good..."

Rotten sits clutching the inevitable can of lager, his legs stretched out before him. He looks, momentarily, abstracted and tired. He runs his fingers nervously through his bright red hair; his mood has changed now from the aggressive punk stance he had earlier assumed and relentlessly sarcastic, he's more open and polite.

His attitude seems constantly to shift from one of defensive conde-scension to passionate concern. His conversation may be scattered profusely with scatological expletives, but he remains abrasively articulate.

Steve Jones sits opposite him; more immediately extrovert in his opinions than Rotten, his characteristic bellicosity is mitigated only by his gruff humour. His contributions to the conversation are more pointed and emphatic. Paul Cook the quietest of the quartet, sits beside him listening more than he speaks.

Sid Vicious is slumped beside John; he's so dreadfully pale and wasted that he makes Keith Richard look like Steve Reeves. He lapses often into a comatose silence that is broken only by frequent statements to the effect that there are certain individuals to whom he would like to deliver "a good kicking". He's a sweet lad, our Sid.

Rotten suddenly jerks forward, staring intensely.

"The Pistols are the best," he says simply. "The only honest band that's hit this planet in about two thousand million years. We've been treated like some kind of fashion parade of a bunch of no-talents. People have said those things for their own reasons.

"And it's very hard to stop that, because when you do an interview with someone they only print what they want to print. You can't control it. So you give up; you just say, 'Shut your face and f– off!' 'Cos it's not worth the hassle of talking to them.'

"Nobody," adds Paul Cook "writes the truth. Especially about us."

"That's right," Rotten continues. "And the worse load of f– b– is from people like Caroline Coon. Always going on about the sociological implications of the Sex Pistols. Makes me cringe. Absolutely DIRE stuff.

"She hates me...I mean, I really thought that people would recognise that what appears about us in the newspapers is b–. But they don't. That's what shocks me about the general attitude of the public. They're excessively stupid. Their whole lives are centred around what the Daily Mirror or the Sun says.

"There was all that crap after the Bill Grundy thing. I just couldn't understand how they could take it all so seriously. I thought it was a great laugh. People are so very gullible. It doesn't matter what anybody thinks about us. It doesn't matter what you think about us. You could go away and slag us off. I don't care. I don't expect anything from anyone."

"Because of what they've read in the national press," Steve Jones observes, "people think all we do is go around giving people good kick-ings, fighting, drinking, f– things up, spitting, swearing ..."

He actually sounds disturbed that this should be the case.

"But we won't change," emphasises Rotten, his eyes glaring. "We'll always tell people to f– off if they try to tell us what to do. That's why we have trouble with record companies. This deal's fine. We don't want to f– this one up...

"We set our OWN direction. We don't follow anyone. And there's no one who can follow us. The rest of those f– bands like the Clash, the

Damned and the Stranglers and all the rest, are just doing what every other band before them has done, it's the same big, fat, hippy trip. Those bands are no different. They make me cringe."

The way John delivers that final word makes my flesh creep.

"I think it's absolutely vile," Rotten speeds on, "when I go to see a band that's obviously trying to imitate us. I think it's absolutely disgusting. That shows a complete lack of intelligence. It shows they have no reason for being on stage.

"You have to do your own thing. You have to be yourself; otherwise you can't offer anything. And if you can't offer anything, you're in the wrong place and you should f– off. You have to be honest. You have to believe in yourself, whatever anyone says or whatever happens. You can't give in.

"That's another reason people hate us: we don't conform to their stupid standards. Like at press conferences, you know, they try to get us to be nice and polite to all the 'right' people. That's dreadful.

"If someone says to me, 'Watch that person, they're in a position to really slag you off,' then I just go up and say, 'You c–, I hate you.' I don't need all that."

"People have described us as a kamikaze band," offers Steve Jones. "But we just play music, we don't crash f– planes. It's just that we don't back down. We just do it.

"The other bands don't have the nerve to follow us. They were all right in the beginning, but now they've signed their contracts they're

Below: **Sid pulls another silly face as John battles with an unco-operative mike stand.**

Above: **Punk's answer to The Glimmer Twins? Sid and John get it on one more time.**

f– up. I feel sorry for them. And now they say that we've f– the scene up. They've forgotten that WE started it. We opened ALL the doors."

"The doors and the windows," says Sid, coming back to life for a moment.

I'd heard the Pistols described as martyrs recently for the reason that they'd sacrificed themselves in the initial assault on the establishment that led eventually to the present commercial success of those bands – like the Clash and the Damned – whom they originally supported.

"That's right," says Rotten. "We helped all them bands in the beginning. We helped them start off. The Anarchy tour, right…WE paid for all that. We gave them hotels, money – the works.

"Well," and here he gives one of his nervously evil little laughs, "I ain't seen any of it come back. We've lost a lot of money. Thousands. And the tax is doing us for 80 per cent of everything we ever got. Which is ridiculous. You saw us squabbling over a quid. It ain't funny. The shortage of money is pathetic.

"But we don't need any sympathy and we ain't martyrs. Martyrs are failures. We ain't failures, 'cos we never give up. They're not going to get rid of us. We'll only finish it the day it gets boring."

"I don't even know the name of the Prime Minister," asserts Steve Jones, "so I don't really see how anyone could describe us as a political band."

"We don't support no one," emphasises Rotten. "Politics is b–."

"We've been discussing the political overtones of the Sex Pistols, as exemplified most significantly by their singles, "Anarchy In The UK" and "God Save The Queen"; as far as I'm concerned the infectious irreverence and spirited venom of these two songs is considerably more appealing than the wearing political stance adopted by, let's say, the Clash.

Rotten agrees and articulates my own feelings when he stresses that music and politics enjoy an uneasy, frequently loathsome, relation-

Left: **A heavily shaded John Lydon chills out with fashion designer Vivienne Westwood (left) and punk 'celebrity' Jordan.**

ship if the political views expressed are incoherent and immature. He's clearly of the opinion that the Clash are incoherent and immature.

"Music," he says, "should be FUN. It's meant to be a relief to working 9 to 5 in a factory. It shouldn't be about some c– on stage yapping about how terrible it is to be on the dole."

"And they've just made a mint. I don't think Clash even know what they're talking about."

"Right," agrees Paul Cook. "People talk about us being Malcolm's puppets. That's ridiculous. The Clash are puppets."

"Malcolm's a good manager," insists Rotten, "but he wouldn't dream of telling us what to do."

"He wouldn't dare," Jones grins. "We'd turn Sid on him to give him a good kicking."

"F– right," quips Sid, without opening his eyes.

"Strummer's no politician. Never was. Never will be," asserts Jones. "I mean that single that he had out with the 101'ers on Chiswick ('Keys To Your Heart'), it was a little love song. Now he's shouting about 'Hate and War'. He don't know what he's on about."

"The Clash ain't go no guts anyway," Sid thoughtfully opines. "They sound as weak as the Damned. Pathetic, the lot of them. That Damned record sounds like an early Searchers album. All tinny. And that Clash album sounds like a folk album. They're going to end up singing ballads, the Clash."

Rotten mentions the new Chelsea single, "Right To Work", and breaks out in a malicious grin: "That's Gene October. Him screaming about wanting the right to work is hysterical. He's got a job. He's in a f group. Ridiculous."

"We take our songs seriously," Rotten comments, "but we don't take ourselves seriously. We believe totally in the songs, though. That's why we play them, and that's why we're prepared to put up with so much aggravation to get them out.

"Yeah, I know I said music should be fun. I ain't contradicting myself. I know we sing about unemployment and all that. You should write about what's happening, but there has to be fun, too.

"Of course, there's no fun in being bored or on the dole. But music should offer a relief from all that. It shouldn't be depressing. If a song's about boredom, it should be about ways to overcome that boredom. It has to be true, but there should be humour. Optimism. And that's not political.

"'Anarchy In The UK' was about MUSICAL anarchy...I don't think you can be a political rock and roll band. It's a loser stance."

It seems an opportune moment to bring up the issue of the Pistols and the National Front, with whom they were associated in a cheap, sensationalist piece in the London Evening News (there have been suggestions elsewhere, too). Rotten, I know, was disgusted and hurt by the piece. It still shows.

"We got f– all to do with the National Front," says Steve Jones first.

"That was someone trying to discredit us and make out that we were for them. It was someone putting the boot in. Just a cheap bit of publicity. My God, that thing in the Evening News made me sick. They said that the National Front used to turn up at our gigs and that's b–. I wouldn't play for the National Front."

He looks at me icily and with a chilling venom proclaims, "I hate them. I despise them. I'm Irish, right, and if they took over I'd be on the next boat back. I believe you should be allowed to live where you want, when you want and how you want.

"If the National Front need a rock group to support they should go

Below: **Don't they look young and (whisper it) healthy? The Pistols pose for a stills photographer during a break in filming a TV appearance.**

after the Clash. They want a Clash movement. Military thing. Like, you know, one of the songs on that album has some stupid lyric about conscription being what we need…that's Strummer on that album. I heard that and I creased up. That's disgusting.

"If you want to join the army, sure – go ahead. But you shouldn't be forced into it. No one should have the right to do that to anyone. That's wrong. Evil."

"We should call the next single, 'We Hate The National Front'," Sid volunteers helpfully.

"If a load of c– like the National Front get into power," says John with cold conviction, "I'm afraid I won't stay around. What's the use in staying to fight? How can you fight an army?…I dunno, though. They might give me a good reason to die. Just get a machine gun and kill as many as possible. Nah, I don't think that would be a romantic end. I don't find anything romantic about dying."

"Neither do I," Sid says after some consideration of the matter. "And I find the idea of being shot to pieces by a million bullets from the National Front really unromantic. We're all going to die from alcohol poisoning anyway…

"I like getting drunk," he then adds on a more cheerful note. "I like getting out of my brain. It's good fun. Ordinary life is so dull that I get out of it as much as possible."

The night before the Sex Pistols were unceremoniously thrown out of the windows by the panic-stricken fuhrers at A&M, says John Rotten, they were told by a paternal Derek Green that they were very fortunate young men; if they had tried to release a record as provocative as "God Save The Queen" in, say, an Eastern European country they would be savagely repressed and would in all probability spend the rest of their days in slave labour in Siberia or somewhere as equally unpleasant.

Be glad and thankful, they were told, that they lived in a free country where freedom of expression was a cherished virtue.

The next day the Pistols were again without a record company.

"We just laughed and said, 'B– to you' and had a big p– up," says Steve Jones when asked for his reaction to that fiasco.

Rotten, however, is less flippant: "Someone at the top put the boot in. We don't know who, but someone doesn't want us to make it. Someone wants us silenced. Someone wants to prevent us from working again. It seems that some of the local councils are lifting their bans, but we still can't get a gig.

"We can't book a hall because we can't get an insurance company behind us. And there's no hall that'll book us without an insurance company, because they think we're mad and that we'll just go in there and smash the place up and walk out the back door, waving a big fat cheque in the breeze. It's bloody ridiculous.

"I mean we were SO disappointed that we didn't get that record out. The record was ready to be released, right? It was going to come out then. We wanted it out then. I think it's a good record. It was disgusting that it wasn't allowed to get out. They signed us up without really knowing what the hell we were about. It was stupid. Pathetic.

"I don't trust anybody any more. I've been let down too often for that. I just keep away from as many people in this business as possible. The deal with Virgin ain't like the record deals we've had with the other companies. These people here are working for us and we like it. With the others we ended up trying to use them as much as they were using us. that wasn't easy, but we had to do it all the same. They don't tell us what to do here. NO ONE tells US what to do."

He's convinced that there exists some kind of conspiracy that's attempting to subvert the potential success of the Sex Pistols. He mentions the attempt to associate them with the NF and the media campaign that continually stresses their obnoxious behaviour.

"I hate that attitude that people have. They think that if you ain't been to university you must be an ignorant lout who doesn't know his own mind and can't form an opinion about anything.

"Some of the most intelligent people I know have come straight out of the gutter. I mean, that goes straight down to boot boys who get fun kicking people. They still have their brains together. They know what they like and dislike. The trouble is, the media poisons them. That's the worst part about it."

Above: **Public reaction to the Pistols' controversial 'God Save The Queen' single in March 1977 was heightened by the fact that Britain was busy celebrating her silver jubilee – as the decorations on this London pub prove.**

109

He despises, too, the continual attempts to associate the Pistols with every outbreak of violence at new wave gigs and elsewhere. He's particularly angry about the band being blamed for the violence at the 100 Club Punk Festival late last year when a girl's eye was gouged out.

"That was despicable. We were blamed for something that happened when we were 200 miles away. That was caused by a fight between the Vibrators and the Damned. But what can we do? We were blamed for it and everybody believed that it was our fault. But this is a fact: wherever we play, when we hit the stage people don't smash each other up. They watch US. They can't take their eyes off us.

"Look, we've got a very varied audience. We've played places where we've had teddy boys dancing at the back. Up north we've had bike mobs to see us. There's been no wars. That's the way it should be; a lot of people having fun together. F– the rest if they won't allow it to happen – THAT'S when you get trouble, when you're trying to stop it.

I wonder whether he was personally frightened by the violence that sometimes attends new wave gigs.

"Wouldn't you be?" he asks simply.

"Most of it is ridiculously posed," he continues. "You get people in the audience saying, 'Come on down here, we'll take you on.' And you look at them and you want to cringe and die, because it is not necessary. They should be having fun. And it's not funny or glamorous being smashed to a pulp. It's ugly and nasty. I've been beaten up frequently, old bean. And it ain't funny…

"You know, sometimes you go out for a quiet drink somewhere and there's a mob in the place and they take a dislike to you because they've seen you face in the papers. And there's nothing you can do. And then it's for real. And it ain't glamorous when it happens."

"You know we get people coming up to us and wanting to take us on 'cos they've heard all about the Sex Pistols," contributes Steve

Above: **Smoking, drinking and 'audience participation' during gigs was always part of the Pistol's snarling stage performances…**

Jones. "Now we ain't going to start on them, but whatever happens we'll get the blame. That's the way it goes.

"Like that Speakeasy thing was just a squabble and it was all blown up and we got the blame. it was a load of b– I mean, if a big guy comes up and starts on me I run…and if he's a little guy I give him a good kicking.

Rotten laughs at the idea that the Pistols, like the members of the rock elite, surround themselves with bodyguards.

"F– that. I hate those c–," he says vehemently. "They're full of lies. Always contradicting themselves.

"Like I was reading a thing about Pete Townshend talking about punk. And I thought, 'WHO ARE YOU? How dare YOU presume to have the right to tell us what it's all about? He half admits that he doesn't understand what's happening on the streets. I don't think he ever knew."

"It's that other c– I hate," interjected Jones. "Roger Daltrey."

"I'd like to give him a good kicking," soliloquised Sid Vicious.

"I don't give a f– for any of them," John continued. "I mean, I never even liked the Stones. Jagger was always too distant. No way could you ever imagine talking to Michael Jagger (he delivers the name with a venomous sneer) like you could talk to someone on the street. And you should be able to. I don't see why he has to have f– bodyguards carting him about all over the place."

"He came down to Sex (McLaren's shop in the King's Road) one afternoon," reflected Sid. "Stood outside for three hours 'cos he was terrified to come inside. And then just as he was about to come in, John slammed the door in his face. He's a f– comedian."

"Ian Hunter's a c– too," observed Steve Jones. "All that talk about coming off the street."

"I know that we frighten these people," Rotten insists. "You read the music papers and they all mention us. This I find very funny. People like Ian Anderson have to slag us off to promote themselves. I find it trivial and silly and childish. Steve Harley's the same.

"You might expect it of US, 'cos that's what were supposed to be like. But they're SUPPOSED to be ever so intelligent. If they WERE intelligent they wouldn't have to say things like that…and it's like they have to be seen at the same places that we go to.

"Like Robert Plant came down the Roxy, surrounded by millions of bodyguards. One of them came up to me and said, 'Robert Plant wants to talk to you. Now, you aren't going to start anything, are you?' And all these heavies are around me waiting for me to have a go at him. And he's twice my f– size. What am I going to do?

"I just looked at him and he's like a real ignorant old northerner, and I felt really sorry for him. The geezer looked so shy. Now how can you respect somebody like that?"

I wondered finally whether Rotten could envisage the 'Pistols one day becoming part of the rock establishment they now so openly despise.

"NEVER," John replied without hesitation, and I found myself believing him. "We're still the only band that doesn't hold press conferences every two weeks and pay for some far out binge for the social elite and grovel around or fly every other reporter in the music press over to New York on a private plane. F– that.

"But we're going to be around. We've got a record out now and we're going to finish the album and we'll find somewhere to play. They won't stop us.

"They can shut us out, but they'll never shut us up."

© Allan Jones / Melody Maker / IPC Syndication

Above: ...even if it was
more usual for Sex
Pistols' stages to
resemble the aftermath
of the D-Day Landings
once they got going.

key recordings

1976 Band sign with EMI – *Anarchy In The UK* single released

1977 After brief stay with A&M, Pistols sign with Virgin and have UK Top 10 hits with *God Save The Queen*, *Pretty Vacant* and
Holiday In The Sun singles. *Never Mind The Bollocks – Here's The Sex Pistols* album tops UK chart

1979 After break-up of band in 1978, *The Great Rock 'n' Roll Swindle* album helps *Something Else*, *Silly Thing* and *C'mon
Everybody* make UK singles charts

1980 Bottom of the barrel is scraped to create the aptly-titled *Flogging A Dead Horse* album. For necrophiliacs only

One of the biggest surprises of 1998-99 was the re-appearance to the world's concert stages and charts of Blondie, the New York band last seen in 1982 when a combination of the near fatal illness of guitarist Chris Stein and an almost complete lack of communication between the other members made their break-up inevitable and a source of relief for all concerned.

Blondie first came together in 1974 when singer Debbie Harry, guitarist Chris Stein, bassist Fred Smith and drummer Bill O'Connor (then known as The Stilletos) decided to change musical direction and name. Initially augmenting the line-up with girl backing singers, the first Blondie settled as Harry, Stein, keyboard player James Destri, drummer Clem Burke and bassist Gary Valentine when Smith left to join Television and O'Connor quit. It was this line-up that recorded the debut Blondie album for Private Stock Records in 1976, an interesting blend of punk-influenced tracks with a heavy indebtedness to Sixties girl groups.

British fans especially liked what Blondie were doing, and their popularity in the UK and Europe led to a deal with Chrysalis in 1977, just as Valentine quit. New arrivals at this time were Frank Infante (guitar) and English bassist Nigel Harrison and it was they who joined the others to make the 1978 album Plastic Letters. This contained two Top 10 UK hits ('Denis' and '(I'm Always Touched By Your) Presence Dear') to see any vestiges of Blondie's punk past buried permanently deep.

The switch to out-and-out pop was confirmed by their choice of Mike Chapman as producer of their Parallel Lines album (also 1978), its wisdom confirmed by the UK No.1 status achieved by both singles 'Heart Of Glass' and 'Sunday Girl'. The disco flirtation of the first named became more pronounced on Blondie's 1979 album Eat To The Beat, which contained three international smashes – 'Union City Blue', 'Atomic' and the Giorgio Moroder-produced 'Call Me', their first US No.1.

While the Blondie hit machine kept churning them out for their 1980 album Autoamerican which produced further US and UK chart-toppers in 'The Tide Is High' and 'Rapture'), matters

had disintegrated in the group's ranks. Harry and Stein were personal as well as professional partners, Stein's health was ravaged by the genetic disease pemphigus, while the other members had begun to resent the media attention the photogenic and articulate Harry was now receiving. That coverage was only intensified during the release of her solo album, Koo Koo and there's no doubt her involvement with Blondie's (apparently) last album, The Hunter in 1982, was more dutiful than wholehearted.

Time (and growing up some) proved curative, however. Chris Stein had survived that life-threatening disease and in 1997 rumours spread that Blondie's members – all of whom had enjoyed steady incomes from the repeated re-packaging of greatest hits compilations in the intervening years – had managed to bury their various hatchets and were seriously considering getting back together. Rumour became reality in late 1998 and the release of Blondie's 1999 album No Exit was the signal for a return of the band to strategic touring and the charts, not least via the hit single 'Maria'.

From hit-making pop icons to feisty, hit-making survivors. Blondie. Who'da thought it?

1 1 4

March 3 1979 Harry Doherty

FEAR OF FLYING

New York. Sunday: Picture this (if you can): Deborah Harry, pin-up Empress of the Lipstick Vogue, stands alone in the kitchen of the modest penthouse apartment she shares with friend and business associate Chris Stein. She wears a bright red sweater and a bewildered look.

She seems to be studying intensely some form of literature. A closer examination reveals that she grips an empty pumpkin pie tin in her left hand while perusing a volume titled The Joys of Cooking.

"Aw ... shit!" Debbie sounds mildly irritated. "It doesn't say if it should be served hot or cold."

She moves towards the cooker, where a pumpkin lies in a pot. she adds a pint of milk. I examine the result and fail to suppress a brief chuckle.

"I wouldn't laugh," she snaps. "*You're* gonna be eating this."

The blonde head with the black streak stoops. Debbie opens the oven door to reveal a roast duck. She stabs it in the breast. "D'you think it's ready?" But before an opinion is offered, the bird is cooling on the sideboard.

"Right," she mutters. "I gotta go out an' look at some clothes." she puts on her Supergirl outfit and slips out into the New York cold. Dinner will be served when she returns. I mean, can you picture this?

Saturday: Realising Harry and Stein's preoccupation with psychic phenomena ("sometimes we don't have to speak to know what the other's thinking") I was sure that they'd appreciate that "Heart Of Glass" is playing, loud and proud, on the radio in the cab which ferries me from La Guardia Airport into New York.

"Phone us as soon as you get in," Chris Stein had instructed me, and Debbie's voice welcomes me when I check in.

"Hold on a minute. I'm just scrubbing the bath." This introduction to the domestic Debbie Harry comes as a shock. It seems interestingly at variance from our usual vision of the lady photographed licking a record on the sleeve of "Picture This".

Subtitle this: breaking down the walls of fantasy.

Debbie summons her mate to the phone. He has, she tells me, risen from his bed this minute. Over the next couple of days, Stein's attachment to the mattress becomes very apparent. "C'mon over," he drowsily blurts. "Dunkley'll be here too." Dunkley? The way he says it implies my knowledge of the person. Andy Dunkley? The Living Jukebox? Nah, couldn't be.

I jot down the address and hit the streets of New York, aiming for the Harry/Stein residence on Seventh Avenue.

4.30 pm: I enter the apartment. I don't know what I expected (it being a penthouse "suite", and this being Seventh Avenue), but what I saw persuaded me that "penthouse" does not necessarily equal "de luxe". Luxurious this was not. Comfortable and homely it is.

On the left is a neat, compact kitchen – the tidiest room in the house, in fact. It would have looked perfectly normal, were it not for the five-foot statue of a nun ominously lurking in a corner.

"Uh? Oh, *that*. Chris bought it somewhere for ten dollars," Debbie explains. "See those marks on it? What happened was that we used to share a place with Tommy and Dee Dee Ramone, and they were so freaked by the presence of the nun that they kept attacking it with daggers, trying to kill it. Eventually Chris had to cover the thing with a blanket."

Next to the kitchen is the living room, which isn't really the living room because it doubles and Chris-and-Debbie's music room. Papers, books and tapes are thrown about the place. A battery of reel-to-reel and cassette machines is flanked by two guitars, a Fender bass and a six-string, on their marks and ready for action should Stein and Harry wish to record demos for the next Blondie album. With studio time booked for the next week, the music room has been used a lot recently.

No, if you want the living room you must advance to the bedroom, which, apart from serving as the sleeping quarters, is transformed in the daytime into Chris Stein's office.

Stein's business acumen has increased considerably in the past year, following management mistakes in the early part of Blondie's career, so as often as not he's holed up in the bedroom, telephone to ear, conducting conversations with record company, promoters, management, publicist and whoever. Occasionally he even conducts business meetings in the room.

In the evening, it reverts to the role of leisure-room, where friends from a very tight circle meet to talk and watch television.

Again, the sparseness of material effects is striking: the furniture is confined to a couple of chairs, a double-bed and, of course, the TV – the main source of entertainment in the household.

So this is the home of Blondie's celebrated sweethearts, an unassuming pad which employs a double lock to hold the madness of the music business at bay, and to ensure that they stay out of the in-crowd. It was once occupied by Hollywood actress Lilian Roth, during

a particularly heavy drinking spell in the Thirties. Its present occupants are very different. In a rare unguarded moment, Debbie will express a wish for more of this life. "I'd like to spend more time fixing up the place. There's so much to do. But we don't have that kind of time yet."

The relationship between Stein and Harry is an intimate kinship that touches whatever they become involved in. Stein has unselfishly accepted that his partner will always hog the limelight, and understands the reasons why, to the degree that he is constantly seeking new avenues to explore her strengths and potential. Rock music was an obvious choice to exploit both the voice and the looks. Now he's encouraging a parallel career for Debbie in movies. For her part, Harry is forever hinting that it's a joint venture; beyond question, she realises that her fortunes turned when she struck up a relationship with Chris.

"That's cos there's nowhere to hang out any more," Stein will reply when I suggest that this life with Debbie in New York seems somewhat reclusive. "We used to hang out in places like Maxi's and CBCG's, but now all we see there is strangers. Also, we got all these people pestering us all the time. But we don't just sit around. Most of our free time is spent working on side projects. Boredom is what causes a lot of hanging out."

Above: **An early shot of Blondie in New York when their music was a mix of punk with echoes of Sixties girl-groups.**

Left: **Still working on their image in 1976 – within a year Blondie would be changing the way they looked and sounded. Could stardom be far behind?**

When I arrive, Debbie is soaking in the bath, preparing for a photo session later in the evening with Mick Rock. Chris, as is his wont, is prostrate on the bed. Sure enough, perched next to him like an attentive psychiatrist, is Andy Dunkley.

Dunkley has dropped into New York en route to South America for a month-long holiday. Somebody must be pumping more than 5p into this livin' jukebox.

Stein, meantime, insists on demonstrating the versatility of his TV set by flipping through a string of channels via a remote-control unit on a bedside cabinet. America is famous for its multi-channelled television system, but Stein gets double the normal number of stations because he subscribes to Manhattan Cable Television.

This afternoon, though, it's pretty boring fare, so, in an unprecedented burst of energy, he struggles off the bed and opens a cupboard to show Dunkley and me a couple of pieces of art. The first exhibit is rolled up like a poster, but Chris calls it "the only real piece of art we have in the place".

He unfurls the roll to reveal an Andy Warhol *copy*. Not an original, mind you. A copy. What I see there is a cow, just like any cow. Except that *this* cow was photographed by Andy Warhol, who has signed it with a dedication to Chris and Debbie. Dunkley – and I don't care what he says – looks as dumb and apathetic as me. "Great, ain't it?" Stein enthuses. "Yeah," Dunkley tentatively agrees. "Great." I maintain a dignified silence.

The second exhibit is a rough of the album sleeve Stein has photographed and designed for the new Robert Fripp release – a "supernatural album".

Stein and Harry have built a solid friendship with Fripp since the ex-King Crimson figure made his home in New York two years ago, and were probably instrumental in reactivating the guitarist at a time when all sorts of stories about his withdrawal from public life were sailing across the Atlantic. He's jammed with Blondie a couple of times, and made a guest appearance on "Parallel Lines", with an off-the-wall solo on the album's strangest track, "Fade Away And Radiate".

Stein is justifiably satisfied with his stab at graphic design on the Fripp cover, especially as it looks certain that it'll see the light of day. He had a couple of dummies (i.e. rough versions) drawn up for the last Blondie album, but they never got past the planning stage. The graphics and photography are part of the "side projects" he referred to earlier.

"Photography is easy to pursue because I'm already set up to do that," he says. "And I went to art school and studied graphics, too, so I'm just utilising what's at my disposal. My mother was a beatnik painter; I've been around artists all my life."

As Chris collects his scraps and puts them away, Debbie makes her first appearance of the day, resplendent in kimono and dripping hair. She is frantically waving a note allegedly carrying a personal message from Gene Simmons of Kiss.

"Meet me for a drink and talk," Gene pines in the note. The girl of his dreams does a crud parody of his vile tongue-wagging role in Kiss.

117

"A phone number for the black book," she mumbles through a rolling laugh. Chris takes it a little more seriously. "You'd better not call him...or else." The number goes into the book all the same.

By early evening, the Harry-Steins are preparing for the photo-session. Decisions, decisions. Debbie is having a furious argument with herself over what to wear, but eventually settles on a beige mini-dress/maxi-jumper with matching wool tights and black heels. Chris has his suit ready, and pulls on a pair of boots that might be described as hob-nails without the nails. Debbie is wide-eyed with disgust.

"Jesus, Chris, you're not wearing *them*, are you?" she screams, staring at his feet in horror.

Chris, lethargic as ever, remains unruffled. "Sure. He's not shooting our feet."

"I hope not," sighs an exasperated Ms. Harry, and we set off downtown to Mick Rock's studio.

It's a strange sensation, standing with Debbie Harry in a main thoroughfare in Manhattan. Stars should not be ignored in the street, but that's what's happening here. In the freezing cold, Debbie shuffles towards the shelter of a shop front, seeking warmth. Meanwhile Chris is stranded out in the iced road, fruitlessly waving for a cab. They motor past. There are a few close things, but Chris loses out every time. Debbie is fed up, and barks: "C'mon, Chris, for Chrissakes." Stein explains his predicament, but Debbie remains unsympathetic. "Ya gotta be

Above: **Fame came quickly for the girl who four years before this 1979 shot was fronting the girl vocal group The Stilletos.**

aggressive. That's the only way you'll get a cab. Be fuckin' *aggressive*."

A few minutes later a cab is driving us towards the photo-session.

The rest of the group, plus girlfriends, are already at Mick Rock's studio by the time we make it. Rock, who used to work for David Bowie, speeds about the place organising the set, having earlier despatched his juniors to collect as many old radios as they could find.

The changing room looks like Take Six in Oxford Street, the boys in the band having brought along their Sunday-best. Nigel Harrison has resurrected clothes from his glitter days with Silverhead. "Mark my words," he warns in a suave English accent, "glitter is returning." After primping and preening, the members of Blondie look so smart that they could pass for models in Freeman's Catalogue.

"Heart Of Glass" can be heard on the radio. Clem Burke loses no time in pointing out to me: "Hear this? This is New York's *number one* disco station."

The significance of that, of course, is that "Heart Of Glass" has attained credibility with the disco buffs. Who, a year ago, would have dreamed that a new wave band would have a number one *disco* single?

The song was written by Stein and Harry and was born out of their fondness for R&B and soul material – plus the influence of the disco phenomenon itself.

"To us, it sounds like Kraftwerk," Debbie maintains. "It's certainly influenced by them. It's just a syncopated sound. It's disco, yet at the same time it's not disco. It's neither. We really like Donna Summer and the Bee Gees. That stuff is good if you're open-minded about it and you don't make a big political deal outta it."

"With me, it's a psychic thing," Stein continues. "It has to do with the beat. The 4/4 rhythm has a calming effect on the listener. It's that heartbeat beat. That's why it's so popular, whereas rock, which has an erratic off beat creates excitement. It's a physical thing. It's biological.

"I like some disco songs, and I don't like other disco songs. It's sorta like an alternative to punk rock. It's a gut emotion. I can't really see disco as being the death knell of live music. Not at all. I think what people object to about disco is the dumb straight people in suits makin' out that they're John Travolta goin' to discos, listenin' to disco muzak and thinkin' they're him. I find that very distasteful, but that side of it is just bullshit and has nuthin' to do with it. I mean people were doin' that to Jefferson Airplane too ..." Listen out for another couple of disco-orientated tracks on the next Blondie album.

The session completed, Debbie and Chris, not usually noted for painting the town red, decide to leave for home; Frank Infanti heads for Max's Kansas City, where the Heartbreakers are staging yet another comeback (or is it farewell?) gig; Burke and Jimmy Destri are Broadway bound to see their former buddy, Gary Valentine, play at a relatively new NY club, Hurrah's.

Hurrah's has been acquiring a healthy reputation with kids and bands alike. It merges rock with disco so subtly that neither audience loses credibility by hanging out there. Its trendy mirrored architecture makes it a safe place for the more fashion-affected kids to visit, while the wide range of bands – the Only Ones made their New York debut there – attracts the earthier audiences.

It wasn't a particularly inspiring night for Gary Valentine, though one wonders why he ever left Blondie in the first place. This gig proved that he is neither a guitarist nor a singer, but there were a couple of good songs that could have been done justice to by a singer of Debbie

Harry's style. You may remember that Valentine wrote "Touched By Your (Presence Dear)". You wouldn't if you heard him sing it. If Gary would realise that his vocation is writing songs, and not performing them, he might find a more fulfilling path.

"Yeah, I know what you mean," Harry later agreed. "There were a lot of ego clashes with Gary, within the band, and that's what led to him leaving. He was always wanting to change things. The difference between us is that I know how to sell a song."

Sunday, 4.30 pm: Debbie is sweating over the cooker while Chris conducts a business meeting – in the bedroom, of course – with a representative from Shep Gordon's office. Gordon is interested in taking over Blondie's vacant management. He has a lot of clout in the States, but Stein is being very cool. Twice bitten, he's third time shy.

Back in the kitchen, waiting for the duck to roast, Debbie pulls out a few Polaroids from the previous night's session with Rock. They look impressive, the boys bunched up around their singer in their high-street suits, holding the radios that the photographer had liberated from market shelves, all set against a striking red background.

"At least we've already got a cover for the next album from that session," Debbie says, noting her own sensuous pose in the shot. "Get out the cheeseboard! The record company wants me to sell my body again."

While she batters the living daylight out of the pumpkin pie, Debbie reveals that she, too, is working on a "secret project", and then is slightly taken aback when I tell her that I know it's a film – and it's not Alphaville.

The project is, indeed, shrouded in secrecy, and both Stein and Harry are unwilling to divulge too much information about it. As the day wears on, I learn that it's a psychological thriller, that it's a low-budget production, that it will only take a week to make (which was instrumental in Debbie's decision to accept the part), that shooting starts the next day ... and that she will play a "tortured housewife".

Left: **The first time Blondie toured the UK, it was in basement punk clubs and university venues.**

She has, it appears, been offered a host of movie roles. She turned down ("Thank God!") a part in Stigwood's Sgt. Pepper's Lonely Hearts Club Band, and is frequently plied with scripts. This one was accepted because of the brief schedule, and because it had an exceptional script that appealed to both Stein and Harry. They also see the venture as a comfortable introduction to acting, which will serve her well when it comes to filming Alphaville, probably some time later this year.

The Alphaville project has come to a temporary standstill, after the introductory blaze of publicity sparked off by an MM front page picturing Harry and co-star Robert Fripp. Stein and Fripp had used the publicity to attract financial backers, and now they're considering the offers. It hadn't, however, originated as a movie project. Stein, having secured the rights to the book wanted to record an album based around it, until a close friend, former Interview editor Glenn O'Brien, persuaded him to go a step further and put it on celluloid.

While Stein views the move into films as an exciting new frontier, his other half remains sceptical about her future under the lights until she feels the temperature.

"It's a whole different sense of timing and pace of working," she muses. "I guess it's much drier, and it's certainly more personal. You don't *need* to have an audience response. You just do it, and if you do it good, you get turned on. It's *that* personal. The director is there, and the crew, but everybody is, like busy, busy, busy.

"I haven't really done any acting before...just a couple of under-

ground videos. Not like this, not like...ah...official. An' it's really complex. You have to choreograph. You have to time. It's the same thing with music – but with music, you have the music to carry you. It's a challenge, and I'm looking forward to it.

"It's so different from rock 'n' roll. There's a lotta things about rock 'n' roll that I don't like. I love being on stage, and I love the excitement, but I don't like the business that much. For some reason, the rock business hasn't *dignified* itself. After the movie industry was around for 20 years, it was dignified. They *forced* themselves to become dignified. They were protected. They could work in certain ways. In rock 'n' roll, a lotta people get misused physically – and a lotta times mentally. The movie industry has all these unions, like the Screen Actors' guild. Those things are very strong. Your working conditions have to be of a certain calibre. But in rock 'n' roll you get constantly faced with very fuckin' wild conditions, y'know. Like, for me a lotta times they seem really rugged – freezin' cold theatres, stuff like that. I dunno if that happens to actors or not.

"Anyway, this is my first experience of doing a movie. If I like it, I like it. If I don't I'll knock it on the head."

Stein is content to spend a lazy afternoon waiting for dinner – a full-scale meal of this sort doesn't happen too often in this household – watching TV, this time switching between sports and films on the cable channel.

On the bed lies a copy of UFO, the magazine which brings up a discourse on one of Chris's many eccentric theories. For instance, he

Above: **A hint that all was not well within the Blondie camp as the solemn group gathered to have their picture taken for the umpteenth time. By the end of their first incarnation, in 1982, only Debbie and Chris Stein were talking to each other.**

believes that the CIA (who else?) have extra-terrestrial beings captive in the White House, an opinion encouraged by an article in this month's copy of UFO.

"The CIA have been involved in so many weird cover-ups," Chris will argue earnestly. "I wouldn't put it past them."

While on the subject of radical theories, it's also worth adding that Stein believes that Crosby, Stills and Nash were planted on an unsuspecting population by the government in the early Seventies to calm the increasing political consciousness and activities of the Sixties. And who'd argue with that?

It turns into an amusing afternoon after of TV and Stein philosophies. The peace is shattered, though, soon after Debbie returns, when she receives a call from a friend who's just finished reading Tony Parsons' and Julie Burchill's The Boy Looked At Johnny and wishes to point out the observations made by this other odd couple concerning Stein and Harry. Debbie calmly puts the phone on the receiver and explodes. Chris wanders out to discover what all the fuss is about. He lethargically returns and flops on the bed, casually reporting: "She wants to sue Tony Parsons."

After a few minutes' thought, he returns to Debbie in the kitchen. She will not be placated.

"I didn't say those fuckin' things," she cries. "He's tellin' lies."

Stein's voice is so soft and controlled that I can't hear his reply. Debbie is outraged by his diplomacy, and attempts a more direct approach to stir his anger.

"Did you see what he said about your fuckin' photographs? He said you're a lousy photographer!"

Chris is stirred, but only because Debbie's outburst is irritating him. "So what? I don't give a fuck what he says."

Stein again returns to the bedroom, giving no clue of the proceeding battle. "Some fuckin' friend that was on the phone," he murmurs.

THE incident emphasises Harry's mistrust and suspicion of the Press. She is loath, these days, to be roped into an interview, and though she was usually the picture of charm in New York, she became decidedly cagey and unsettled if a discussion moved towards any seriousness.

Blondie's relationship with the papers, and particularly the British papers, has deteriorated rapidly over the last year, the rot ironically coinciding with the band's outstanding success in Britain. Stein, for instance, puts the recent rumours of a split down to "one of our enemies spreading malicious gossip. A lot of stuff that's written about us has a high percentage of inaccuracy."

Nevertheless, Stein is the more tolerant of the two, showing an implicit appreciation of the power of the media, and an anxiety to exploit it whenever possible.

"Some of them have obviously turned on us cos we're too successful. We're outta the grasp of power-mad critics. It makes them very nervous when they know they can't make or break you any more. The bigger you get, the more imaginative the lies they'll print. It isn't that we get misquoted a lot. It's just that it's taken out of context. It's different here, though. The American press is less opinionated, on the whole, and more musically analytical."

Debbie cools down and, while carving the duck, doubtless thinks only of Tony Parsons.

During the evening, it should be reported, Debbie's hair changes colour – from blonde to light brown with the first rinse, to slightly darker brown with the second. For the movie, you understand. Stein is impressed.

Hey, that's really good," he raves. "It makes you look younger."

Debbie doesn't know what to make of that one.

MONDAY 7.30 am: "Make-up call for Ms. Harry."

7.30 pm: At the home of Debbie Harry and Chris Stein.

Harry: "Nervous? This mornin' I was scared shitless. I was gonna call you up. I was almost in tears."

Stein: "Why? D'you think you couldn't do it?"

Harry: "Yeah, I thought 'Oh shit. Here I am. I can't do it.' Like, I was really freakin' out. That was it. I was really fucked up."

Stein: "An' what happened? You did it, didn't you?"

Harry: "Well, y'know, I would feel how freaked out I was and then I would just say to myself 'You can't let this happen! You gotta do it. What're you gonna do? Quit?' An' I just had to talk myself back into doin' it."

Stein: "So then what happened? Didn't you do it? Whaddya worryin' about?"

Harry: "So then in the afternoon I just beat the words into my head. I just studied the script."

Stein: "What couldn't you do? Remember the lines?"

Harry: "Yeah. Like, I was havin' terrible trouble. I couldn't choreograph the words an' the movin', put the endin's at the right time or the beginnings. I was so fucked up."

Stein: "You were a little nervous. What's the big deal?"

Harry: "*Dennis* could do it right away."

Stein: "Well, he's done movies before."

And it goes on.

In the course of the evening, with Debbie completely exhausted after a hard day's work, we talk more about the "side projects". Debbie says that she was interested in producing a group, the B-girls, but the plan was abandoned when the lead singer and the guitarist had a fight. Movies now take care of Debbie's spare time.

Stein, however, is taking on as much as he can handle. Apart from photography and graphics, he's also been producing an album for a friend, violinist and electronic musician Walter Steding, and at the mention of his name heads for the tape deck to play the result of the collaboration. It's a rather far-fetched version of "Hound Dog", with a solo by Robert Fripp.

Steding, according to Stein, is the antithesis of Blondie's pure pop. They first met a couple of years ago, when he supported Blondie at places like CBGB's and Max's Kansas City.

"Producing him is great because there are no preconceptions whatsoever, and there are no references to music or anything else that I can think of except to jazz and that isn't deliberate. it's sorta like psychedelic jazz. It has a good sense of humour, too, which appeals to me. it satisfies my desire for abstraction. Blondie's music is much more regimented and mapped out carefully.

"I should say, too, that there's a definite trend now towards free-form rock and jazz in New York. Even the B52s, who play tight, have these weird abstractions on top of the driving rhythms. It's a backlash against the regimentation of punk rock. It's like you play faster and faster – and finally you can't play any faster, so you just play erratically."

Other members of Blondie, too, have been involving themselves in solo projects. Jimmy Destri has been producing an excellent local band

Above: **Cool amidst the frantic angst of punk rock, an icon of the era.**

have the right kind of hook that can be grabbed by the media. Bands like Kiss and Rush *have* to tour constantly, because they can't get the right type of media coverage. That doesn't necessarily mean it's moronic, but it's a lifestyle that we don't adhere to. We want to use the media – which is there to be used, after all.

"Being on stage is great. What I don't like about touring is the rest of the day. You spend an hour having a good time, and you spend 22 hours sleeping or lazing about a bus. That's a real drag. I mean, you're never not tired on a tour. You're always tired because you always gotta get up too early."

Maybe they didn't like the lengthy tours because their relationship is one which doesn't allow for participation in the on-the-road raving that many bands maintain keeps them sane.

"Well, it makes it a lot easier when you have somebody to bounce off. Now that we have a little more money, when we do tours of the States the boys take their girlfriends with them, too. It's more fun. It's a better atmosphere."

Many bands think that it's taboo to take girlfriends on tour.

"Yeah," Stein says. "But everybody has cool girlfriends in Blondie."

Before I leave, Stein has one more treat in store, a visit to an underground television programme that's beamed on cable TV. He's genuinely excited by the prospect. TV Party, as it's called, goes out every Monday night at 11 pm, and is masterminded by Glenn O'Brien. It is, truly, Alternative TV.

Chris explains that it's a sort of community venture and that the studio, off East 53rd Street, can be hired for 40 dollars an hour. It's available to any crank who has some message for the nation; one night there was a woman so in love with her goldfish that she acquired the studio to tell Manhattan about them. She had a potential audience of half a million.

A couple of weeks back, Debbie – who decides tonight to rest at home – went on TV Party and gave lessons on pogo dancing. It's that sort of programme.

When we arrive at the studio, the audience and artists are mingling. They come in all shapes, colours and sizes – the lunatic fringe, Stein calls them. As the hour approaches, the studio is a scene of unrelenting chaos, with the calm O'Brien presiding, but when the clock strikes 11, a loose band of Stein, Walter Steding, a bassist, a percussionist, a sax player and a singer play and sing the first thing that comes into their head. So *this* is free-form jazz.

O'Brien launches into his introductory spiel. Michael Aspel he is not. "Cold enough for ya? Welcome to the station that doesn't say 'cold enough for ya?'"

And it goes on, with spontaneous anecdotes and a guest appearance by Peter Hammill, who looks as it he's just stepped into another planet (which, of course, he has).

Stein is called upon by O'Brien to give a few words. He imparts his theory of extra-terrestrial beings at the White House. Steding calls for more venues in New York, mentioning that CBGB's has gone downhill (an opinion with which the audience vociferously agrees).

The hour flies by, and Stein dismantles his equipment in a corner of the studio.

"You were asking about the people we hang out with," he says, casting an eye over his eccentric court.

"Well, *these* are our friends."

called the Student Teachers, as well as working on his own material, while Clem Burke was recently playing with Chris Spedding. Within the framework of Blondie, Stein sees it as a very healthy practice.

"It's easier for me to create things now, because I feel like there is really an audience and people will look or listen to whatever I do. We always wanted Blondie to be a multi-media commune. It's not supposed to be just a band. Actually, we're gonna go into religion pretty soon...

"We view it as a long-term thing. You see, if I'm bald I can't appear on an album cover, but I can still *produce* records and stuff. All the boys in the band are worried about their hair. I'll bet Joe Strummer would worry if he was bald. Some people can pull it off, like Eno can do it gracefully. Actually, Debbie should shave her hair off. That'd be great."

Framing Harry and Stein within Blondie can be a delicate matter, especially when the issue of internal conflict is raised. They argue that most of the problems have been eradicated now that the various members have settled into their own apartments, and now that they are looking for a new manager. The claim to be in complete control of the situation.

But I'd guess that there's still a certain amount of friction within the band. In some ways, Harry and Stein have a different outlook on rock 'n' roll than the rest of the band. For instance, some of the band are anxious to get out on the road gigging, while Stein and Harry are reluctant to drag their bodies across the United States.

They don't deny that there are problems. "All these projects act as a valve and give us a lotta satisfaction," Debbie says. "There are so many strong personalities within the band that you have to find a channel to release the rest of the energy, otherwise you get a lotta bickerin'."

Stein once stated, in a Rolling Stone interview, that touring is "for morons".

"That was misconstrued. What I meant is that if a band has to tour incessantly, it's not really for morons but it's just for people who don't

© **Harry Doherty / Melody Maker / IPC Syndication**

Above: **A record company shot of (left to right) Destri, Burke, Harry, Stein and Infante.**

key recordings

1976	Blondie sign with Private Stock and release, er...*Blondie*
1978	Now signed to UK-based Chrysalis Records, band release *Plastic Letters* and score with hit singles *Denis* and *(I'm Always Touched By Your) Presence Dear*. Produced by Mike Chapman, *Parallel Lines* includes chart-topping *Heart Of Glass* and *Sunday Girl*
1979	Disco rules as *Eat To The Beat* becomes first US smash and Giorgio Moroder produces No.1 *Call Me*
1981	Writing is on the wall for Blondie as Debbie Harry releases the solo album *Koo Koo*
1999	Back, proud and on form, *No Exit* proves that there is life after break-up

Until Robert Nesta Marley, the outside world had little or no idea of the wealth of talent waiting to break out of the West Indian island nation of Jamaica. There had been odd Jamaican artists who'd scored one-off single hits, but they'd been viewed as little more than interesting novelties. Bob Marley would change all that.

Marley grew up in the tough Trenchtown district of Kingston, his early musical education gained from street sound systems pumping out a mixture of calypso, bluebeat, ska and American soul. Like many of his contemporaries Marley readily embraced the new hybrid which sprang from this chaos and became known as reggae.

It was singer Jimmy Cliff who recommended that Marley see Leslie Kong, who produced his debut single, 'Judge Not (Unless You Judge Yourself)' in 1962. Within two years Marley had become leader of The Wailin' Wailers, then a vocal group whose often-changing personnel was stabilised by Marley, Bunny Livingston and Peter Tosh. With Clement 'Sir Coxsone' Dodd now producing, by 1966 they'd become a full-blown band and had scored local hits with 'Put It On','Simmer Down', 'Love and Affection' and 'Rude Boy', the latter a glorification of Trenchtown's streetwise delinquents.

Financial imperatives (he'd married Rita Anderson early in 1966) forced Marley to leave for America and a string of temporary jobs. He also recorded for small US labels, but these would languish in their vaults until everything with the name 'Marley' on it became invaluable to collectors. Back in Jamaica, in 1967 Marley started his own Wailin' Soul label, one of whose first releases was Reggae on Broadway, an album by American singer Johnny Nash, who would return the favour by recording hit versions of Marley's 'Stir It Up' and 'Guava Jelly' in 1972.

By 1969 Marley and the Wailers had converted to Rastafarianism, whose practitioners are dedicated Bible readers and believe that regular smoking of 'ganja' (marijuana) is sacramental. This last-named aspect of the religion cut no slack with Jamaican authorities who'd jailed Bunny Livingston for 14 months when he was found with a giant stash in 1967.

Now produced by Lee 'Scratch' Perry, The Wailers released two fine albums on their newly-formed Tuff Gong label in 1969 (Soul Rebel and Soul Vibration) and scored big hits with the singles 'Duppy Conqueror', 'Small Axe', 'Soul Rebel' and '400 Years'.

In 1972, Chris Blackwell, the Jamaican-born head of Island Records, signed The Wailers to his international label and work began on Catch A Fire, an album which – when it was released in 1973 – transformed Marley's life forever. Touring Britain and the US on the back of a comprehensive marketing campaign, he achieved a cult status helped when Clapton included 'I Shot The Sheriff' on his chart-topping 461 Ocean Boulevard album and George Harrison told journalists that The Wailers were the best thing he'd seen "in ten years".

There would be one more album by The Wailers (Burnin', also in 1973) before Tosh and Livingston tired of the emphasis being put on Marley and quit to pursue their own careers. Marley replied with his Natty Dread album in 1975 to give the new-named Bob Marley and The Wailers their first UK chart appearance. Then, when a 'live' version of 'No Woman No Cry' (a song featured on Natty Dread and highlight of the aptly-titled Live!) made its way into the UK Top 30, Marley really was on his way.

His US breakthrough came in 1976 with the album Rastaman Vibration. Even though its follow-up, Exodus, was not as successful in America, the title track proved a hit single around the world. In 1977 he returned with another international hit, 'Jammin' and, a year later, with 'Is This Love'. There would be four more albums to come – Kaya and the double-live Babylon By Bus (both in 1978), Survival (1979) and Uprisin' (in early 1980) – throughout which time his popularity and influence grew enormously.

Any active role Marley could have played in Jamaican politics were put firmly aside in 1976 after seven gunmen burst into his Kingston home and seriously injured him, his wife and his manager, Don Taylor. Marley's support of African civil rights would be recognised in 1978 with his reception of a Third World Peace Medal.

On October 8, 1980 Marley was rehearsing in New York, prior to embarking on a major US tour with Stevie Wonder, when he collapsed. Rushed to hospital, he was told he had lung cancer and a brain tumour. While Marley began treatment in a German clinic, Stevie Wonder rush-recorded and released 'Master Blaster (Jammin')' as a tribute.

In April 1981 Bob Marley was too ill to attend in person and receive Jamaica's Order of Merit from the prime minister and asked his son, Ziggy to accept it in his place. Aware that he had little time left, Marley flew to Miami to be near his mother, and on May 11 died at the Cedars of Lebanon Hospital. He was 36 and deserved the full state funeral he was accorded ten days later in a Kingston packed to overflowing by thousands of grieving citizens.

Bob Marley made an indelible mark on musical history. The impact his music made was reflected by the hit albums and singles which followed his death and the fact that, even now, his name is the still the first to come to mind when anyone says the word 'reggae'.

Bob Marley June 12 1976 Ray Coleman

'DON'T DEAL WITH DARK THINGS'

Don't want success. Success mean nuttin'. Plenty people been successful, but dey still living dead – Bob Marley.

It's no ordinary rehearsal room, the doorless out-house in the garden of Bob Marley's house in Hope Road, Kingston, just a few minutes along from the Prime Minister's residence.

The Wailers practise here, in a room about twice the size of the average British lounge. What makes it extraordinary in atmosphere is the unmistakable feeling that when the musicians are in here, playing and smoking and planning a concert or an album, it's as if nothing had ever happened and they are still jamming purely for fun, as they did ten years ago. With few cares or considerations beyond the next tune, the new

single, and not the faintest prospect of world tours and hit albums. A drum kit lies idle, an empty guitar case here, a chair or two...but what's this?

A running order is scribbled and stuck to the wall, reading as follows:

Revolution/Natty Dread/So Jah Seh/No Woman/I Shot The Sheriff/Talking Blues/Road Block/Bellyfull/Jah Live/Trenchtown Rock/Nice Time/Concrete Jungle/Kinky Reggae/Midnight Ravers/No More Trouble/Bend Down Low/Get Up Stand Up/Rat Race/Bumin' And Lootin'/Stir It Up/Duppy Conqueror/Slave Driver/Rock My Boat/One Love/Thank You Lord.

On another wall, an article of faith: a portrait with the words: "His Imperial Majesty, Emperor Haile Selassie, King of Kings, Lord of Lords."

Incongruously, a sticker is pinned beneath it: "Album Of The Year – Natty Dread."

Bob Marley lives here, works here, plays here and if there's one thing absolutely endearing about the whole Jamaican-Rastafarian/ Reggae story as it reaches its peak with Bob Marley's tour next week, it's this: what you see, and what they say, is all there is.

Below and right: **Bob Marley and the original Wailers (Peter Tosh, Bunny Livingston, Carlton Barrett and Aston 'Family Man' Barrett) pictured in Jamaica before their music made reggae an international force. The departure of Tosh and Livingston in 1974 left Marley free to enlarge the band and begin his climb to superstar status.**

Previous page: **Soul vibration incarnate – Bob Marley lets fly.**

Left: **As anyone who saw them will testify, Bob Marley's gigs were never laid-back affairs, as UK photographer Ian Dickson captured here.**

There's no hiding behind poses, and the uncluttered sound of their music runs synonymously with their personalities. The rehearsal room is the opposite of pretentious.

Marley is hard to reach. Even his friends say that strangers, particularly white ones, should not go to his house unless accompanied by a face which Marley recognises. It's virtually impossible to make an appointment to see him, because he appears not to recognise schedules, even for himself. But eventually on that hot evening, he appeared from the table tennis room in his house and walked me outside, saying he would think better with some air.

His house is large and old and rambling, and bears the vibrations of a commune. People drift in and out, by car and on foot, and he waved to them all, while remaining seated on the steps.

The house is a positive statement by Marley. Opposite, there are some terrible new apartments which look like prison cells, and Bob continually laughs at the fact that they have bars up, protecting them from burglars. "No way to live, no way to live!" he keeps saying. "Must run home like mind. Keep open."

Thus, Marley's home, Island House, in Hope Road, Kingston, is open to all-comers. Especially Rastafarians.

As the Marley/Wailers success gathers momentum, so their allegiance to Rastafarian principles becomes more concentrated. Every other sentence of Marley's speech is punctuated by a reference to Jah (God) and as he drew harder on his cigar-sized spliff (joint), repeating: "Righteousness must cover the earth like the water cover the sea," I had visions of a sermon rather than a conversation, and certainly fading hopes of a lucid conversation.

And yet it's too easy to dismiss the obsession with Rasta as excluding their attachment to reality. It's impossible to catch, first time around, every word and nuance of what Marley is saying, but his drift is quite simple to understand, and while he keeps returning to his declarations that commercial gain is not his aim, he is acutely aware of what is happening around him. His mind moves very quickly indeed, and his powers of observation are uncanny.

I asked him first about his evident need to smoke ganja (herb), of which he partakes a pound a week, and why the smoking of it was so dovetailed into his Rasta beliefs.

"Herb is the healing of a nation," he said quietly. "When you smoke, you don't frighten so easy. Herb bring all brethren together, all thinking alike and that's why they lock you up when you smoke herb, because it makes people think the same way, but if people don't smoke herb they think different from each other, can be told what to do and get...confused.

"In Babylon we give thanks for herb, and if we didn't have herb to educate us, we be educated by fools who tell us to live like funny, like in Babylon. Herb is the healing of the nation. Bible say that. Herb come out of the ground!"

Did this contempt, then, for materialism and Babylon (Western culture) and even for organised society represent Black Power, and did Bob feel his music was preaching TO white ears, or to blacks about whites?

"My music fight against the system. My music defend righteousness. If you're white and you're wrong, then you're wrong, if you're black and you're wrong, you're wrong. People are PEOPLE. Black, blue, pink, green – God make no rules about colour, only society make rules where my people suffer and that why we must have redemption and redemption is now.

"Against white people? Couldn't say that. I fight against the system that teach you to live and die."

So his music existed for propaganda? He laughed at the seriousness of the word. "No. If God had-na given me a song to sing, I wouldn't have a song to sing. So it's not MY music, from my soul, doing these things, saying these words. I don't know about propaganda but in telling truth, and I don't deal with the wrong things of life, and I don't want to know them because as soon as you know them, you...know them, and because you're not perfect you might try to change.

"Don't like the idea of propaganda, that's not how I-and-I see it. Don't deal with dark things."

And yet many of his songs, I said, were laced with stabs at various inequalities. 'Bellyfull', for example, was surely a commentary on the starvation of some as compared to the abundant wealth of others?

Not exactly, Marley answered. It was more subtle than that – your belly's full, but we're hungry for your LOVE of your brethren. Food's in your stomach, but cannot you see there is more to living than filling it? Where's the love for your brethren? No, he averred, it wasn't entirely a materialistic commentary, more a sad declaration of the bancruptcy of believing that everything ended with self-gratification.

Above: **Preacher Bob. "In Babylon we give thanks for herb..."**

But he was obviously not playing a role. Asked if he felt any responsibility as the most popular star reggae had produced, he said: "I don't think about it, you know. Too busy working.

"People come to me, say: 'Bob Marley, big international artist' and I laugh. I don't know what that mean. If it mean more people listen, enjoy music, then good. That's all."

Still, he had been watching the adoption of reggae by others, and he liked Johnny Nash's 'Stir It Up', a world hit version of the Marley song, and he was interested in other incursions into the style, mentioning Paul Simon's 'Mother And Child Reunion' ("Nice").

"See, dem American players come down here and play with Jamaican musicians who are very friendly. Make good records. It happens all the time."

So there was no determination to keep reggae as a wholly private scene, and Jamaica was happy for the world to go to Kingston and join in?

"Nah, world cannot take it," Bob replied immediately. "This is one of them things the world cannot take. It's like gold is gold and silver is silver, and what is...imitation can be seen t'be imitation.

"So the real thing, nobody can take it away from here. You have to really come in to this thing at our time to have the feel, y'know. It's art, y'know, art. Not just a purposeful thing, but from knowing.

"That's why I-and-I know nobody can take it. They can go anywhere and play funky and soul, but reggae – too hard, reggae. Must have a bond with it. The real reggae must come from Jamaica, because other people could not play it all the while, anyway – it would go against their whole life. Reggae has t'be...inside you."

Marley was now trying to get himself to define reggae music as clearly as possible, and the nearest he could get was to say it was like jazz.

"Jazz – a complete music," he declared, still smoking. "Reggae complete too. Reggae is funky, but it's also different from funky, and sometimes I think funky soul music goes little too far in what it tries to do. Reggae music is simple, all the while. Different from soul as well. Cannot be taught, that's a fact."

It relied on a mental attitude, he explained. If he was depressed and was going into a studio, he could not make music properly. But then, it might easily have something to do with the people and their vibrations. He felt – well, not uneasy in the company of non-Rastafarians, but not relaxed either. He wanted to stress, though, there was no antipathy towards white non-Rastas.

"Well, I say give a man a chance if he's not Rasta. The Bible full of stories of people not treated right for not believing. Problem not with people who are not in touch with Rasta, but with people who are once Rasta and then have left it and have to go back to it. These can be difficult and...confused people."

Propaganda for Rastafarianism was something he admitted, if not for black repression. Are you trying to make audiences outside Jamaica appreciate what Rastafarianism stands for?

Below: **An avid soccer fan and part-time player, one of the media stories of the time said that Bob Marley's fatal cancer had begun with a foot injury incurred during a kick-about.**

130

Above: **The fervour and intensity Marley brought to live performances was a gift to photographers all over the world.**

"Yeh, mon. Rasta Man Vibration gonna cover the earth! Jah say: until the philosophy which places one race superior and one race inferior is finally and permanently discredited and abandoned, then we won't have no peace. Babylon believe in divide and rule, but Rasta one way only, the right way, and we can do it but it take longer. We have redemption now, nobody can stop it..."

Marley said he read a chapter of the Bible every day, and based his belief on that, including his diet. He is a vegetarian, although that is not a prerequisite of Rastafarianism. He didn't drink, he said, because it was obvious that pumping chemicals into his body would make him ill. "A little wine, sometimes," he reflected.

"The reason people drink is because they want to feel how I feel when I smoke. Everybody needs to get a little high sometimes, just that some people get high on the wrong thing. Herb does grow. How much do I smoke? Plenty."

Could someone be a Rasta and not smoke?

"Yeh...but if you believe in Rasta and fight against the herb, you are wrong. Herb needs to be understood properly, but, in hands of Rasta it is the best healing of a nation."

Smoking is highly illegal in Jamaica, however, and Marley repeats his view that society is frightened of people thinking the same way.

"Vampires!" he roared. "Most people are negative out there, but Rasta people think positive. Most people in Babylon want power. Devil want power. God don't want power, but Devil need power, 'cos Devil insecure."

Insecurity never bothered him. Even when he travelled outside Jamaica he remained confident, secure, positive.

The only country he would contemplate settling in, except Jamaica, was Africa – this was naturally bound up with his Rasta convictions – but even without the prospect of settling there, he planned a trip there soon.

Friends say they dread the day Marley goes there, because he's such a highly-charged, sensitive man that it is bound to change his entire attitude, one way or another, towards his beliefs.

He said the system taught people that they must live and die, but he and his brethren did not agree. Furthermore, they were totally opposed to the worshipping of material goods to the point where the people in 'Babylon' (Bob's all-embracing word for the centre of the world's problems) died working for material objects which would do nothing to enrich their lives.

It wasn't that he personally renounced materially useful things: bicycles, cars, were OK in the Rasta creed, but they were merely a means to an end. "If somebody gave me a spaceship, I would give it back to him because I could not use it," Marley continued.

He pointed to that ugly block of new houses opposite and laughed, sadly. "Those people over there are working to live in a situation not good, but the system educates them to think that is the end of their life," he said.

"People not taught to be at peace with themselves. Education all wrong. Put you in a bracket where you earn enough money to pay for THESE things!" (He pointed at the houses again).

"Well, you have to be a Rasta man to beat the system, and when they can get a Rasta man in jail, they do, and then they try to get you back there. Everyone wants the biggest this, the biggest car, refrigerator, crazy, mon – this is the system I keep talking about..."

He started to sing 'Rat Race'.

What about the race for the title of the biggest reggae band in the world, then? Did he concede such a contest existed?

"Can't say that," he offered, convincingly. "I-and-I, my brethren, only answer to myself and Jah. If de Wailers are in some race, we must have been put there by somebody, but not us."

How about the future of the band, Bob? Does it plan to change, progress in any foreseeable way?

"When I feel that the job has been done that I-and-I have been sent to do, I-and-I pack it up," he stated firmly.

When would that be?

"When I feel satisfied and when Jah tells me I am finished with this work. It might be at the end of the American visit, or the English visit – I will know that when as many people as possible have learned what we have to say."

When the system is challenged?

"System bound to go," he answered.

The personal manager of Bob Marley is Jamaican-born Don Taylor, who has worked with Tamla Motown in Detroit, and especially closely with Marvin Gaye, Little Anthony, Martha Reeves and Chuck Jackson.

He's managed Marley for a year, and says he was warned against taking on Bob by locals who described Marley as a "problem, difficult character."

"What you must remember," said Taylor one day as he contemplated the escalating Marley story yet again, "is that Bob's sharper than all of us.

"Right now, he's getting to the position he was in ten years ago, of not trusting people and that's a pity. Lots of people hang around the studios, for instance, saying they are broke and asking him for ten dollars just like they used to.

"He always used to give friends dollars if they needed it, but now the whole world seems to be joining in. Maybe it's because there's jealousy in this town because Bob's the only one who made it, and people are out to take him for a ride. This is real bad, y'know – they should realise that he's made it possible for everyone to make it.

"Instead, people are talking behind his back and speaking all this crap about selling out. Listen, the same guys who knew Marley when he was in Trenchtown are talking behind his back now, and it's sickening..."

Bob Marley, he declared, knew all about the rats and roaches of Trenchtown living. "He also knows all those old slogans about no money, no jobs, no future. Well, Marley's GIVING them a future."

Flying out of Kingston next day aboard Air Jamaica, I asked the hostess her views on reggae, Rastafarianism and Bob Marley. She was about 25, a black Jamaican.

"Rastafarianism? Oh, it's quite popular, but only among the very young here. I don't think reggae will ever catch on much. It's really dance music for the young. What would you like to drink?"

132

Above: **Bob gives the time of day to Peter Tosh and Michael Philip Jagger, chairman of the Dartford, Kent branch of his international fan club.**

Above: **Another day,
another sold-out gig.
Bob and The Wailers
head for a London
stage door, watched
by a raincoated
photographer and a pair
of the city's constables.**

key recordings

1969   Lee 'Scratch' Perry produces *The Wailers* debut album, quickly followed by *Soul Rebel* and *Soul Vibration*

1973   Signed to Island Records, The Wailers release *Catch A Fire* and the equally combustible *Burnin'*. The rest of
             the world catches up with Jamaica

1975   *Natty Dread* is first album billed as Bob Marley and The Wailers

1976   America succumbs to Marley's magic as *Rastaman Vibration* and *Exodus* give him his first major US hits

1978   His powers at their peak, Marley delivers the double-whammy of *Kaya* and *Babylon By Bus*

1980   *Uprisin'* is the last album released in Marley's lifetime

If there can be said to be anything constant in Neil Young's long career, it's that he has never been consistent. His forays into many diverse musical styles are charmingly eccentric. Not always successful, sometimes oddly obtuse, his unpredictability is, paradoxically, what attracts his many most fervent fans. Young apparently decided many years ago that life on the straight and narrow was not for him. There were too many interesting sideroads to explore, even if many proved to be dead ends.

Born and raised in Toronto, Canada, Young switched from high school rock to the folk circuit before moving to Los Angeles in 1963 with bassist Bruce Palmer. They teamed up with Stephen Stills, Richie Furay and Dewey Martin to form the very successful Buffalo Springfield, when Young's keening vocals and blossoming songwriting skills first gained international attention.

Signing a solo record deal in 1969, Young released one unsuccessful album before recruiting Crazy Horse as his backing band. Their first collaboration with Young, the 1969 album Everybody Knows This Is Nowhere, boasted at least three classics in 'Cinnamon Girl', 'Down By The River' and 'Cowgirl In The Sand', and sold more than a million copies in the US alone.

Joining David Crosby, Stephen Stills and Graham Nash to create CSNY in 1970 and enjoy superstar status, Young also continued to work with Crazy Horse. His After The Goldrush album was another international hit, aided in no small part by the impact of songs like 'Only Love Can Break Your Heart' (a US Top 40 single) and the dramatic 'Southern Man', while the 1972 set Harvest – the third in a row to go platinum – repeated its US success by reaching the top of the UK charts while 'Heart Of Gold' gave him his first US No.1 single.

In his first detour from predictability, in 1972 Young produced Journey Through The Past, an autobiographical documentary and soundtrack album which barely bothered the charts and shelved for 18 months his anguished Tonight's The Night set (a moribund tribute to Crazy Horse drug fatalities Danny Whitten and roadie Bruce Berry) while releasing the tame live album which teamed him with The Stray Gators, David Crosby and Graham Nash.

CSNY were reunited for one track of Young's 1976 album Zuma, but it was Long May You Run (billed as The Stills-Young Band) later that year which saw Young return confidently to the charts. Two more albums in 1978 – American Stars & Bars and the triple retrospective Decade – were only the warm-up for the successful acoustic offering Comes A Time and the multi-million seller Rust Never Sleeps. This saw Young re-united with Crazy Horse, something that would continue with the 1979 Live Rust double album and Neil's production (under the alias 'Bernard Shakey') of an in-concert, on-the-road movie.

The 1980s saw Young experiment even more, from the strong country feel of his 1981 album Hawks & Doves to the synthesiser doodlings and vocoder distortion he employed on Trans. He also tried his hand at old-style rock'n'roll (Everybody's Rockin' in 1984) and hard country (Old Ways in 1985), before returning to more consistent form – and the company of Crazy Horse – for the best-selling and critically acclaimed Ragged Glory in 1990.

Five new albums winged their way to Young's fans during the 1990s, the best of which were undoubtedly Unplugged (in 1993) and 1995's Mirror Ball, a set which saw him confidently rocking out with Pearl Jam. The first encapsulates Neil Young's continued ability to sing beautiful songs with hair-raising emotional intensity, while the second shows why anyone who thinks Neil Young is a spent force should be forced to spend a spell in thumbscrews.

Write him off at your peril...

Right: **There's a passion in everything Neil Young does, whether he's singing a ballad (as here in the late 70s) or tackling some hard rock magnum opus.**

Previous page: **The Crazy Horseman of the Apocalypse – Neil Young in typical sartorial disarray. Shopping for clothes has obviously never been a priority for the man from Toronto...**

September 14 1985 Adam Sweeting

LEGEND OF A LONER

Looking back 10 years or more, Young can now put his well-documented bleak period into a longer perspective. After "Harvest" had clocked up sales running into millions, Young's fans were horrified by the release of the double album "Journey Through The Past", a bitty and meaningless "soundtrack" for Young's rarely-seen film of the same name. After the album came out, the film company refused to release the movie, to Young's continuing disgust.

Next came the nerve-shredding live album "Time Fades Away", a dingy and macabre affair notably devoid of the pure melodies beloved of his soft-rockin' aficionados. Young, feeling boxed in by commercial success, had steered away from it. The chart performance of "Heart Of Gold" had brought him a lot of things he found he didn't want.

"I guess at that point I'd attained a lot of fame and everything that you dream about when you're a teenager. I was still only 23 or 24, and I realised I had a long way to go and this wasn't going to be the most satisfying thing, just sittin' around basking in the glory of having a hit record. It's really a very shallow experience, it's actually a very *empty* experience. "It's nothing concrete except ego-gratification, which is an extremely unnerving kind of feeling. So I think I subconsciously set out to destroy that and rip it down, before it surrounded me. I could feel a wall building up around me." To add insult to injury, his next studio recording was the harrowing "Tonight's The Night", though with a perversity that was becoming typical of him the latter wasn't released until *after* the subsequently-cut "On The Beach". Both albums stand up strongly to this day. Both use the rock format as a means of redemption and rejuvenation, the very act of recording (no overdubs) serving as therapy.

"'Tonight's The Night' and 'On The Beach' were pretty free records," Young pondered, lighting another unfiltered Pall Mall. "I was pretty down I guess at the time, but I just did what I wanted to do, at that time. I think if everybody looks back at their own lives they'll realise that they went through something like that. There's periods of depression, periods of elation, optimism and scepticism, the whole thing is... it just keeps coming in waves.

"You go down to the beach and watch the same thing, just imagine every wave is a different set of emotions coming in. Just keep coming. As long as you don't ignore it, it'll still be there. If you start shutting yourself off and not letting yourself live through the things that are coming through you, I think that's when people start getting old really fast, that's when they really age. 'Cos they decide that they're happy to be what they were at a certain time in their lies when they were the happiest, and they say, 'that's where I'm gonna be for the rest of my life'. From that minute on they're dead, y'know, just walking around. I try to avoid that."

One of the key tracks from "On The Beach' was "Revolution Blues". a predatory rocker in which Young adopts the persona of a trigger-happy psychotic, eager to slaughter Laurel Canyon's pampered superstar residents. Reflecting on the song prods Young into some unsettling areas. "That was based on my experiences with Charlie Manson. I met him a couple of times, and er ... very interesting person. Obviously he was quite *keyed up*."

Gulp. Before or ... *after* the Sharon Tate killings?

Left: **He's just an old folkie at heart – Neil relaxes back-stage with a warm guitar and a harmonica harness. Only the shades suggest he's one of the world's most successful and influential rock stars.**

"Before. About six months before. He's quite a writer and a singer, really unique – very unique, and he wanted very badly to get a recording contract. I was at (Beach Boy) Dennis Wilson's house when I met Charlie. Couple times.

"The thing about Charlie Manson was you'd never hear the same song twice. It was one of the interesting things about him. He had a very mysterious power about him which I'm hesitant to even fuckin' *think* about, it's so strong and it was so dark, so I really don't like to talk about it very much. I don't even know why I brought it up."

Young stopped talking for a moment. Thought we'd lost him, but he continued. "There is a saying that if you don't look the devil in the eye you're alright, but once you've looked him in the eye you'll never forget him, and there'll always be more devil in you than there was before.

"And it's hard to say, you know. The devil is not a cartoon character, like God is on one side of the page and he's on the other. The devil lives in everyone and God lives in everyone. There's no book that tells you when the devil said to God 'fuck you' and God said (makes raspberry noise). All those books that are written are just one person's opinion.

"I can't follow that, but I can see these things in other people. You can see it and feel it. But Manson would sing a song and just make it up as he went along, for three or four minutes, and he never would repeat one word, and it all made perfect sense and it shook you up to listen to it. It was so *good* that it scared you."

A couple of years later, then, Young wrote "Revolution Blues" – "well I'm a barrel of laughs with my carbine on, I keep them hopping till my ammunition's gone"... So how did the superstar community take it, Neil? "Well, see, I wasn't touring at the time, so I didn't really feel the reaction to 'On The Beach'. Then when I went on the road I didn't do any of it, so..."

He did, however, perform the song on the Crosby Stills Nash & Young reunion tour, to the discomfiture of the others.

"David Crosby especially was very uncomfortable, because it was so much the darker side. They all wanted to put out the light, y'know, make people feel good and happy and everything, and that song was like a wart or something on the perfect beast."

When it came to the release of "Tonight's The Night", Young again incurred the wrath and disbelief of people who thought they knew him fairly well. The album had been recorded with a Crazy Horse reconstituted after the death of songwriter and guitarist Danny Whitten, a close friend of Young's who'd given him early encouragement in his career.

Whitten had been due to go out on tour with Young, but was too heavily dependent on heroin to cope. Young sent him home. The same night, Whitten died of an overdose. "Time Fades Away" documented the subsequent tour, while "Tonight's The Night" was made in memory of Whitten and Bruce Berry, and CSNY roadie who also died from heroin.

Young remembered the day he'd taken "Tonight" into the offices of Reprise, his record company at the time. "It was pretty rocky," he grinned. "I would describe that as a rocky day. They couldn't believe how sloppy and rough it was, they couldn't believe that I really wanted to put it out.

"I said 'that's it, that's the way it's going out'. It's a very important record, I think, in my general field of things. It still stands up. The original 'Tonight's The Night' was much heavier than the one that hit the stands. The original one had only nine songs on it. It was the same takes, but the songs that were missing were 'Lookout Joe' and 'Borrowed Tune', a couple of songs that I added. They fit lyrically but they softened the blow a little bit.

"What happened was the original had only nine songs but it had a lot of talking, a lot of mumbling and talking between the group and me, more disorganised and fucked-up sounding than the songs, but there were intros to the songs. Not counts but little discussions, three and four word conversations between songs, and it left it with a very spooky feeling. It was like you didn't know if these guys were still gonna be alive in the morning, the way they were talking. More like a wake than anything else." Why did you take it off then?

"It was too strong." said Young slowly. "I was really too strong. I never even played it for the record company like that. We made our own decision not to do that. If they thought 'Tonight's The Night' was too much the way it came out – which they did, a lot of people – they're lucky they didn't hear the other one."

It was here that Young hit the lowest patch, spiritually, of his career, probably of his life. His impatience nowadays with the hippie generation, and his endorsement of a right-wing President, believed by many to be a

Above: **Creator of one of the most distinctive guitar styles in modern rock'n'roll, Neil found new impetus for his tougher work with Crazy Horse in 1969, before he teamed up with David Crosby, Stephen Stills and Graham Nash.**

dangerous lunatic, can probably be traced back to the traumas around the time of "Tonight's The Night". Until then, the ride had been more or less free. Was it, I queried, a case of Whitten's death being not only a personal tragedy, but a metaphor for a generation and a way of life? Or death? "It just seemed like it really stood for a lot of what was going on," Young answered. "It was like the freedom of the Sixties and free love and drugs and everything...it was the price tag. This is your bill. Friends, young guys dying, kids that didn't even know what they were doing, didn't know what they were fucking around with. It hit me pretty hard, a lot of those things, so at that time I did sort of exorcise myself."

Did you feel guilty that perhaps you and people in your position had encouraged that?

"Somewhat, yeah, I think so. that's part of the responsibility of freedom. Freedom to do what you want with not much experience to realise the consequences. I didn't feel *very* guilty, but I felt a little guilty."

It's fitting that Young's latest re-emergence in public with yet another shift in musical direction should coincide with a wave a new groups who acknowledge a debt to his part work. Green on Red's Dan Stuart freely admits that their "Gas Food Lodging" LP was heavily influenced by Young's epic "Zuma" collection ("if you're gonna steal, steal from the best," as Stuart puts it). Jason & the Scorchers play "Are You Ready For The Country", the Beat Farmers turn in a welt-raising treatment of "Powderfinger", and Pete Wylie's just cut a version of "The Needle And The Damage Done" as an anti-heroin gesture. And Dream Syndicate's Steve Wynn will reminisce about Young and Crazy Horse any time you like.

Above: **Giving his all in the mid-70s with Crazy Horse bassist Billy Talbot. Some of Neil's best work was achieved with that band during a 15 years-long association, in concert and in the recording studio.**

With half the material for a follow-up album to "Old Ways" already in the can, Young is in the middle of a renaissance of sorts. Not even the AIDS terror can dent his confidence.

"It is scary. You go to a supermarket and you see a faggot behind the fuckin' cash register, you don't want him to handle your potatoes. It's true! It's paranoid but that's the way it is – even though it's not just gay people, they're taking the rap. There's a lotta religious people, of course, who feel that this is God's work. God's saying, y'know, 'no more buttfucking or we're gonna getcha'," Young cackled dementedly.

"I don't know what it is. It's natural, that's one thing about it. It's a living organism or virus, whatever it is. I hope they find something to stop it. It's worse than the Killer Bees." Young, obviously, isn't making a play for the Gay vote. They probably don't hold with that sort of thing in the country. But his conception of the entire universe is, to say the least, unorthodox.

"I'm not into organised religion. I'm into believing in a higher source of creation, realising that we're all just part of nature and we're all animals. We're very highly evolved and we should be very responsible for what we've learned.

"I even go as far as to think that in the plan of things, the natural plan of things, that the rockets and the satellites, spaceships, that we're creating now are really... we're pollinating, as a universe, and it's a part of the universe. Earth is a flower and it's pollinating.

"It's starting to send out things, and now we're evolving, they're getting bigger and they're able to go further. And they have to, because we need to spread out now in the universe. I think in 100 years we'll be living on other planets."

On a more earthly plane, Young's excited about the prospect of playing a benefit for the people of Cheyenne, Wyoming, whose houses and land have been devastated by a freak sequence of natural disasters. Young's band and equipment will be airlifted in for the show, by National Guard C130 transport aircraft and by private jets loaned for the occasion by some giant corporations.

"There's something different about it," Young mused, "having the government help us get there so we can help the farmers. The National Guard's gonna help us load and unload, get in and outta the place, help us set up the stage. It's interesting."

But it's something else, above and beyond his this-land-is-your-land preoccupations, that gives Neil Young his lingering aura of menace and strange purpose. You can feel it when you talk to him, and it permeates all his best music. He sees it something like this.

"I've got a few demons, but I manage to co-exist with them. The demons are there all the time y'know, that's what makes you crazy, that's what makes me play my guitar the way I play it sometimes. Depends on the balance, how strong the demons are that night, how strong the good is.

"There's always a battle between good and evil in every second in your life, I think. In every judgement you make both sides are represented in your mind. You may hide the bad side, but it's there."

Above: **Have guitars, will travel. Only for this song, during one of the many solo acoustic concerts he's given down the years, Neil Young opts to accompany himself on the banjo. He is also, as you probably know, a pretty nifty pianist too. It's called talent.**

key recordings

1969 *Everybody Knows This Is Nowhere* heralds the arrival of a great team: Neil Young and Crazy Horse. The album sells a million in the US, while singles *Cinnamon Girl*, *Down By The River* and *Cowgirl In The Sand* are all hits

1970 While working with Crosby, Stills and Nash, Neil has solo hit with *After The Goldrush*, still with Crazy Horse

1972 *Harvest* is third Neil Young album to go platinum

1977 A triumphant return to form with *American Stars & Bars*, while the triple retrospective, *Decade*, gives Young another million-seller

1979 Back with Crazy Horse, Young tours the US and releases *Rust Never Sleeps* album and movie documentary

1981 Back to the country with a team which includes former Band drummer Levon Helm, Young releases *Hawks & Doves*

1990 Crazy Horse back in the saddle for this year's Young classic, *Ragged Glory*

1993 One of the greatest in-concert albums ever as Neil Young appears *Unplugged* with a host of long-time musical buddies

1995 Neil Young and Pearl Jam? It worked beautifully on *Mirror Ball*

If any one artist can be said to have completely dominated the world rock music scene in the 1980s, it was Bruce Springsteen, a man who leaped from the obscurity of New Jersey clubland to filling most of the world's biggest stadiums, selling untold millions of records and becoming the iconic representation of America's blue-collar workers.

Born to a working class family of Dutch extraction in 1949, Springsteen began playing guitar and writing his first songs at the age of 13, his music owing a huge acknowledged debt to 1950s rock 'n' roll giants, not least Phil Spector's massive-sounding productions.

Springsteen had, by 1972, assembled a band capable of playing all night long, if the mood took them. His manager, Mike Appel, talked the legendary Columbia Records producer John Hammond into attending an audition session. He promptly signed Springsteen up, unusually allowing singer and manager to produce.

The resulting Greetings From Asbury Park, NJ (1973) and The Wild, The Innocent And The E Street Shuffle (1974) revealed a powerful and imaginative lyricist/composer capable with a fascination of life on society's murkier fringes.

While neither sold well, the buzz surrounding Springsteen's climaxed with top rock critic Jon Landau describing Springsteen as "the future of rock 'n' roll." With Landau replacing Appel behind the studio glass Springsteen produced Born To Run in 1975, a much richer sounding and dramatic collection of songs. Backed by a huge international PR operation, Springsteen became the first entertainer to appear on the covers of Time and Newsweek magazines simultaneously as Born To Run raced to No.3 in the US album charts. Bruce Springsteen had the world at his feet.

He also had Mike Appel on his tail. Artist and manager had fallen out and Appel consulted lawyers. Served with an injunction which stopped him recording for almost two years, Springsteen enlarged his E Street Band with guitarist Steve Van Zandt, and hit the road running.

Springsteen created a three-hour show that left sell-out audiences limp and bootleggers delighted. Meanwhile, the man they now called 'The Boss' had the pleasure of seeing his income benefit from hit covers, most especially Manfred Mann ('Blinded By The Light'), Patti Smith ('Because The Night') and The Pointer Sisters ('Fire'). When his beef with Appel was finally settled, Springsteen was able to record again.

Darkness At The Edge Of Town, his 1977 come-back, was more restrained than many had expected. Springsteen began work on his next album even while his exhaustive touring schedule continued unabated. In 1979 all his experience poured out on the brilliantly diverse double album The River. The album hit No.1 in the US and sold vast amounts in every country with electricity. With his live show now a massive four-hour epic, Springsteen toured the US and Europe.

He then sprang a surprise by releasing the solo acoustic (and ultra-sparse) Nebraska in 1982. Released with little fuss, it still lodged in the upper reaches of the US and British charts for six months.

Springsteen's recording career reach its pinnacle in 1984 when Born In The USA began a two-year residency in the US charts, spending seven weeks at No.1. Seven of the album's tracks became hit singles while the title track achieved patriotic anthem status, even if the lyrics actually dealt with a Vietnam veteran's disillusionment with his country of birth.

Springsteen raided his own archives for the 40-track Live: 1975–85 which was released in 1986 and gave him another worldwide smash. So, too, was the 1987 album Tunnel Of Love after which Springsteen lent his weight to the Amnesty International Human Rights Now! world tour with Sting and Peter Gabriel.

For much of the 1990s Springsteen appeared content to chill out with his wife, Patti Scialfa and his son, who was born in 1990. The albums that he did release (including Lucky Town and The Ghost of Tom Joad) displayed a repeated concern for society's losers and victims.

Just when his fans must have despaired of seeing The Boss strut his stuff on big stages again, Columbia released 18 Tracks, a box-set of previously unreleased material, in early 1999 and Springsteen – plus the E Street Band – began a world tour in Europe.

At the time of writing, that tour is still underway, breaking box-office records across America. It's just like he never was gone.

September 30 1974 Michael Watts

LONE STAR

It rained torrents that week in Texas, but the outlook never seemed less than fine. We were down there for a christening, anyway, albeit a little late in the day.

The baby, you see, has been bawling for our attentions, and most of us have been a little slow to notice. And then, it's a very HUNGRY baby we have here.

So Texas it was, though it could have been anywhere, because Bruce Springsteen is some baby, all of 25 years old and pretty seasoned as far as these things go; you figure he'll have the crowds on top of their seats anyplace he turns up.

He wants a shot at the big title, as they say, and in turn a growing number of people would like to see him take that crown which has been bobbing from head to head of every rock and roll champ in the past two decades.

In their minds he's the logical contender, the new golden boy of rock 'n' roll, who's finally emerged from the fastnesses of New Jersey bars and campus halls to bid for the public's heart.

You talk to almost anybody in New York and what do they say? "Bruce Springsteen! Oh, sure, he's great. But, sugar, you've seen NUTHIN'. You shoulda been there TWO YEARS AGO when he was playing at the Student Prince in Asbury Park. THAT was really somethin'."

And so on, blah, blah, blah. New Yorkers always like being like that after the event.

But in Texas, that big, lone star state brooding southwest on the map, where the news takes a while to filter down, it's hard to be blasé, especially when the rain is falling in gut-buckets.

"Springsteen, you say? Jewish fella?" We-ell, no. Of Dutch origin, actually, a Catholic, but we'll let that pass.

It's not their fault. Bruce Springsteen has only just begun to break big anywhere, to touch that vital psychic nerve of a mass audience which sets the ball rolling, and no one can be absolutely sure why it's happening now, though those who've seen him lately instinctively feel his rapport with the goddess of fortune.

Two years ago, however, when that benign spirit John Hammond signed him to Columbia Records, the press mostly snickered up their sleeves about the "new Bob Dylan". Springsteen replied with his manic-euphoric grin, and then they wrote him off as some kind of Dr. Demento.

"Madman drummers bummers and Indians in the summer with a teenage diplomat" – they always picked up on that first, and wildly off line from his first album, 'Greetings from Asbury Park, N.J.' and dismissed the rest as junk in some sort of summary tribunal.

After all, surely you had to be a nut, gobbling bennies, or some misdirected/informed Dylan disciple to write like that, didn't you?

To his credit – or perhaps he was just oblivious – Springsteen hung

Right: **Springsteen's early shows were a revolutionary blend of raucous, down-and-dirty roadhouse rock and Phil Spector bombast that soon found an audience eager to share his vision.**

Previous page: **All hail The Boss! For a man who once said he'd never play stadiums, Springsteen has never had any trouble filling the world's biggest arenas.**

on in, sustained by kind words from worshippers who had seen him in his long-haired, bar-band days back in Asbury and thereabouts, plus new fans who were jolted back by the fierce, jumping current of his personality, with its foggy mumblings and impenetrabilia, the feisty stance of the street punk, and those lyrics that leapt at the inner ear with their roll-call of weird, vibrant characters – Wild Billy, Crazy Janey, Rosalita, Weak Knee Willie and the whole steamy essence of Latin street-life that has wafted out from the kitchen of his imagination.

He stuck to it the only way a musician can – he kept on playing even though other bands took fright at him and wouldn't, increasingly, use him as a support in case they were blown away – and a double difficulty here, because he was opposed anyway to gigs with heavy rock sets and their attendant zombie audiences.

Finally, he had a job getting booked anywhere outside New York and New Jersey. But he didn't seem unduly bothered because, as he often said, he'd as soon play to 15 people as 1,500 if the music was right.

Although the second album, 'The Wild, The Innocent And The E Street Shuffle', sold more than the first, Springsteen had still not really registered as the major artist Columbia and John Hammond had prophesied, and Hammond – everybody always brought this up – had been the guy who brought Dylan to the label a decade before.

The presence of the Minnesota Kid did seem in all truth to loom uncomfortably over any young unfortunate who had aspiration,

Left: **For a man who's always thrived on putting on long stage shows, Springsteen spent a surprising amount of his early career hiding his light under this woolly bushel – it was as central to his image as occasional beards and an endless supply of black T-shirts.**

even circumstantially, to the crown.

Just because he was new, and he had the beard and the hair...it was too bad, it really was, and him not even Jewish. Springsteen, in fact, only owned a few Dylan singles – being too shy to ask his record company for the catalogue – and he'd never even seen Dylan perform, since Bobby hadn't made it to Asbury before the motorcycle disaster.

They still said he'd been influenced by him – well, if you were healthy at all, he reasoned, you'd better be influenced by him!

And then, in the middle of this year, the numbers appeared to click in the perfect combination. No longer playing to chick peas and shell steaks at Max's Kansas City, that downtown pitch for wide-eyed tourists, he and his E Street Band were booked in July into the posh Bottom Line Club, Greenwich Village's finest and the kind of place where CBS president Goddard Lieberson might feel more at home.

In the space of a couple of nights the boast of his manager, Mike Appel, that this scruffy kid with the perpetual grin was the "finest actor/artist in the history of rock 'n' roll" could no longer be laughed off on the rock gossip circuit, but had to be fed for analysis into the critical computer.

A top-notch American rock critic had already come out with his own strip of ticker-tape proclaiming Springsteen as "the future of rock 'n' roll." In New York at least nobody laughed after that, nobody said it was "Bellevue rock" anymore. At concerts girls threw red roses to him in a Spanish love tryst, stages buckled from too many vociferous feet.

And a lot of people began remarking, "do you remember that time we went out to New Jersey, and there was that band...?"

To be fair, it was certainly true that Springsteen's performance had developed in a year since he was Upstairs at Max's.

At New York's Avery Hall in October, what once were mannerisms had flowered into a perfect synchromesh of rock 'n' roll ballet – theatrics without the tricks, movements and dances assimilated from old Sixties soul revues, bits of stage business with the drummer and the black tenorist, a gift for mimicry, and this big, dramatic whisper that Springsteen employed as one weapon in his vocal armoury – a whisper roughed out hoarse and attractive, played off against an acoustic piano and a violin at certain sections in his performance.

More than ever, too, it was apparent that his musical roots were embedded in the thundering symphonies of Spectorland, secured especially in the styles of Spector's girlie groups: in the Crystals and Ronnie and the Ronettes, several of the girls themselves from New Jersey, of course. One of his proudest possessions, it later emerged, was a signed colour photograph of Ronnie Spector.

Springsteen's heart, evidently, was back there in the Fifties and early Sixties. His poetic intellect had absorbed the songwriting advances of the Sixties and Seventies – those knotty problems of metre and internal rhyme – but he intuitively anticipated in his new audiences the response for that uncluttered, emotional freshness embodied in a song like 'And Then He Kissed Me'.

The number, in fact, with which he closed his Avery Hall show that night was the old, joyful rabble-rouser, Gary US Bonds' 'Quarter To Three'.

In those few months since the Bottom Line performances his album sales have started to pick up in America, especially those of his second record, which has gone past the 80,000 mark. Still, that isn't too great; by big league standards it's even a failure.

So the people who know about these things are forever badgering

him to bring in a big-time producer instead of Mike Appel, someone like Richard Perry, maybe, or Bob Johnson, or...Phil Spector.

Springsteen says no, summoning a rueful smile for his elders and betters. He and Appel managed it okay together, as far as he's concerned. All his records had been commercial, he thought, and no sounds had gone down he disagreed with.

Although there's a smell of burning somewhere, he remains very loyal to Appel, while Appel announces, in very precise tones, that his artist's "presence on stage dwarfs any musical attempt on vinyl. Any album is a disaster in comparison."

His record company, meanwhile, bites its nails and waits for the third album in the early part of next year.

Other artists, maybe, will break his songs first. David Bowie has recorded 'Growing Up' and 'It's Hard To Be A Saint In The City', the Hollies have done '4th Of July Asbury Park', and Allan Clark 'If I Were The Priest'.

But Springsteen doesn't want to be just a fat cat on some publisher's shelf. He's looking for the main action.

OF these musical politics, however, the good people of Austin, Texas, know nothing, though the name of Bruce Springsteen is well-remembered from a gig last year at the Armadillo World Headquarters, a big 2,000-capacity club that likes to think of itself as a Fillmore in a city with pretensions to the cultural cosiness of old-time San Francisco.

Austin, situated on the Colorado River in the Texan interior, if that's the phrase, plays home to Doug Sahm and the 40,000-student University of Texas, and once, indeed, to Charles Whitman, who from the top of a tower near the main drag rifled 18 people to death. Kinky Friedman, another Texan, and a Jew to boot, wrote a catchy ballad about it; that's one way to achieve immortality.

During the day a travelling rock band in this city might occupy itself

Above: **The Springsteen Whisper** – 'roughed out hoarse and attractive, played off against an acoustic piano and a violin...'

looking through a number of thrift shops for old 45s and 78s on Dial, Duke/Peacock, Josie and other, more arcane, labels.

But at night, after a cloud-burst, the visitor is greeted only with streets dripping empty and miserable, surfaces black and shiny, with the neon strips of hamburger joints little more than cold comfort.

We find Springsteen late at night in the Fun Arcade on Main Street, which is where one would have expected him arriving in a small town.

He's literally running from game to game – from the pool tables to the pin-football, at which the Tex-Mex kids are so adept – to Pong (the official name for "television tennis"), and on to Air Hockey, a two-player game that involves slamming the puck between goalmouths across an air-cushioned tabletop.

He's a small guy, about five foot seven, with a deceptively rumpled, sleepy face – deceptive because he's winning at all these games.

Tufts of curly hair grow out from under a grey cloth po'boy cap, his skin is sallow, and the beard is scraggy. But with his rubbed jeans, beat-up leather jacket, and this hat tipped raffishly over one eye, he becomes at second glance something quite charismatic...a pool hall hustler, a Fifties runaway, floating cool with his hard-earned savvy, the kind of character that Kerouac would immediately have recognised and set down.

A peculiarly anachronistic air clings to Springsteen. After observing him a few moments shooting pool and rattling up big scores with such intensity, I start to think that he should've been a Beat poet himself, hopping on boxcars around America, sharing a bottle of wine with ol' Ti Jean and the hobos out in the yards and then writing down his fleeting sensations, each rush of thought, on scraps of paper he stuffed about his clothes.

That was another age, when electric guitars weren't so common, but Springsteen still gives off this heady whiff of pristine romance, of nostalgia for the wide-open America that this rock generation has never known, some outlaw quality of adventuring that cuts right across all this business of middle-class white boys leaving school to sing black men's music.

And again, the well-thumbed line comes straight to mind, that nobody ever taught him how to live out on the street. Because he already knew, knew instinctively.

On the Thursday morning, when the New York Times calls the Sheraton Inn in Austin, Springsteen turns to the man from CBS and asks if he's really got to do the interview.

"It's only ten minutes out of your life."

"But why?"

"It can help you. They want to do a big story."

Springsteen brightens at a sudden thought. "You got the wheels, right? Okay, let's go out and play. Let's go get some hamburgers" – his favourite food, since fancy cuisine makes him uncomfortable.

He treats the CBS man to a hoarse, compulsive chuckle. His voice has a husk on it like a kernel.

"You really should talk to him. It is the New York Times."

There is a pause before he grumbles assent. "Aw, okay."

Springsteen avoids interviews if he can, apparently not out of bolshevism or with any attempt to envelop himself in mystique, but because he finds it hard to adjust to the brittle game of question and answer, of careful probing, smart deceptions and double-guessings that are supposed to elicit some approximation of the truth.

He is too real to put his faith in the glamour of headlines, too mindful of his privacy to undervalue his personal feelings at the sight of a notebook or tape recorder. This attitude is really a corollary of his dislike of rock stardom, which he professes to find as meaningless, as most rock stars are unappealing to him.

They're jokes, hoaxes, gyps, he's fond of saying, because every other person can be one if he's willing to surrender himself to a public relations man.

"They're just people who wanna crawl back in the womb," he will say, "people who have built their own reality and are afraid of reality itself." Being a rock star was letting yourself be controlled, and that way you cheated yourself.

So no, he doesn't ever want to be a big, hyped-up rock star, playing at Madison Square Garden, where kids will need binoculars to see him. "I hope somebody shoots me offstage," he says, "if they ever see me there, because then I'll deserve it."

The band, guys who've been out on the road for some years, several of them spent with Springsteen, are less sure what's involved. The organist, for one, Danny Federici, a taciturn, sandy-haired man who also played with Bruce in a group called Steel Mill back in the old Jersey days.

"I don't know what to make of the whole thing," he says. "I don't even know what to think of the way the audiences respond. I know Bruce is good, I know that, but I don't really understand what it is, or how they let it all out the way some of the people do for our concerts."

Still, it's essentially Springsteen's responsibility. He supervises the music as totally as he orchestrates the audience's emotions, and the E Street Band is a group in which personal expression has to be sublimated in the collective effort in which there's a group sound and infrequent soloing, since one of Springsteen's musical ideals is the sound-mesh that Dylan achieved on his electric albums.

Only Danny, briefly, gets a large slice of the spotlight, just as it was Al Kooper alone who was allowed to rise out of the mix on 'Highway 61'.

Springsteen has picked them all carefully. The bassist, Garry W. Tallent, has been with him since '71 when Bruce led another band of Jersey renown, Dr. Zoom and the Sonic Boom. The pianist, Roy Bittan, arrived in September after long-time keyboardsman Davey Sancious became too idiosyncratic with his prepared piano pieces and iconoclastic Debussy style, while the present drummer, Max Weinberg, was auditioned around the same time.

He's a number one pupil of Pretty Purdie and, among other former occupations, an ex-Broadway pit player (The Magic Show and Godspell), showbiz experience that Springsteen particularly utilises in his rapid number of time switches and off-the-cuff routines.

Right: **A new style in hats when his career began to take off. It was one like this that the MM's Michael Watts and five others bought in Texas when his feature on Springsteen was being written.**

But the main man is Clarence Clemons, a big, imposing black tenorist who was a football player in the Cleveland Browns until he got a leg injury, and who once held down a spot as one of James Brown's Famous Flames.

Clarence also sings harmonies, and he's a kind of foil for Springsteen, this huge dude, standing front left setting of the diminutive singer – Clarence in his white suit, black shirt and hat, with the shades, counterpointing this skinny, hungry-looking kid who looks as if he's been leaning on fire hydrants all his life.

The band is as tight as the fingers on a hand, all living within ten miles of each other in New Jersey, near the beach and not far from Asbury Park, just so's rehearsals will be easier to arrange.

On Thursday at the Armadillo there are no visiting dignitaries, but the audience is greater than the previous evening's, a crowd of tall Texan gals and young longhairs in dirty-cream cowboy hats cocked back on their heads, in their hands huge pitchers of pale beer which they slop in the glasses of whoever is standing near.

It's a crowd that wants to boogie and crack those empty cans of Lone Star beer under their scuffed boot-heels in this large barn of a joint, warm but still redolent of the rainy night outside.

So they're unprepared and somewhat off-balance when Springsteen walks out in his battered duds with little, scholarly Roy, the pianist, and Suki, who just happens to be the wife of his sound engineer, Louis Lehav, and spent time in the Israeli Youth Ork – this slight, tiny blonde, a heart-stealer in rolled-up denims and boots, a thumb-nail sketch of charming, fragile femininity, who crooks a violin in her shoulder.

And Bruce, in his muscle tee-shirt with his hair haloed by the lighting, a tender John Garfield characterisation with one hand fingering the veins in his arm, eyes hooded in shades, Bruce starts in on his uptown drama of Spanish Johnny, sad-eyed Romeo figure, looking for a sweet word from his girl, all the sounds of the city in the song, with the violin like a breath of night wind across the West River.

And the cowpokes, even if they're all maths students, most likely at the university, cease their crunching and slurping. "And from out of the shadows came a young girl's voice, that said: 'Johnny don't cry'…"

Springsteen whispering over the mike in a long moment of total magnetic concentration, until on the last piano note, a single delicate droplet, the crowd bellows out its huge roar of rough approval.

And from that instant Springsteen has them, Austin and Texas, by the horns, all out to ride the emotions off 'em.

He always performs this single song, 'Incident On 57th Street', as his opening number, and then brings on the rest of his band: Clemons, clutching his gleaming horn; Garry Tallent, vaguely Leon Russell with his flowing brown hair and beard; Max's face virtually obscured by the hovering cymbals; and Danny on last, the sandy moustache with its hint of truculence, sitting right across the stage from Roy Bittan.

They ease out with the familiar Crystals oldie, altered naturally to 'And Then She Kissed Me', and then Bruce's own 'Spirit In The Night', Clemons and Tallent on the harmonies, a rasping big band sound, Weinberg driving and hopping them along, Bruce skinny-legging it around the stage, and the audience fully twitching now, caught in the spell of the event.

The music is truly overwhelming, a wild, heady mixture of lyrical mosaics refracted through a warm glow of nostalgia, memories of nights spent listening to the radio under the bed covers, when music was undiluted and young, the same almost forgotten stab of joy, but undeniably Seventies R&B, the music brought keen and wailing into the present times and suggesting at every other turn the influence of jazz and Latin sounds.

The measure of its exciting effect is its refusal to be pinned down, but for me at least it touches some particularly sensitive chord, submerged deep in the rubble of the subconscious, that's exhilarating but also disturbing, because it's rarely exposed so completely.

I listen to Springsteen like I used to listen to Dylan, John Lennon and Chuck Berry – as though a life depended on it and no more can be said than that.

Just one impressive factor about Bruce Springsteen is his encyclopaedic knowledge of rock 'n' roll and the intuitive use to which he puts it. Eddie Cochran brushes shoulders with the Crickets and Bo Diddley, Phil Spector appears all over the place, and in the live version of 'Rosalita' he throws

Left: **Springsteen does not seem able to give less than 110 per cent once the spotlight lands on him.**

off a Four Tops riff. On 'Sandy' he even uses Federici on accordion, possibly inspired by the Beach Boys' 'God Only Knows'.

But the noise and smells of street-life crowd in on him. I shut my eyes and I can see those dirty New York yellow cabs, nosing in wolfpacks down the hot asphalt on Eighth Avenue, the charred stink of bagels in the air. Manhattan or the tackytowns of New Jersey, he hasn't wandered far from either.

"It's hard to be a saint in the city," he sings with an edge of pride, a sentiment chock-full of New York attitudinising.

Tough cops, bar fights, jukeboxes, pimps, alleyways, Harleys, greasers, filthy denims, circuses, boardwalks, Spanish razorboys, trains and tenements – this is his literary stomping ground.

Springsteen, born in Freehold, New Jersey, lives these days in an outlying district of Asbury called West End. Asbury Park is a seaside town in Eastern New Jersey, with a population about 50 per cent black and crammed in the summer with tourists who haven't got the money to go to Atlantic City up the coast.

It was the usual story. His mother had bought him a guitar when he was nine, but he hadn't taken it seriously until he was 13, around the tail-end of that golden age of rock 'n' roll, and just before the Beatles arrived to whip up every white kid's latent fantasy of success in the adult world.

Elvis, the Chiffons, Sam Cooke, the Shirelles, Chuck Berry, the Isley Brothers – every night he went home and put those babies on the record player, seeking out the release promised in the black grooves.

Rock 'n' roll, he swore, was what kept him from going nuts, but it was the genuine, horny old stuff he dug. The Beatles were pop, and the Rolling Stones he stopped buying after 'December's Children'. Something to do with the fancy production.

He was in and out of various bands, even making nightly trips to the Cafe Wha! in Greenwich Village, but his first important group was Child.

Danny Federici was another member, Bruce was 18, and the band went off to San Francisco and cut a four hour tape for Bill Graham's Fillmore Records – so good, according to Federici, that Graham offered their manager 2,000 dollars to sign, which wasn't considered enough.

They came back and changed their name to Steel Mill, playing heavy rock, and picked up a reputation in the Jersey towns, where they could play to two or three thousand people a time for 500 dollars and 50 per cent of the gate, even without a record company.

He wrote a lot more in those days. Every weekend the band had a new repertoire. And he was into the image, sexy with his shoulder-length hair and his guitar slung low, low down. Until one night it wasn't enough any longer. They were a big local act, and yet one evening Bruce walks out onstage and he doesn't feel it any more, it's almost as if he were parodying himself, and there and then he decides to bust it up.

It was hard on Federici. His wife had just left him and there was Bruce saying it was all over. He still has a mental picture of himself stuck in his hallway with his suitcase, trying to figure where to go next. The next two years he never played for anyone unless they paid him upfront, he felt so hurt.

As for Springsteen, he set up another band, Dr. Zoom and the Sonic Boom, which included Garry Tallent and practically everyone else he knew who could play an instrument. He was still searching for the right vehicle, and then hitched his name to a ten-piece band loaded with horns and R&B riffs, that eventually whittled itself down to seven, and then five.

They had been friendly for a long time with Looking Glass, seen how

they hit the jackpot with 'Brandy', a Number One American single, and wondered why they weren't hitting it, with Bruce writing these great, colourful songs – and wondered especially why Tinker, Springsteen's manager from way back, hadn't ever clinched that record deal.

A vote was taken, and one morning Springsteen went sorrowfully back to the surfboard factory where he and Tinker lived, and delivered the black spot. The guy was fixing his truck, underneath it. He didn't say a word.

It was through him that Springsteen met Mike Appel.

BY the time we've all boarded the group bus that Friday morning, ready to leave a very rained-out Austin, a rather unnerving change has swept through the whole party.

Five or six of us are wearing hats like Springsteen's, bought in town from the Texas Hatter and pulled down low over one ear in the true style of the Depression era, so that we resemble young Okies, or the Little Rascals, depending on your imagination.

Springsteen looks amused at his groupies, but he never says a word. From this point, leather jackets, jeans and caps, beat up and lived in, become something of a uniform.

Above: **Riding high on the international success of his Born To Run album, Springsteen and the indomitable Clarence Clemons receive the applause of another ten thousand or so acolytes.**

The bus pulls out at midday on its 200-mile trek to Corpus Christi, a town on the Gulf of Mexico which combines, one is led to understand, the palm-treed pleasures of a resort with the financial income of oil refineries.

Just above Springsteen's bunk, where he's curled up in a blanket, a single red rose hangs from the roof, a tribute cast by an admirer at the Tower Theatre in Philadelphia. But Bruce is suspended in his own uneasy limbo, drained of sleep by the previous two days' performances. He dreams he's being driven across a rough landscape and up a huge mountain, slowly and terrifyingly, because the incline is vertical. And then it stops, and he's poised, safety resting on a clenched breath, his body almost upside down, jagged edges below...

When he awakens, sweaty and anxious, to cars speeding by on the highway, he fishes around for an explanation of the dream. "And the mountain was called Success, right?" grins one of the party.

He explains that during a performance he has to fulfil two needs, the physical and the emotional, and that sometimes you do one, sometimes the other, but usually you fall short on both.

Inside himself he envisions these little gates, and throughout the performance he goes through each one until BOOM! – the big release! But always there's another one there, always just one, and the intensity of the feeling burns in his stomach, needing to be released, because performing is the only thing he ever does in his life and he has to go all the way with it.

His philosophy is, you have to drain yourself, your band and your audience, and in its place the performer leaves something else, an indefinable something. But for all parties it's the sense of release that's important. Music is simply the modus operandi.

"Because," he will elaborate, "a movie, music, a book – whatever – everybody uses these things to satisfy a need. Creating is a release in itself. Everything's a release.

"That's what it's about in this society – you gotta get released," laughing at his own intensity. "That's what everybody wants, that's why the audience come, man. They don't come to say, 'hey, you're great!' or to be jived with rock stars and stuff – they mightn't even know why they come – but they come to get release, to be set free.

"They think they're gonna get something they need, and it's gotta be more than just jump up and down and 'boogie, boogie!' What happens is that people cheat themselves and they don't know it. I would never cheat myself. If you don't cheat yourself you don't cheat anybody. You can never play too much, for example, there are never too many encores.

"If you can't let me do an encore let me smash a chair or somethin'. I don't know if here's ever enough of a release. Maybe it comes when you die, the Ultimate Release..."

IN Corpus Christi that night, where he's topping the bill over old Sir Douglas Quintet organist, Augie Meyer, the local cat from San Antonio, he does four encores, even though here are only 300 people in the 1,700 Ritz Theater.

There's been no airplay on him, no announcements, no advertising. As a word of mouth he's a whisper down here in darkest Texas...but the audience is ecstatic, going totally bananas in this bare, white-bricked theatre that was built back in the 1920s as a vaudeville hall.

And Springsteen gushes, coming off really high, saying, "No, man, it doesn't matter how many there are. Sometimes it's even better when there's not a lot there. You get off yourself and the band."

He knows that next time he played there it would be full; but it's

152

unlikely there will be a next time. For this is an altogether grey, creepy town. Several years ago a hurricane blew in from the Gulf and took Corpus away with it, and though the physical scars have been patched up, in spirit it's only one graduation from a ghost town.

So much for sun-kissed beaches. The resort has shut down for winter, the air is clammy and cold.

So no-one was unhappy to leave that alien town for Houston, a wide, expanding sprawl of a city, not unlike Los Angeles in its centre-less architectural concept. Sitting, later, in his Houston hotel room, Springsteen can look back on his Corpus performance and say, "I had a good time, but right now it seems like a kind of a void. It didn't seem complete enough."

If only he could have done a final encore, he broods, the show in the Houston Music Hall might have come close to the perfect emotional dissolve that he's seeking. But the management's fear of the unions prevented them from performing and he wanders off dejectedly as the audience swarms out, upset that he's not physically spent, that there's energy left with no place to go...

So, late this Saturday evening, in Houston's downtown Holiday Inn, Bruce Springsteen is slowly shaking off his post-performance blues and equalising his emotions.

He's saying that when he gets back to New Jersey he has to make a lot of changes in the band, to get more depth. He feels he's just on the perimeter of what he should be doing.

But perhaps inside he's remembering that night years ago when he walked out on-stage and suddenly found he was only parodying himself, that it had become a bore. He's only too aware now of how he needs that shiny hit record to sustain his momentum, that elusive combustible which will break open another door for him, just as he once stepped through a door that took him into rock 'n' roll and off the streets.

And yet change is all around him. He spends long weeks on the road now. He will see less and less of Asbury Park which, though no millionaires' row, has been a big source of inspiration for his music. He's rarely written on the road before, but he will have to adjust. His consciousness is developing. He has to work it all out.

He's a guy who might have gone bad, or just become a bum, but found this little seed within himself and learned what makes it grow, till he's filled up inside with lots of different goodies.

Everybody has it but most people just never figure it out. Springsteen says his father was one of those. "And there are guys still out there, guys my age, guys a lot older."

So with this perspective he sees his function, his role, if he has any at all, as one of trying to show people some quality, some emotion, that is real, and the way he tells it is less pompous than it sounds.

He says, "You've got to be able to see yourself for what you are, and not until that can you improve on what you are and be what you want to be. But people throw it away for a hoax, the Big American Hoax. For me, I can't deal with life in reference to governments and politics. I have to deal with it on a personal level.

"If you look at Bob Dylan, that's what he was doin'. 'Blowin' In The Wind' was all right, but I don't like it half as much as 'I Want You', 'Like A Rolling Stone' or anything on 'Blonde on Blonde'.

"'I Want You' – that's it, that's the ultimate statement you can make to anybody. What else can you say? And that's the greatest lyric in the song, those three words, in the whole damn song! I put that on, man,

Right: **The calm before yet another storm. Springsteen checks out the acoustics of one more cavern, soon to be filled by the faithful.**

and I get blown away, I get blown down the street, 'cause there's no hoax there, it was real, real as hell."

In his own songs Springsteen tries for that same honesty, searching however wildly for some clear picture of himself. "I don't know what I'm writing from," he says, "but the main thing I've always been worried about was me.

"I had to write about me all the time, every song, 'cause in a way you're trying to find out what that 'me' is. That's where I choose where I grew up, and where I live, and I take situations that I'm in, and people I know, and take 'em to the limits."

But in pursuing this self-discovery, away from the stage he's grown self-contained, untouched by people in the final analysis. Although easy and friendly, not a bit aloof, he's still a lone star, moving on his own independent trajectory. He's into none of the musician's usual trips – doping up, drinking and heavy womanising. The girls he meets on the road he never turns into groupies, to be discussed with appropriate lip-smacking noises on the bus next day. Dope was not even important to him as a teenager.

"People do it because their friends do it," he explains carefully, "and at the time I didn't have any friends in Asbury...I had a guy I'd see once in a while, and a girl, but outside of that there was nobody. I wasn't in that circle.

"Consequently, I was oblivious to a lot of social pressures and stuff within the scene, 'cause I was on the outside, on the outside looking in...until I started to play and then people come closer to you. You don't go to them, they come to you."

He pauses, his hands rumpling through his hair. "But by then it was too late. I was totally involved in what I was doin', and I had no need for anything else, or for anybody. I was there, and that was it, for me."

He gets up and turns the television off and then goes back to the bed, where he sits cross-legged.

"You know, you have to be self-contained. That way you don't get pushed around. It depends on what you need. I eat loneliness, man. I feed off it. I live on a lotta different levels, y'know, because I've learned to cope with people, which is – be cool all the time, I can do that because...I've got too much going on inside to be upset over things that are trivial to me.

"So I've learned to really flow with it on the surface. I can roll with the punches. It's a way of getting along."

Still, he's in the ring now, moving up the rankings, with other managers fastening their beady eyes upon him. Suddenly it's become a big deal, and he needs all the help he can get. He and Appel battle it out together, managing on a shoestring until The Breakthrough arrives.

One day he wants to have that big pile of money, wants to hold a million dollars in his hand, just to see what it's like. And come that day he's promised himself he'll ride in a limousine and go to some spiffy high society do where they'll have to announce him.

Then – thinking dutifully – there's his mother who's worked every day since she was 17, and she's old now. He'd like her to stop – his old man, too. Oh – there's all kinds of dreams wrapped up in that million bucks. But mostly he knows what he wants, and it's to do with an attitude.

"I wanna be able to spit on the floor when I like," he says with passion. "I just wanna be in control. I don't wanna be controlled through the air, man. I wanna spit in the air..."

In the early hours of Sunday morning we confront ourselves at a celebration party held in Roberto's home, a large wooden-frame building set back from the road amidst tall grass. The rain has stopped momentarily, but the vegetation on the drive swishes heavily.

Inside it's a great melee, with people crushed drunkenly together. Ice rattles in a big tub holding cans of beer. Over in one corner several people play gin-rummy on a big, battered old table. There are cigarettes stubbed out in the potato salad. The party is on its last legs...

It's well after 3 a.m. when Roberto, mad Chicano that he is, portentiously raises his hand and calls, in thunderous fashion, for silence. As the hubbub cuts out he draws Bruce to him and makes a little speech about how honoured he is to have such a rising star in his home, he, Roberto.

And while Springsteen looks sheepish, the guests raise their cans of beer to him for a brief moment. Then someone coughs and the party limps to its close.

Later, in the car back to the hotel, Springsteen says, "Do you know what he gave me?" And he pulls out of his pocket Roberto's absurd Lone Ranger mask. We all have a good laugh at that, and then we head for the nearest hamburger joint, because Bruce is feeling very hungry by now.

© Michael Watts / Melody Maker / IPC Syndication

Below: **The Boss wields his guitar in earnest. He learned his first chops at home, playing along with his favourite records and never bothered with formal lessons.**

Above: **The E Street Band letting loose with their mighty roar. Springsteen and 'Miami' Steve Van Zandt trade licks, watched admiringly by Clarence Clemmons and bassist Garry Tallent. Keeping it hard and steady is drummer Roy Bittan.**

key recordings

1973	Signed to Columbia Records by John Hammond, Bruce and manager Mike Appel produce *Greetings From Asbury Park, NJ*
1974	The same team make *The Wild, The Innocent and The E Street Shuffle*
1975	Rock journalist Jon Landau assumes control for *Born To Run*
1979	His career in overdrive, Springsteen releases *The River* double-set
1984	*Born In The USA* begins its two-year stand in the US charts and Bruce becomes 'The Boss'
1986	Bootleggers weep as *Live 1975–85* makes their efforts redundant
1995	Social awareness time as Bruce explores America's underbelly on *The Ghost Of Tom Joad*
1999	He's back! *18 Tracks* signals the return of The Boss and The E Street Band

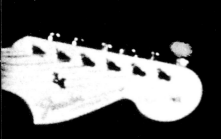

e l v i s   c o s t e l l o

Once in a while an artist emerges who fits no neat pigeon-holes or categories, does not look like stars are 'supposed' to look, yet manages to reach the top by dint of sheer talent. Elvis Costello (real name Declan McManus) is one such rarity – a consummate songwriter and composer who has matured into an accomplished live performer.

Born in London in 1954, Costello moved to Liverpool with his mother when her marriage to big band singer Ross McManus broke up. A computer operator for a cosmetics firm by day, in his late teens he took his mother's maiden name to play folk clubs as DP Costello. By 1976 he was fronting a country-rock band, Flip City and getting used to his songwriter demos being rejected when the newly-formed Stiff Records offered him a deal.

Label boss Jake Riviera suggested he adopt the name 'Elvis' (for the hell of it) and work with Nick Lowe, Stiff's house producer (because it made sense). The first album they made together (My Aim Is True) saw Costello backed by US country-rock outfit Clover, minus lead singer Huey Lewis. While his first three singles failed to chart, heavy airplay and a healthy buzz helped the album reach No.14 in Britain.

Now backed by The Attractions, Costello toured the US for the first time in December 1977, having left Stiff to join Riviera's new Radar Records. 'Watching The Detectives', his last Stiff single, gave him his first British hit. Costello returned to America for more dates and by March 1978 My Aim Is True was in the US Top 30 album chart.

On a roll, Costello released This Year's Model in May 1978 and the landmark Armed Forces a year later, the latter distinguished by the hit single, 'Oliver's Army'. In 1981 he visited Nashville to record an album of country material with producer Billy Sherrill (Almost Blue), but was back on track again in '82 with the outstanding Imperial Bedrooms. His 1983 and 1984 albums Punch The Clock and Goodbye Cruel World reinforced his status as a superlative songwriter. During this time he also produced albums by Squeeze, The Specials and The Bluebells and – through The Pogues – met Caitlin O'Riordan, his future wife.

Fifties rock'n'roll was the inspiration behind Costello's 1986 album King of America, but a reunion with The Attractions and Nick Lowe in the same year resulted in the disappointing Blood And Chocolate. After collaborating as songwriter with Paul McCartney for the latter's Flowers In The Dirt album, in 1989 Costello was back on form for Spike, worked with ex-Byrd Roger McGuinn and in 1991 co-wrote the music score for the controversial hit British TV series, GBH.

That year also saw him back to form with Mighty Like A Rose, while his search for new musical horizons was realised in 1993 in his collaboration with the classical Brodsky Quartet and the release of The Juliet Letters. The rest of the 1990s saw him release three further solo albums (Brutal Youth in 1994, Kojak Variety in 1995, and All This Useless Beauty in 1996), compose more soundtrack music and embark on a number of other collaborative projects, the most successful of which saw him team up with Burt Bacharach for the 1998 album, Painted From Memory.

While his past record labels have flooded the market with compilations of old hits, Costello himself appears content to live and work in Ireland, preparing whatever new music his mind can devise. Only one thing is certain: it'll be interesting listening.

158

May 20 1989 Allan Jones

SONGS OF LOVE AND HATE

The beloved entertainer answers my call to his room with a croak. He's not up yet. I'm not surprised. We've been up most of the night, drinking our fool heads off at a party celebrating the Irish Music Awards. We'd driven back to Dublin in the haunted hours before dawn, drunk and rowdy, no doubt convinced that we were having the time of our lives. This morning we feel like death, of course, bones growing out of our heads, tongues turning to chalk, hoarse-voiced and delirious.

On the phone now, to Costello, in the lobby of his hotel, I'm shaking, wracked by nausea, chills and fever. Costello sounds as bad as I feel, which is as bad as it gets. He asks for 15 minutes to pull himself together. I tell him we'll give him 30 and meet him in the bar, where Sheehan and I have beers for breakfast. Costello joins us, looking like he's been dragged all night across scrubland, naked, by his heels. We all proceed to feel very sorry for ourselves, and then we go up to Costello's room, heads still pounding, every nerve end flayed and twitching.

We talk late into the afternoon, too tired almost to quit. Drinks keep arriving. Pretty soon, I'm getting drunk again. We try to remember when either of us last felt quite so bad, and Costello remembers when it was always like this for him – endless tours, fuelled by drugs and too much booze, every day a hangover, a stumbling through entire seasons, strung out on alcohol and narcotics; hell, after the novelty had worn off, leaving only the habit and the debris.

"I really thought all that nonsense had reached a kind of peak when were in Holland doing 'Get Happy!!'," Costello says, his voice chipped at the edges with exhaustion, "when were literally writing songs on the way to the studio from the bar. But later, it was just as bad. Probably worse. When we were in Nashville for 'Almost Blue', there was a film crew with us, making that 'South Bank Show' documentary. While they were filming, it was all very serious, and I'd be making all these ponderous statements about why I was making this country album, which everyone seemed to think was a completely lunatic thing to be doing. But as soon as the cameras stopped rolling, it was 'Right – *more drugs*, where's the f***in' drinks?' Screaming our bloody heads off, because we were just so completely f***in' *out* of it.

"A lot of people think that album sounds so depressed because I was drinking so much at the time. But there were other things that con-

tributed to that, things were happening in my private life that I don't really want to talk about. It wasn't just drinking. I mean, I was drinking a lot in f***in' 1978. But I was having a better time then. It's when you're drinking and you're *not* happy, that's when you've got to worry. That's when it's gonna affect the way you look at things, because you're probably drinking for the wrong reasons. And *that*'s when things start to get warped and you don't think anything through.

"I remember Nick Lowe once said to me, he said, 'You know, I just don't understand you. You *fight* every drink or any drugs you take. You fight them all the time. You're trying to stay straight all the way through it.' And I still do it. I'll never admit that I'm drunk. But we all drink. And sometimes it's for the right reasons...to let your mind off the leash for a while, and have a bit of fun, and then you don't mind if you make a bit of a prat of yourself, like last night. And it doesn't matter if you end up shouting at people, or have a punch up or whatever, as long as you wake up the same person. It's when you *don't want* to wake up the same person that you've got a problem.

"And I think I maybe went through that for a while. There were times when I'd feel every moment as bad as I do this morning. Times when you'd wake up, feeling like you were knocking on heaven's f***in' door and there'd be nobody there to f***in' answer you. Those were the worst times..."

There was a general feeling back then that you were purposely f***in' up your life to give you material for your songs.

"I think I did that for about a year," Costello says, tired now and showing it. "At the very most. And then I began to mistrust the results. Because if you do that, it's like when they pour acid in rabbits' eyes or something. What does it prove? It proves that it hurts the animal. Very smart. It's unnecessary research. And I guess I did some unnecessary research for a while. And then I'd write something that would scare the

Left: **An early publicity shot of Elvis in classic rock guitar hero pose. His adoption of such a distinctive (and until then, unique) forename was always bound to result in a furious and publicity-making media debate. And so it proved, and another Elvis headed for stardom.**

hell out of me…Like, there's a couple of things on 'Get Happy!!', than when I read them back, I just scared the hell out of myself. And I thought, 'Uh-uh…better not think any more about *this*…it's going too far…' Because you can think *too f***in' much*, you know, and it gets a bit f***in' *evil*."

Did you ever during this period think you were going too far, becoming *too* personal, too explicit, pouring too much venom, rage and spite into your songs?

"Maybe in retrospect…I can recognise sometimes where I maybe went over the line. But then again, I was never really that specific. I mean, people who really do pay too much attention for their own good have tried to peg certain songs to certain people. It's like a game, isn't it, that started in the early Seventies with people like Joni Mitchell. People always wanted to know who those songs were about. And people have tried that with me, and it's always been wrong.

"The fact is, those songs were never merely *confessional*…Even if you're satisfying your own selfish desire to put somebody down in a song or praise them, it isn't important that everybody knows who you're writing about or the specific emotional situation that provoked it. The song should have a universal appeal, otherwise it doesn't serve any purpose. It becomes merely self-indulgent. Like 'Let me tell you some more secrets about myself…' It's all me me me. And that just gets really f***in' painful after a while. But then you get people saying, 'Well at least it's honest.' But *is* it? Is it honest to go around going, 'Look at my open sores.' I don't think it is. I think it's just f***in' indulgent."

Do you feel resentful, then, that people still dig through the bones of your songs, looking for the explicitly autobiographical in your writing?

"No, I don't *resent* it," Costello laughs, setting off a bout of wheezing. "I just blame John Lennon. It's the 'Plastic Ono Band', that album started it all. After that *everything* was supposed to be f***in' confessional. The early Seventies were full of all these people baring their f***in' souls for public scrutiny. There were records whose authenticity depended on the confessional aspect, and if you read certain magazines and the background interviews, you knew who these songs were about.

"And that for me always used to spoil it. Particularly when you found out what *dickheads* some of the people were that they were writing about. I'd rather have them be like Smokey Robinson songs, which could be about anyone. I don't think it's important that people know who 'Alison' was actually about. It's none of their f***in' business. It's a *song*. 'I Want You' is a *song*. It doesn't matter who it's about…"

People still automatically assume it's addressed to Cait…

"Yeah," he says wearily. "But it's just nonsense. It's just a song. It's a *really well written song*. It's also very personal, but you don't have to know the whole story to be touched by it…It's like people might say this new record is *less* personal because most of it's written in the third person. That's just as misguided. It all came out of *my* head, so how can it *not* be personal, you know…But there are still people, yeah, who want everything I've done documented and explained…but we're really getting into something else here.

Above: **A posh outfit for a posh event. No rebel, he, Elvis has always been prepared to suffer strangulation by bow tie if the occasion demands, and it obviously did on this particular night.**

"Like I say, it's all in the past…none of it means a damn. You can't go digging around for ever in the past. It's history. Let it go. It's what I'm doing *now* that counts. *That's* what I want people to realise."

We were in Dublin to talk about "Spike", as if it hadn't been talked about enough already. The album arrived in February, in a blizzard of promotional activity unprecedented in Costello's career. For the first couple of weeks of the album's release, he was everywhere. You couldn't pick up a magazine, turn on the radio or television without finding Costello waxing lyrical about the record.

It got to the point eventually where all this public salesmanship seemed evidence almost of a desperate attempt by Costello to revive an interest in himself and his work, increasingly marginalised in the Eighties, and to recapture the commercial ground he'd lost after the enormous commercial success of "Armed Forces" in 1979. There were times, though, when his cheerful bluster seemed positively ingratiating.

"I certainly didn't feel that way," Costello bristles when this is brought up. "I think it's important to remember that the last 10 years with Colombia in America were often really frustrating. They just didn't know how to promote us. They'd run out of ideas. And by the end, I think they'd just given up, especially after 'King of America', which they didn't have a f***in' clue what to do with, and 'Blood And Chocolate', which they hated and subsequently just f***in' *buried*.

"So this was our first one with Warner Brothers, and obviously you've got to accept the fact that the record company has nothing but horror stories from the past about you, and I simply didn't want to get off on the wrong foot with them and end up having to go through the same old f***in' battles just to get a f***in' record in the shops.

"So when the impetus came from America for me to promote the album, I said I'd do it. There was nothing *ingratiating* about it. As for being desperate – you can't *force* people to put you on the covers of magazines or on the television or the radio or whatever. That was *their* choice. And it just proves to me how f***in' *dull* everything must be right now, if someone with my tenure in the business can just reappear after three years and get that kind of attention. I mean, it's no big f***in' deal.

"But it amazed me, the ease which on the one hand you can come back and command the centre stage, just by saying you're there, and secondly still be regarded as someone outrageous. But what else is happening? In England, there's a cult a week for some band that's gonna save us all, and then you never f***in' hear of them again. It's very easy and I suppose attractive to get excited and emotional about the Darling Buds or somebody. But after a while, you can keep up with who's the latest flame.

"And who's outrageous anymore? Like I was just in a radio station somewhere in America, in the south, quite a mainstream station. And this guy said, 'Sometimes I just have to let my hair down and get outta here, go over to my old college station and play as much Nick Heyward as I like!' And with all due respect to Nick, he's *not* Jimmy Reed. I mean, I think Nick Heyward's made a couple of nice records, but he's not the wild man of rock 'n' roll. But he was this guy's definition of outrageous…And if that's indicative of the present climate, it's maybe not so curious that I still get some attention. And it's maybe why anything I do, not so much in England, but particularly in the States, seems to them to be effortlessly weird.

"So to get over to *them* the fact that the record isn't all *that* strange, you sometimes have to fill in a little of the background. You know, I've run into this a lot. People build up such preconceptions or they just associate you with one thing and they can't hear anything else you do. It's like they're looking at a painting you've done, upside down. Unless you can change their point of view, they're never *gonna* see.

The last time I was in Dublin with Costello, we ended up drinking in some gaudy nightclub where the fluorescent throb and gash of neon lit us in garish hues and strobes flashed, epileptic and deranged. Bono

Right: **Doin' the Townshend Windmill. Even though he's remarkably free of mannerisms on stage, not even Elvis can resist the odd flail at a Fender.**

arrived just after us. His appearance among the heathen throng was almost papal. First the crowd parted in front of him, reverent, adoring, as he advanced across the club. He settled at a table opposite us and looked around the room with the empty, dead stare of someone who'd long since lost the plot; a distant, cold glare that saw very little and understood even less. He could have been on another planet, and probably was. He was quickly surrounded by a sea of smothering supplicants, eager to pay their respects, kiss the hem of his coat, be touched by his presence, blessed by his righteousness.

"F***in' place," Costello muttered into his beer, "is turning into Lourdes."

We were at a table on a corner of the dancefloor, trying to make ourselves heard to each other above the infernal thud of the disco. Now that you're closer to us, you can hear that we're talking about "Blood And Chocolate". Costello is telling me that he had been convinced that this was the record that people had been waiting for him to make since "Get Happy!!", a return to the classic Attractions' sound, the record that at a stroke would revive his faltering commercial ambitions, thoroughly thwarted for most of the decade. This was outrageous. "Blood And Chocolate" is the most extreme and brutal of all Costello's albums. It sounds like it's been ripped screaming from the clefts of bedlam. In the bland, conservative climate of late-Eighties pop, it was a howl from an outer darkness. It stood no chance of being a hit. So when Costello tells me that he thought it would return him to the mainstream, I don't believe a word. A year later, though, in Dublin again, Costello is sticking to the same story.

"I honestly wasn't being ingenuous," he says. "I knew in America, especially, they took a huge gasp of breath when we did 'Almost Blue', and although 'King Of America' was one of those records that got me great reviews, Columbia just couldn't sell the f***in' thing…So I did have the notion when we came to do 'Blood And Chocolate' that in the States at least, they'd throw their hats in the air and cheer. I really did think it was the album they'd been wanting me to deliver. Because there were elements of it that I thought were stereotypical. It was like an older, grumpier version of 'This Year's Model', which I was pretty sure they'd go for. As it turned out, they did to it what they'd done to the two or three records before it. They buried the f***in' thing.

"In retrospect, I think we underestimated how f***in' *harsh* it sounded. But that was the mood we were in. We wanted it live and we wanted it loud, and we achieved that at the expense of everything else. I mean, we tried to do a ballad on that record, a really pretty song called 'Forgive Her Anything', but we physically couldn't play it. It sounded like we were playing with boxing gloves on. It needed too delicate an arrangement for the sound we'd contrived. And we got to really fighting about it. Like, 'It's your f***in' fault, you playing too f***in' loud.' 'No, I'm not. You're playing to f***in' *fast*.' It was like the f***in' Troggs. But there was nothing we could do with it. That sound we had, there was just too much barbed wire in it. I was just too f***in' *ferocious*."

Given the subsequent split of the Attractions, was "Blood And Chocolate" meant to be a kind of last hurrah?

"Not intentionally. The idea was just to get together again and make a record. Originally it was gonna be an EP, a one-off thing, a bit of an undercover job, just to put the fun back into playing together. Because by then everything had got a bit askew. There was a lot of bad feeling that because of the way things turned out, the Attractions ended up

playing on only one track on 'King Of America', and the internal politics surrounding that record weren't too pleasant. And I don't think I handled it very well. But neither did a couple of the group. It just got unnecessarily ugly, you know. Like you were there that night at the Duke of York's when I had that row with Steve. That's the sort of thing that was happening. People were being set up against each other. And I hate all that shit, and I didn't want everything to fall apart in acrimony, so the main thing was just to get back together instead of bickering. The thing was, I had no idea it was gonna turn out to be so extreme. But I love it. I think it's one of the two or three best records we made together.

Releasing two six-minute singles from it, "Tokyo Storm Warning" and "I Want You", didn't seem to be the most thoughtful commercial strategy. Were you just being perverse?

"No…I really thought they were the best two songs on the record. There were maybe a couple of others that could have been singles. 'I Hope You're Happy Now' might have been a hit, or 'Blue Chair'. But I couldn't see the wood for the trees over that one. You know, I sometimes tend to get too self-conscious about pop music. When I've got a good pop song, I have difficulty actually doing it properly. I somehow want to f*** it up. And I think the idea sometimes of releasing the obvious poppy track from an album as a single is patronising…"

Doesn't "Veronica" fall into that category?

"No," Costello says firmly, prepared to defend this one to the hilt, whatever the damage. "That's *unashamedly pop music*. You know, with that, I've come back to the way I was thinking when we did things like 'Oliver's Army'. I'm loath to say the word, because the minute you say something's subversive, it's not subversive any more…But there is a trick to it, you know, where you can slip something out that takes people a while to figure out what it is you're actually singing about. With 'Veronica', if people had realised straight off that it was about an old woman, they might have thought it was too maudlin and just shut it off. Whereas the whole point of the song is that there is some hope and defiance in the character. So I think it's really good that it sounds like it's about a *young* girl, instead of it being a ponderous thing about an old woman, or something self-consciously dramatic like 'Eleanor Rigby'. Which is a great record, but you immediately know it's about this strange person. Whereas the idea with 'Veronica' isn't to patronise the character. It's said with love. So I like the idea that the music is really kind of bright and pretty. It's the prettiest record I've made in ages."

"Veronica" is one of two tracks on "Spike" written with Paul McCartney. Another of their collaborations, "My Brave Face", has just been released as the ex-Beatle's new single; more are to follow on McCartney's forthcoming LP, "Flowers In The Dirt". We had talked the previous evening about the collaboration, and Costello, getting drunk, had worked himself into a rare old fit about the jaundiced view some people have of McCartney: he'd even been told that working with him somehow devalued his own critical standing.

"That's true," Costello says the morning after, nursing a hangover, feeling fragile but feisty. "People was actually told me that. But f*** 'em. They're people who wouldn't know a good piece of music if it boned 'em up the arse."

So what was your immediate response when the call came from the McCartney Empire? Did you think you were on to an easy earner? Were you flattered? Suspicious?

"It might sound facile," Costello says, "but I didn't think about it in
any of those terms. I just thought, 'Let's give it a go.' And it was all very
unselfconscious – no big deal. We just got on with it. Occasionally, I'd look
up and think, 'Oh, hell, it's *him*.' Because he really – don't laugh – he really
does look *frighteningly like him*. The same was true of Orbison. He's one
of those people who look exactly like you expect them to look. You
know, I think of him like a Buzz Aldrin or somebody. Somebody who's
been to the moon and back. Nobody – none of us in whatever part of
the business we're in – none of us can conceive what it must be like to
have been through what he's experienced. It's a unique experience,
probably, in the 20th century to be him. And that's not making too big
a thing of it.

"And the fact that he's so easy going about it all just seems to rile
people. I mean, he could be a mad person, he could have reacted to
what he went through in any number of ways that could prevent him
now from being as straightforward and normal as he apparently is. The
very fact that this guy has sort of *glided* through life and been very well
rewarded is the cause, I think, of most of the flak he gets. It's just f***in'
envy, that's what it is when you get right down to it…"

And he hasn't been shot, so he's not a legend.

"Absolutely," Costello says, heaving forward. "And he's uncomfortably
undramatic about this thing he's been through. But, you know, he has
been through it all, through more things than you could probably imagine.
So why does he have to live up to somebody else's fantasy of who he is?
I think that's a completely unreasonable demand to make of anyone.

"It's like these people who criticise him for being too rich or too
famous. What the f*** has it got to do with them? It's just crap, you
know. Why don't they just shut the f*** up and let him get on with his
music. I also think that people who criticise him for being sentimental
are talking a lot of shit as well. Because in any other line of work, if a
man of 46 wasn't sentimental about his kids, they'd think he was a
f***in' *sociopath*, you know. He's a married man, he has a nice life.
What's the f***in' matter with that? F***in' hell, just because he's
famous they want him to be at the barricades all the f***in' time. It's
just stupid. He's just a really good musician, probably one of the best
there has been in a long time…it's absolutely coming out of his fingers,
you know…and if he doesn't want to use that musical talent to say
world-changing things, that's *his* f***in' business."

"Blood And Chocolate" struck more than one commentator as a
protracted musical identification with the troubled genius of John Lennon.
When the invitation came to work with McCartney, was there maybe a
feeling that you were being cast in the role that Lennon once played?

"No," Costello says quickly. "Lennon's obviously not around to be
fallible or great or whatever – some bastard shot him – so in America,

I think they're sometimes obviously fitting up a lot of people for the role. And I think it's a dangerous thing. In America, some really neurotic critics are trying to fit me in those shoes. And I think it's f***in' irresponsible. You know, COME ON. DRAW A F***IN' TARGET ON MY BACK…"

Costello has been through all this before, after the notorious Columbus incident he received nearly 200 death threats in a week.

"Don't remind me," he shudders. "Don't remind me."

The afternoon draws on. We are both feeling as parched as f***. Costello orders another round of drinks. We talk about some of his other recent collaborations, most notably with Roy Orbison, whose version of the radically re-written "The Comedians" was the undisputed highspot of Orbison's posthumous "Mystery Girl" LP. Before flying out to Dublin, I had belatedly caught up with the "Roy Orbison And Friends: A Black And White Night" video of the commemorative concert in Los Angeles, at which Orbison was backed by an all star cast including Elvis Presley's Taking Care Of Business band (the TCBs, featuring Glen D Hardin, Rut Tutt, Jerry Scheff and legendary guitarist James Burton, who appeared on "King of America"). Also on the show were Costello, Tom Waits, Jackson Browne, KD Lang, Bonnie Raitt and Bruce Springsteen.

So what was it like, Elvis, clocking in behind the Big O?

"Well, it was very hard to be in *awe* of him," Costello says. "He was just very gentle, a little removed, perhaps a bit bemused by all the attention, but quite moved by everyone's enthusiasm. Because basically it was a big pain in the arse doing the show. I mean, it looked a lot of fun when they cut it together, but I have to say the production people had very little consideration for the musicians, including Roy.

"Basically, they didn't have a f***in' clue. In the end, T-Bone took a lot of the heat and he ended up telling them what to do, otherwise they would've had musicians leaving in droves. Because there was one point where there was nearly a rebellion. Even with all deference to Roy, I think there was a point where some of the musicians were ready to walk, because there were a lot of ugly political things going down that could've been avoided if they'd been a bit more sensible. And what you see is this really good-natured show, so it really goes to show how much people dug him, because they all put that behind them. And a lot of the credit for that has to go to the TCBs, particularly, even through they were the ones most taken advantage of.

"Like, Rolling Stone came to take pictures and they didn't even ask James Burton to be in the shot. The guy from Rolling Stone didn't even recognise him. It was sort of, 'Right, we'll have Roy in the middle, and Bruce, you sit this side of Roy, and Elvis, you sit on the other side…' I said, 'What does this make me? The Holy Ghost or God the Son?' Because that's what it looked like…the f***in' Holy Trinity, with Roy as God the Father, you know…'"

The show brought you into immediate contact with some people like Springsteen, about whom you've often been less than flattering…

"Let's be frank," Costello laughs. "They were people I've often been downright f***in' *rude* about. In fact, I've usually slagged them off, which I think is fair enough. I have my opinions about them and they probably know what they think about me. They might get a little outraged sometimes, but I don't give a flying f***, you know."

So how did you hit it off with old Bruce?

"I thought Bruce wasn't too bad," Costello says, and I can only think the drinks are having an effect. "I mean he didn't come until the day of the show. But he turned up, no entourage, no bodyguards, no manager, no roadie. Carrying his own guitar as far as I could see. And I assumed he knew the songs so well he could just busk it. But I have this nice little image of him…Where we did the show was at the Coconut Grove, in the Ambassador Hotel, where Robert Kennedy was shot. The Grove is in a kind of basement at the back, and the kitchen just behind the stage is where he got shot. Place was like something out of the f***in' 'Shining'…Anyway, all the boys were crammed into one dressing room. And you couldn't move for all these baskets of fruit. It's *Hollywood*, you know, so every f***er on the show gets a basket of fruit with nuts and f***in' cheese…And, anyway, we're all packed in there, and it suddenly reminded me of when I was a kid and I used to go to the Joe Loss shows with my dad…all the guys in the band, standing around in their underwear, smoking…It was great. We were really like the Orchestra… And just before we were due on, I looked around and there's Springsteen. He's got a Walkman on, and he's got his electric guitar and he's got the chart of 'Only The Lonely', and he's looking really intense and worried. And suddenly he went, 'Oh f*** – that's how it goes.'

"But I thought he played great on the show. He played his guitar solo, didn't he? That *one* guitar solo that he does. He plays with his *eyebrows*, have you noticed that? And there were a couple of songs where he has to trade off guitar parts with James Burton, and everybody thought he was really gonna be out of his depth. But he didn't try to outflash Burton. You can't, let's face it. So he played his one note solo and he played it very emphatically, like he really meant it. And James came back with this ridiculously fancy like that he does and gave Springsteen this look, you know, 'Top *that*, boy.' And Bruce is going, 'Oooooh, *shit*…back to the one note solo…' I thought it was pretty cool."

Costello is by now in a pretty expansive anecdotal mood. I ask him about Van Morrison, who appeared with him the last time he played the Albert Hall.

"I think what I really admire about him," Costello says, "apart from the fact that he makes the most incredible f***in' records, is his *single-mindedness*. People go on about him being difficult, but he does it *his* way and if you can't accept that, then go somewhere else. I don't think he's gonna cry. He's tougher than that. He really is tougher than the rest. He's in a class of one, and if you don't like it then f*** off, you know. There are only like two or three people with his kind of singular identity in rock 'n' roll. Like, Lou Reed, Dylan…"

You met Dylan once, didn't you?

"I've met Dylan a few times, yeah," Costello says. "We had a strange conversation once, I remember. I met all his kids once in a parking lot in Minneapolis. He came to this party with all his sons. Lined them up like they were on parade, and I had to shake hands with them. He said, 'This is Jesse, he knows all the words to "Pump It Up".' And I thought, 'Now there's something wrong with this statement, Bob. He knows all the words to "Subterranean Homesick Blues" is what you probably mean.' Jesse was a punk fan. I don't know how old he is now, but then he was into the Clash and people like that. I think he thought his dad was a bit old-fashioned. Maybe he's since realised that his dad was a bit more happening than Mick Jones, you know. I hope so. I mean, I love old Mick, he's great. But Bob's always been a bit more happening than Mick, let's face it."

What do you talk to someone like Dylan about? the *weather*?

"Actually," Costello says, "yeah. With somebody like Dylan or Van, they say they're unpredictable souls who can be rude to people. So I figure if they just accept you and you just talk in ordinary conversation about the weather or something, it means they're giving you somehow more credit than they would to someone they don't really have time for. I mean, you hear all these horror stories about these people, but you've got to remember that there are plenty of people who want a piece of them and they make unreasonable demands on them. And there are a few people that have tried to make those demands of me, so I'm aware of the fact that if you start like getting in on them and it's like, 'C'mon, Bob, where ARE the Gates Of Eden?' you'd expect to be shown the door. I'm always mindful of what it's like when somebody get on *my* case. Sometimes it's well-meaning, but you really just can't answer their questions, because you can't *think* like them. They've got their perspective on what you do and you just can't get into it."

The night before the interview Costello had appeared at the Irish Music Awards. He and Christy Moore had done a version of "Dark End Of The Street", an old Costello favourite. It was a moment of sober beauty in an otherwise unremarkable pantomime. The front rows of the audience were full of wriggling Brosettes who glared at Costello with furious indignation. Turns out later that they are howling mad with him for being less than kind to Bros on a recent radio show. After the show, some of them cornered him in a local pub.

"It was funny as hell," he says. "They all wanted my blood for slandering Luke by suggesting that he might be something less than a Titan. I just felt a bit sad for them. Because this, you know, is the extent of their musical excitement, this rather dull group. And they were going, 'Tell us you really don't hate them.' And I'm going, 'I don't *hate* them, I just don't *like* 'em. I'm not *supposed* to f***in' like 'em. *You're* supposed to like 'em…' It was all a bit pathetic, really, because they'll all be embarrassed in four years' time that they were ever Brosettes. It's like, where do you meet Bay City Rollers' fans these days…And Bros will be

forgotten in the long run, because they don't represent anything particularly worthwhile. It's like Michael Jackson. He'll be forgotten in 50 years. He'll be like this person who statistically was famous, like Al Jolson or Rudy Vallee, but nobody'll remember him. He's just a facsimile of excitement. And because there's no substance to what he does, and because he's sold his soul to a corporate identity, which is actually bigger than he is, in the long run I think he'll be swallowed by it. It's like Whitney Houston, I think it's downright sad that somebody as good as her will take a billion dollars from Pepsi to sell herself down the river. She's just turned into this cabaret singer. You look at her and it's like the light's gone from her eyes. She's just another victim of the Pepsi Vampires."

So who are the strong, Elvis, who's to be trusted? Who's *angry* any more?

"I dunno," Costello says wearily, exhaustion creeping up on him like a slow tide. "It does seem at the moment that there's no real willingness to test anything. But it's not surprising really. All the mannerisms of rebellion in music seem to have been used up. You only have to look at Guns 'N' Roses to realise that. Cait got their album, you know, and it's f***in' terrible. It's like an Outlaws record or something. 'I'm goin' down the road with my geetar and I'm a baad mutha f***er…' F*** *off*, you little twat. It's about as rock 'n' roll as f***in' David Nixon. The thing is, you can't keep leaping out of the cupboard going boo to people. It's not frightening any more.

"And the funny thing is, the *real* wildmen are still unacceptable. I'm not talking about someone like Johnny Rotten. He's completely acceptable. He's just like Quentin Crisp. He's an English eccentric. But *Jerry Lee Lewis*, man. I saw Jerry Lee, and he's still f***in' unacceptable to most people. T-Bone went for a meeting with him, because he's been working on a film they're doing about him. And they went to this really chi-chi Hollywood café, and this little waiter comes up and goes, 'Hi, my name ith Cwithtopher and I'll be your waiter for tonight. Is there something I can get you?'

"And Jerry Lee says 'Yeah. What about something blonde, 21 years old with big f***in' tits.' Just starts straight in, you know. Brilliant. And someone like that, they're always gonna be on the outside. He's definitely the real thing. And there's really no one else around who's that unique, that singular. I don't see anyone like that around anymore. I see a few interesting eccentrics. Morrissey. Michael Stipe. Johnny Lydon. Myself, maybe. But those heavy metal bands who think they so f***in' outrageous. I just think, 'F*** off, pal. You don't even own the territory.'

"Because I look back at some of the things *we've* done, and it's no f***in' contest. I mean, we've had our f***in' *moments*, man. And they don't even come close."

© Allan Jones / Melody Maker / IPC Syndication

Above: **Marriage to Caitlin O'Riordan and the relative sanity of a home in Ireland have helped Elvis expand his musical horizons. Besides collaborating with the likes of Burt Bacharach, he has also explored the roots music of his adopted homeland.**

key recordings

1977	Newly renamed Elvis signs with Stiff and Nick Lowe produces *My Aim Is True*. As Costello enjoys first hit single *(Watching The Detectives)* he also becomes a Demon
1979	Elvis at his militant best for *Armed Forces*
1983	*Punch The Clock* punches another hole in the charts
1989	Costello collaborates with Paul for McCartney's *Flowers In The Dirt* album
1991	Still smelling fragrant, Elvis releases the fine *Mighty Like A Rose*
1993	Costello goes classical with The Brodsky Quartet for *The Juliet Letters*
1997	Warners release definitive *Extreme Honey: The Very Best of The Warner Bros Years*
1998	Sublime songwriting rules as Elvis teams up with Burt Bacharach to create *Painted From Memory*

The six brief years that Nirvana spent together making music and mayhem left us with one bona fide rock icon/martyr (in singer Kurt Cobain), three fascinating albums that defined not only the grunge culture they typified but the so-called 'MTV generation' for whom they became heroes, and a wealth of legends to prove that the tradition of rock'n'roll excess was still alive, if not well.

Coming together in Aberdeen, Washington in 1988, Nirvana's founder members (guitarist/singer Cobain, and bassist Krist Novoselic) worked with a number of other drummers before settling on Dave Grohl, one-time member of the Ohio group, Scream, in 1990 to create the outfit that would prove so successful.

It was with drummer Chad Channing that Nirvana recorded their debut single, 'Love Buzz'/'Big Cheese' for the Seattle label, Sub Pop Records, and while a second guitarist, Jason Everman, was featured on the sleeve picture of their first album, Bleach, in 1989, he played on none of its sessions and had left by the time it was released. The underground buzz that Bleach created led to an extensive touring schedule for Nirvana, and it was after European dates that Channing left, his place being taken briefly by Dan Peters, from Sub Pop labelmates Mudhoney. It was Peters who played on Nirvana's 1990 single, 'Sliver'.

Grohl joined just as Nirvana signed with Geffen Records and the trio's first album for the label, Nevermind, became a US No.1 in early 1992 and a worldwide hit. A startling album, it marked the arrival of an intriguing outfit capable of writing songs that transcended the norm, while the Top 10 success of their single 'Smells Like Teen Spirit' proved an ability to reach a far wider audience.

Cobain's much-publicised affair with Hole singer Courtney Love was cemented in 1992 by their marriage and the arrival of a daughter they named Frances Bean. Tabloid headlines followed allegations that Love had continued to use heroin while pregnant. The stress of this, his enforced assumption of the role as a kind of spokesman for the so-called 'Generation X', and a

recurring, painful stomach condition combined to lead Cobain to increase his own drug abuse.

The production of Nirvana's next album, In Utero, with Steve Albini was marked by disagreements between Albini, the band and Geffen Records, who disliked the deliberately 'low-fi' approach Nirvana were taking. Whatever, In Utero proved that Cobain was still delivering excellent songs and it followed Nevermind into most charts around the world. But Cobain's increasingly errant behaviour climaxed in him collapsing into a drug-induced coma while on tour in Italy.

Whether or not it was – as later conspiracy theories suggested – a failed suicide attempt, Cobain was flown back to Seattle. It was there, on April 5, 1994, that he killed himself with a shotgun. In the hysteria which followed his death and funeral, Geffen released the Unplugged In New York album recently recorded by Nirvana for an MTV special. They would also release two compilation sets (Singles in 1995 and From The Muddy Banks Of The Wishkah in 1996) to meet the overwhelming demand that still existed.

Krist Novoselic formed a new band, Sweet 75, in 1997 while Dave Grohl and Pat Smear (who'd played second guitar on some later Nirvana dates) formed the excellent Foo Fighters.

Neither, it's safe to say, could hold a burnt-at-both ends candle to Nirvana.

July 11 1992 Everett True

CRUCIFIED BY SUCCESS

The interview with Nirvana takes place in a dressing room on the edge of a river in Stockholm. The day is cloudy, with occasional flashes of sunshine. People are drinking coke, and, in Krist's case, red wine. Krist and Dave are sitting on one couch, Kurt on another. A bowl of chilli-roasted peanuts and some fruit nestles on the table. Someone's smoking.

The band seem awkward in each other's presence, slightly wary of one another. When Krist speaks, his eyes are looking anywhere but in Kurt's direction. When Kurt speaks, he does so almost defensively, as if he feels a need to justify himself in front of Krist. When Dave speaks, you know he can feel the uneasiness, but he's trying to ignore it.

Apart from a brief spot on Swedish TV earlier today, this is the first interview Nirvana have given as a band for a long while. This might account for the subdued atmosphere – although many people have pointed to Nirvana's success as creating cracks, friction within the band. Certainly, Kurt seems warier than when I last met him – photographer Steve Gullick has to go through a ridiculous rigmarole of hoods and bleached hair and agreements later on before he's allowed to take any shots.

The noise you can't hear is support band, Teenage Fanclub, sound-checking for tonight's show. Nirvana's concert is lacking in any real excitement or emotion, although the encore is inspired. It seems they still have some way to go before playing arenas becomes second nature to them. It's obvious the band aren't happy with this state of affairs, but equally obvious that they aren't prepared to compromise their principles just to make people feel easier.

"We're going into the studio as soon as we get back to Seattle," says Kurt. "What I'd like to do is to go into Reciprocal with Jack Endino (the engineer on 'Bleach'), and rent exactly the same equipment as was there when we recorded 'Bleach'. We record the songs with Jack on an eight-track, record them somewhere else on a 24-track with Steve Albini, and then pick the best."

So you're aiming for a rawer sound on the next album?

"Definitely less produced," says Krist.

"As long as it doesn't sound like 'Nevermind'," adds Kurt.

Why? Are you fed up with it?

"No, I really like that album," Kurt replies. "And it doesn't matter what kind of production it has because the songs are good. But it would have been better rawer. It doesn't sound very original."

"We don't want to find ourselves in Slayer's situation," Dave explains, "where the same people produced their last three records and they all sound identical. That's stupid."

When you talk about how different you want your next record to sound, isn't there an element of wanting to challenge your audience about that statement? (The implication is that, because Nirvana have become fed up with their audience, they want to alienate them.) Kurt denies this.

"It's not like that," he says. "It's more like challenging ourselves, making a record exactly as we want to. Whether our audience likes it or not doesn't matter. We don't want to be writing 'In Bloom' for the next five years."

"Maybe the next record will be the one where we can judge how much impact we've actually made," Krist wonders aloud.

"Yeah, but we know that at least 50 per cent of people who like us now aren't going to like our next record if it has a lot of abrasive, inaccessible songs on it," replies Kurt, scornfully. "If they do...man, that proves our theory that you can shove anything down the mainstream's throat and they'll eat it up."

"But that's what I thought of our second record as being," interrupts Dave. "Something way less produced, where we can push the sound even further and see if we can get a noisy LP on the charts."

"But do you think that would happen?" Kurt asks him. "Let's pretend we haven't released 'Endless Nameless' yet, and it's our first single off the next album – if people bought it, wouldn't it just prove that they like us just cos it's cool to?"

"No," Krist replies. "That argument just doesn't hold any water. They wouldn't be that mindless."

Right: **Moving too fast for the camera to catch him, Kurt Cobain performed on stage the way he lived his short, explosive life – at the speed of light.**

Above: **For once, the streetwise punk image was not created by stylists or public relations whiz-kids. With Kurt Cobain, what you saw was what you got – raw and undiluted.**

(NB: "Endless Nameless" is the 10-minute long noise-fest grunge track which appeared on limited quantities of "Nevermind", and on the B-side of "Come As You Are".)

Do you think you'll have another single as big as "Teen Spirit"?

"No," states Kurt, firmly. "We haven't written any songs as good – or as poor – as that. We might write one right before we finish recording the album, because 'Teen Spirit' was written just weeks before 'Nevermind', but we're not going to try.

Kurt disappears momentarily to find a cigarette. Someone (the promoter? a roadie?) pokes his head round the door, looking for Alex, Nirvana's exuberant tour manager. The strains of Teenage Fanclub's "The Concept" drift in through a window, glorious in the early evening air. Dave cracks open another can.

Earlier, a bunch of us had gone for a stroll down by the river while Kurt and Courtney traversed the town, looking for Nirvana bootlegs to liberate and then give to kids wearing official Nirvana tee-shirts. One seller became freaked out and started yelling at Courtney – but there was no repeat of the ugliness in Ireland, where Kurt was reportedly punched by a bouncer after going to stop an altercation between security and a fan.

Right: **Kurt with daughter Frances Bean, soon after her birth in 1992. Sadly, her arrival was not enough to halt Cobain's continued slide into increased drug abuse, depression and self-inflicted death.**

It's apparent that there are two distinct camps in Nirvana: the newly-wed couple – and everyone else. Still, that's no reason to start believing all the malicious stories that have plagued Nirvana, and, more particularly, Kurt Cobain, since the band's rapid rise to the top. Drugs? What the f*** does it have to do with you, punk?

Krist stretches his legs, and sighs. This is gonna be a long interview. Kurt comes back and we continue.

When I saw your static performance in Oslo two days ago, I kept thinking back to what Kurt told me last year: "We're not going to be proud of the fact there are a bunch of Guns'N'Roses kids who are into our music. We don't feel comfortable progressing, playing larger venues."

"We can't," Krist agrees. "We've always treated people with that mentality with a little bit of contempt and cynicism, and to have them screaming for us ... Why are they screaming? What do they see in us? They're exactly the same kind of people who wanted to kick our arse in high school."

"It's just boring to play outdoors," explains his singer. "I've only just gotten used to playing large venues because the sound is at least tolerable. But, outside, the wind blows the music around so much that it doesn't feel like you're playing music, it feels like you're lip-synching to a boom box recording. Plus, these festivals are very mainstream – we're playing with Extreme and Pearl Jam, you know? Ninety per cent of the kids out there are probably just as much into Extreme as they are into us.

"I try every night," he continues, "but I just can't fool myself. I'm not going to smile and pose like Eddie Van Halen, even though he's a miserable drunk. That doesn't mean it'll be that way next month (Reading), but that's how it is, right now."

Do you feel any responsibility?

"For what?" Kurt asks.

The masses. The people who bought your record. Because you've been given this power to use.

"To me," Dave begins, tentatively, "our main responsibility is not to pretend to be something we're not. I don't think pretending to be a professional rock unit really works. If we're gonna have a shitty show, then let's have a shitty show. I can see there's a lot of responsibility playing massive shows, but other kinds? I don't know."

"It's rock'n'roll to be irresponsible," Krist adds.

I know.

"Once you start considering this to be a responsibility, it becomes a burden," muses the drummer.

Silence.

We've reached a brief impasse. Kurt starts leafing through a crap metal rag and spots a picture of Melvins (his early mentor) to his delight. Courtney sticks her head round the door to ask if we've seen Siren, because Inger Lorre slags her in it. Someone throws her a copy.

Dave starts telling me about the interview that they've just done for Swedish TV.

"THEY thanked us for saving rock'n'roll," he laughs. "For throwing a bomb into the rock'n'roll establishment."

Do you feel you've done that?

"Maybe we blew a paper bag up and popped it," sneers Krist.

From where I'm standing you don't seem to have changed very much. Murmurs of agreement come from the assembled.

What do you hate most about being famous?

"Kids with Bryan Adams and Bruce Springsteen tee-shirts coming up to me and asking for autographs," Kurt says. "When people in the audience hold up a sign that says 'Even Flow' (a Pearl Jam song) on one side and 'Negative Creep' (a Nirvana song) on the other."

Silence from the other two.

Okay. What's the best thing about being famous?

"You know, that's a really good question," answers Kurt, ironically.

"We might get some perks here and there," his bassist ventures. "A free drink or two, maybe."

Do you get many groupies?

"When I was about 12," replies Kurt, "I wanted to be a rock'n'roll

Below: **Lest we forget, Nirvana was a three-piece – the Ohio-born drummer Dave Grohl (left), and the Seattle-based duo of guitarist-singer Kurt Cobain (centre) and bassist Krist Novoselic, captured in early, happier, days.**

star, and I thought that would be my payback to all the jocks who got girlfriends all the time. But I realised way before I became a rock star that that was stupid."

"Maybe it's flattering to all these heavy metal bands, but we find it kind of disgusting," adds Dave, Nirvana's only unmarried member.

How about drink?

"I came into this tour with a fresh perspective," Krist muses. "I used to get stressed out, drink a whole lot and react to everything. Now I just go with the flow."

"I've always loved the spontaneity of being frustrated and pissed off…" Kurt challenges him.

"…and drunk," finishes Krist. "Oh yeah! I've had some of my best inspirations intoxicated – it's a different reality. It's like living in a movie or a cartoon, where your subconscious takes off. That's where all the good stories come from. But it's such hell on your body."

Has the sudden fame appreciably changed your lifestyles?

"Definitely," responds Kurt, vehemently.

"It hasn't changed mine," his bassist disagrees. "I can still go down to Safeway, buy fruit and vegetables, walk around town. I don't care if people stare at me or whatever."

"You don't?" Kurt asks him. "At all?"

"No," replies Krist. "and the more they see me, especially in Seattle, the more…"

"Oh yeah, eventually they'll get tired of sniggering at you and talking behind your back." Kurt finishes the sentence for him. "Well, I've been confronted by people wanting to beat me up, by people heckling me and being so drunk and obnoxious because they think I'm this pissy

rock star bastard who can't come to grips with his fame.

"I was in a rock club the other night," he continues, "and one guy comes up, pats me on the back and says, "You've got a really good thing going, you know? Your band members are cool, you write great songs, you affected a lot of people, but, man, you've really got to get your personal shit together!' Then another person comes up and says, 'I hope you overcome your drug problems.' All this happens within an hour while I'm trying to watch the Melvins, minding my own business.

"There were about five or six kids sitting around, very drunk, screaming 'Rock star! Rock star! Oh, look, he's going to freak out any minute! He's going to have a tantrum! He's going to start crying! Then this other guy comes up, puts his arm around me and says, 'You know, my girlfriend broke up with me and took my Nirvana album, so you should give me $14 to buy a new CD, cos you can afford that now you're a big rock star.' And I said, 'Gee. That's a clever thing to say. Why don't you f*** off?'"

"But you have to ignore them," Krist warns him, "or it becomes an obsession. I have dreams about being nude in public, and I interpret them as worrying about sticking out. Forget it! It can become a preoccupation. I was like that, too, when I used to see someone famous…"

"Yeah, but did you pitch them shit?" Kurt interrupts him.

"No," Krist replies. "I didn't, but that incident you mentioned seems to be pretty isolated.

"It's not isolated," snarls Kurt. "It happens to me all the time – every time I go out, every f***in' time. It's stupid. And, if it bothers me that much, I'm going to do something about it. F*** it, rock doesn't mean that much to me. I still love to be in a band and play music with Krist and Dave, but if it means that we have to resort to playing in a practice room and never touring again, then so be it.

Krist and Dave fall silent. The mood in the room has turned dark.

"I have to hear rumours about me all the time," the singer growls, "I'm totally sick of it. If I'm going to take drugs that's my own f***in' prerogative, and if I don't take drugs it my own f***in' prerogative. It's nobody's business, and I don't care if people take drugs and I don't care if people don't take drugs.

"It all started with just one article in one of the shittiest, cock-rock orientated LA magazines," he continues, "where this guy assumed I was on heroin because he noticed that I was tired. Since then, the rumours have spread like wildfire. I can't deny that I have taken drugs and I still do, every once in a while. But I'm not a f***in' heroin addict, and I'm not going to…"

He trails off, momentarily wordless.

"It's impossible to be on tour and to be on heroin," he begins again. "I don't know any band that could do it, unless you're Keith Richards and you're being given blood transfusions every three days, and you have runners going out and scoring drugs for you."

Kurt glowers with anger.

"I never realised that mainstream audiences react towards mainstream rock stars in this manner, because I've never paid attention before," he rails. "I don't mean to complain as much as I do, but it's a load of shit. It's really stupid. I've had days where I've considered this to be a job, and I never thought that would happen. It makes me question the point of it all. I'm only gonna bitch about it for another year and, if I can't handle it after that, we're gonna have to make some drastic changes."

© Everett True / Melody Maker / IPC Syndication

Below: **The woes of the road – sometimes it all got too much for Kurt. "It's impossible to be on the road and to be on heroin," he protested, vehemently denying that he was a junkie.**

Above: **Towards the end you didn't need glasses to see that time was almost up for Kurt Cobain and Nirvana. On April 5, 1994, it was.**

key recordings

1989   Seattle's Sub Pop Records release Nirvana's *Bleach* for grateful members of Generation X

1992   Now one of America's hottest live bands, Nirvana switch to Geffen for US No.1 with *Nevermind*, which includes classic
single *Smells Like Teen Spirit*

1993   Steve Albini takes the producer's chair for the stripped-down *In Utero*

1994   Kurt Cobain commits suicide, but *Unplugged In New York* gives Nirvana another international hit

1995   Singles album meets undiminished demand for Nirvana product...

1996   ...while *From The Muddy Banks of The Wishkah* closes a fascinating chapter in rock history

index of artists

ACKNOWLEDGEMENTS

Corbis UK Ltd/**Bettmann** 20, 25, 29, 33, 49, 123, 147, /**Philip Gould** 98-99, 110 left /**Hulton-Deutsch Collection** 60, 102, 104, /**Neal Preston** 63, /**Roger Ressmeyer** Front Endpaper, Back Endpaper, /**Bettmann**/ **Amalie R. Rothchild** 10, /**©S.I.N.** 32, 100, 108, 170, 173 Bottom Right, /**Bettmann**/ **UPI** 11 Bottom, 141.
Gered Mankowitz/**copyright Bowstir Ltd.** 1999 51.
Nat Finkelstein/**The Photographers Gallery, London, UK** 16-17, 18-19, 68.
Barry Plummer 22, 66, 70, 75 Top Right, 109, 114, 116, 120, 130, 146.
Redferns/**Richie Aaron** 105, 106, 111, 140, 150, /**Paul Bergen** 4-5, 61, 154, 175, /**Chuck Boyd** 90, 97, /**Garry Brandon** 139, /**Fin Costello** 151, 155, /**Ian Dickson** 58, 59, 67, 78-79, 83 right, 128, 132-133, 159, /**Erica Echenberg** 82-83 Centre, /**Dave Ellis** 71 /**Mick Gold** 86-87, /**Robert Knight** 53, /**Elliott Landy** 15, 88, /**Michel Linssen** 2-3, 43, 84, 85, 96, 134, 142-143, 167, 174, /**Andrew Maclear** 30-31, /**Michael Ochs Archives** 14, 57, 124-125, 127 Top, 131, /**Keith Morris** 160, 162, /**Rb** 42, /**David Redfern** 40, /**Ebet Roberts** 82 left, 103, 121, 122, 141, 169, /**S&G Press Agency** 26, /**Donna Santisi** 118, **Jurgen Vollmer** 27, /**Val Wilmer** 23, /**Charlyn Zlotnik** 37, 161.

Retna Pictures Ltd 149, /**Robert Altman** 136, 137, /**Adrian Boot** 117, 126, 127 Bottom, /**Andrew Catlin** 164, /**Charlyn Zlotnik** 75 Bottom Left, /**Jill Furmanovsky** 80, /**Gary Gershoff** 163, /**Jak Kilby** 56, /**Photofest** 12, /**Neal Preston** 138, 152, /**Michael Putland** 28, 36, 38, 44-45, 46, 48, 52, 73, 77, 132, 144, 145, /**Ed Sirrs** 171, /**Ray Stevenson** 50, 115, /**G. Hanekroot**/**Sunshine** 1, 34-35, 64-65, 76, 93, 95, /**Kees Tabak**/**Sunshine** 156-157.
Rex Features 94, /**Chris Foster** 54-55, 62, /**Harry Goodwin** 119, /**Dezo Hoffman** 92, /**Richard Mitchell** 8-9, /**Sheila Rock** 129, /**Peter Sanders** 11 Top, /**Ray Stevenson** 101, 107 /**Stephen Sweet** 172, 173 Top Left, /**Dick Wallis** 113
The Special Photographers Library/**David Wedgbury** 47, 89